The Manga Guide to
JAPANESE FOOD

Everything You Want to Know About the History,
Ingredients and Folklore of Japan's Unique Cuisine

HIROSHI NAGASHIMA

TUTTLE Publishing

Tokyo | Rutland, Vermont | Singapore

Contents

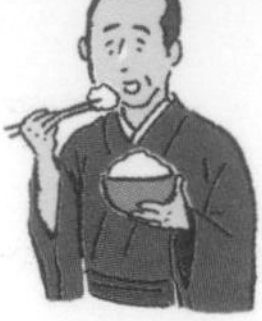

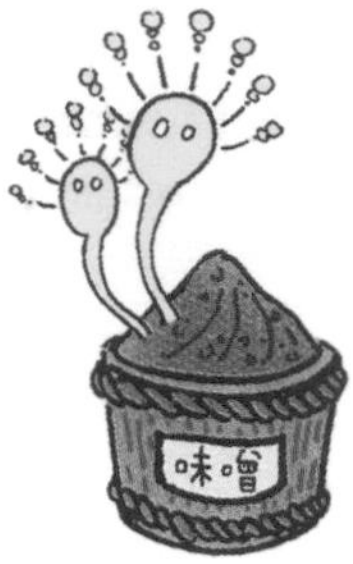

味噌

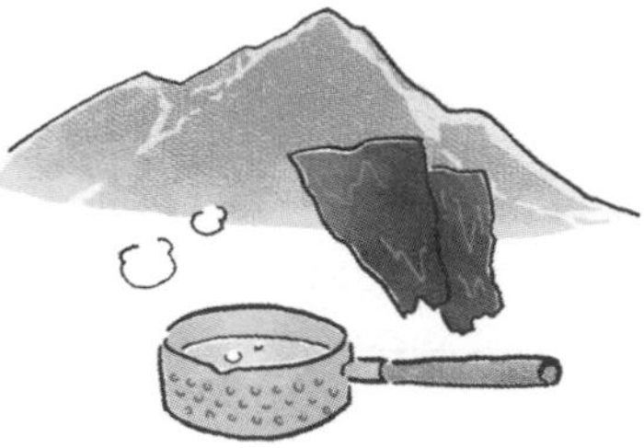

PART 2

A Brief History of Feast Foods and Sushi

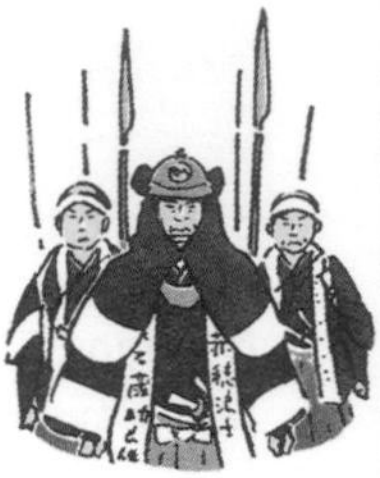

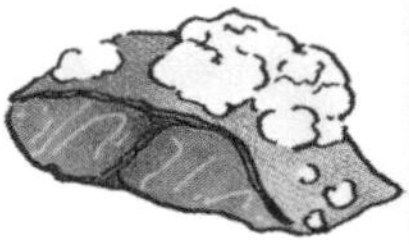

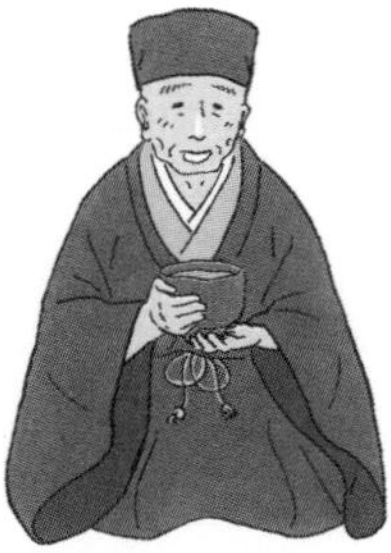

PART 3

Putting It All into Practice

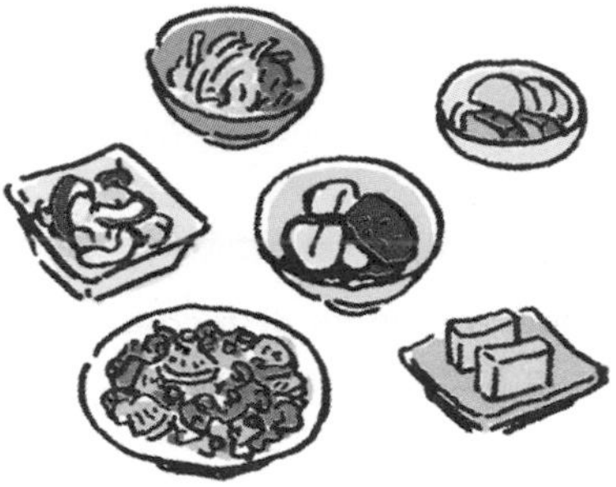

The Elements of Kaiseki Cuisine

Tableware and Food Presentation

Dining at a Traditional Japanese Restaurant

Afterword

Why Japanese Cuisine Fascinates Chefs Around the World

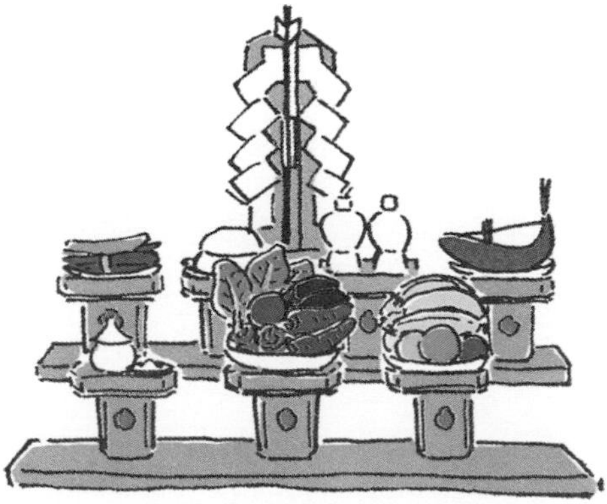

Why I Wrote This Book

Japanese food is attracting attention around the world. According to statistics from the Ministry of Agriculture, Forestry and Fisheries, there were 156,000 Japanese restaurants overseas in 2019, up 30 percent from 2017 and approximately sixfold from 2006.

In 2013, "Washoku, traditional dietary cultures of the Japanese, notably for the celebration of New Year" was added to UNESCO's list of Intangible Cultural Heritage, and interest in Japanese food culture has continued to grow steadily since then.

Despite this international excitement, I have to wonder whether we Japanese people know enough about our own traditional food culture. Many books have been published on Japanese food culture and history. However, most are not easy to understand or accessible. This book arose from my desire to introduce Japanese food culture to a younger generation in an easy-to-understand manga format.

Tradition and history may seem unrelated to daily life. But take a moment to ask yourself what makes plain white rice taste so good, why Japanese people eat special foods for the New Year, or why cutting is so important in Japanese cuisine. When you start digging, you'll discover there's always a reason, usually one deeply related to Japan's geography and climate. Everything starts to make more sense once you learn how past generations created and passed down their food culture. You may be surprised and even moved by the ingenuity of these earlier generations. The act of preparing and eating food is part of a unique culture connected to science, folklore, ideology, economics, society and more. There is so much to learn!

In this book, I have tried to introduce ideas that get to the essence of Japanese food culture, with a focus on topics other than cooking techniques. Because we live in a global era, I have also incorporated comparisons to the food cultures of other countries. I hope this book will help you think more deeply about Japanese food, and the future of what and how we eat.

— **Hiroshi Nagashima**

Since Japanese food was added to UNESCO's list of Intangible Cultural Heritage in 2013, the term "washoku" has been widely used to refer to Japanese food culture. This book focuses on food prepared by chefs, and therefore uses the term "Japanese cuisine" instead.

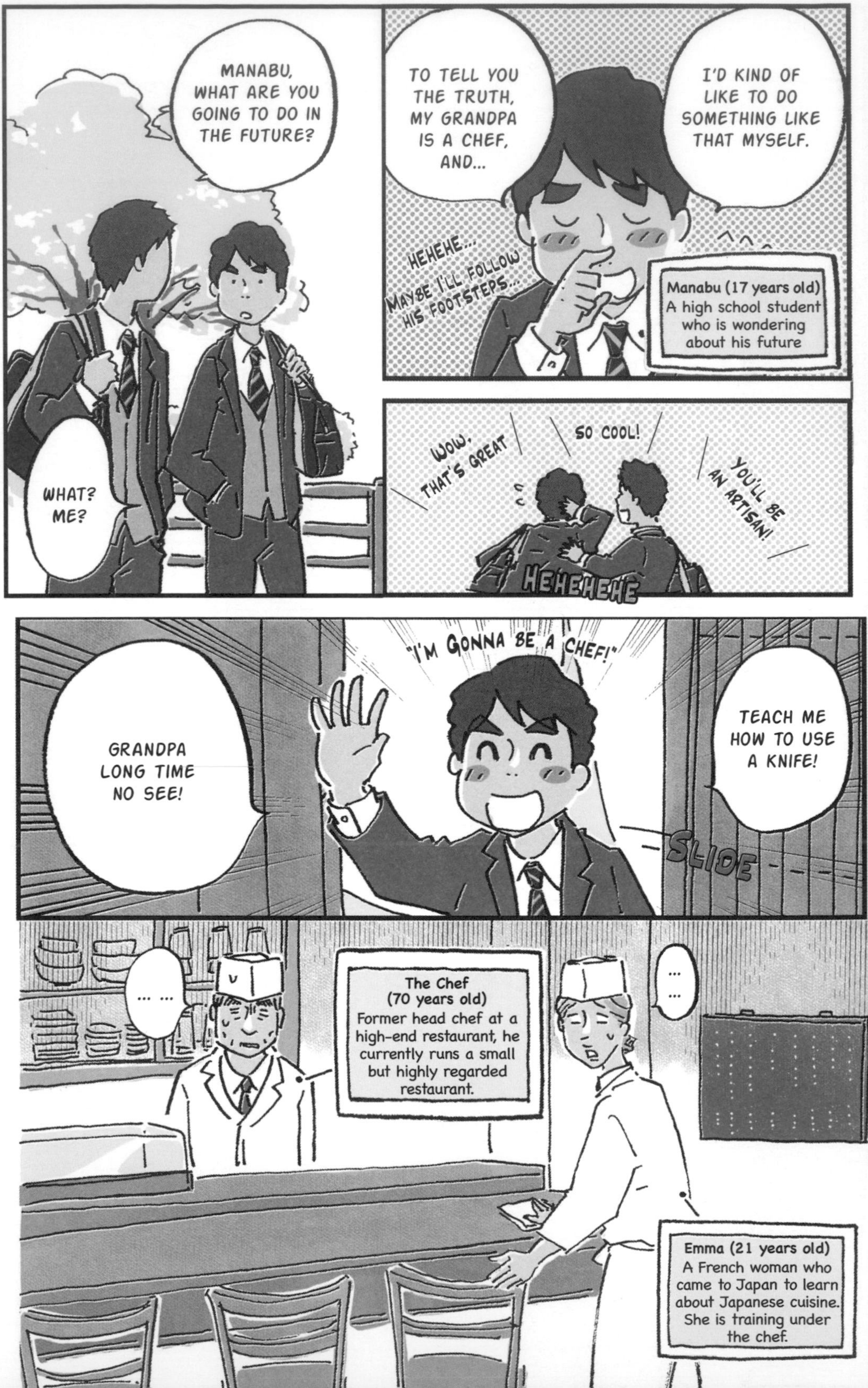
MANABU, WHAT ARE YOU GOING TO DO IN THE FUTURE?
WHAT? ME?
TO TELL YOU THE TRUTH, MY GRANDPA IS A CHEF, AND...
I'D KIND OF LIKE TO DO SOMETHING LIKE THAT MYSELF.
HEHEHE... MAYBE I'LL FOLLOW HIS FOOTSTEPS...
Manabu (17 years old) A high school student who is wondering about his future
WOW, THAT'S GREAT
SO COOL!
YOU'LL BE AN ARTISAN!
HEHEHEHE
"I'M GONNA BE A CHEF!"
GRANDPA LONG TIME NO SEE!
TEACH ME HOW TO USE A KNIFE!
SLIDE
... ...
The Chef (70 years old) Former head chef at a high-end restaurant, he currently runs a small but highly regarded restaurant.
... ...
Emma (21 years old) A French woman who came to Japan to learn about Japanese cuisine. She is training under the chef.

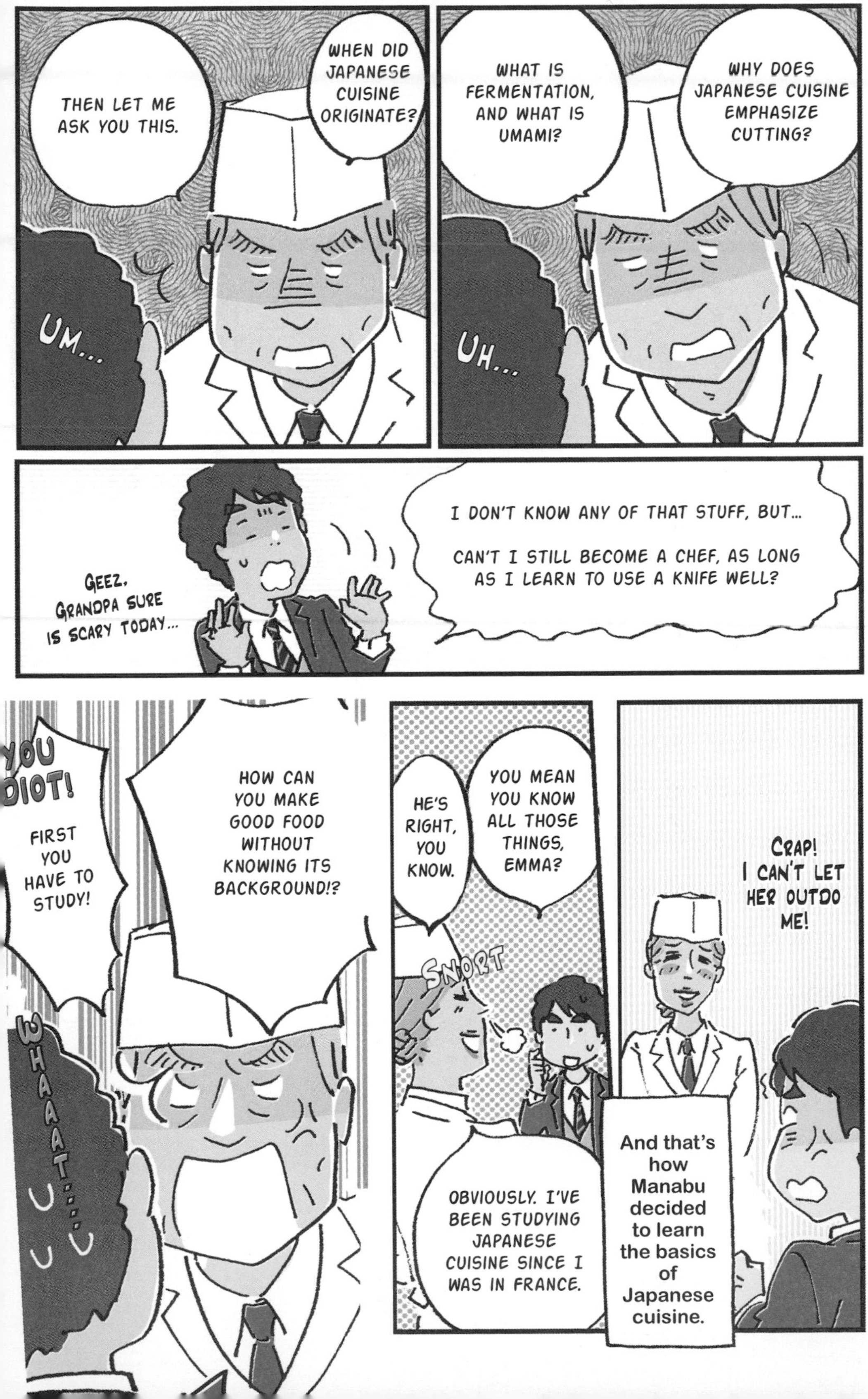
THEN LET ME ASK YOU THIS.
WHEN DID JAPANESE CUISINE ORIGINATE?
UM...
WHAT IS FERMENTATION, AND WHAT IS UMAMI?
WHY DOES JAPANESE CUISINE EMPHASIZE CUTTING?
UH...
GEEZ, GRANDPA SURE IS SCARY TODAY...
I DON'T KNOW ANY OF THAT STUFF, BUT...
CAN'T I STILL BECOME A CHEF, AS LONG AS I LEARN TO USE A KNIFE WELL?
YOU DIOT!
FIRST YOU HAVE TO STUDY!
HOW CAN YOU MAKE GOOD FOOD WITHOUT KNOWING ITS BACKGROUND!?
WHAAAAT...
HE'S RIGHT, YOU KNOW.
SNORT
YOU MEAN YOU KNOW ALL THOSE THINGS, EMMA?
OBVIOUSLY. I'VE BEEN STUDYING JAPANESE CUISINE SINCE I WAS IN FRANCE.
CRAP! I CAN'T LET HER OUTDO ME!
And that's how Manabu decided to learn the basics of Japanese cuisine.

IT WOULD BE GREAT IF I COULD ANSWER QUESTIONS FROM FOREIGNERS ABOUT JAPANESE FOOD.
I WANT TO LEARN FROM THE GROUND UP WITH MANABU. I'M CURIOUS HOW JAPAN'S FOOD CULTURE COMPARES WITH EUROPE'S AND AMERICA'S.
THE ORIGINS OF JAPANESE CUISINE ARE DEEPLY ROOTED IN JAPAN'S GEOGRAPHY, SO LET'S START THERE.

Part 1

The Eight Pillars of Japanese Cuisine

- The Story of Rice
- Pure Water, Delicious Food
- Japan's Wooden Tableware
- Seafood on All Sides
- Food for the Gods
- The Importance of Cutting
- Fermenting for Flavor
- Umami, the Fifth Flavor

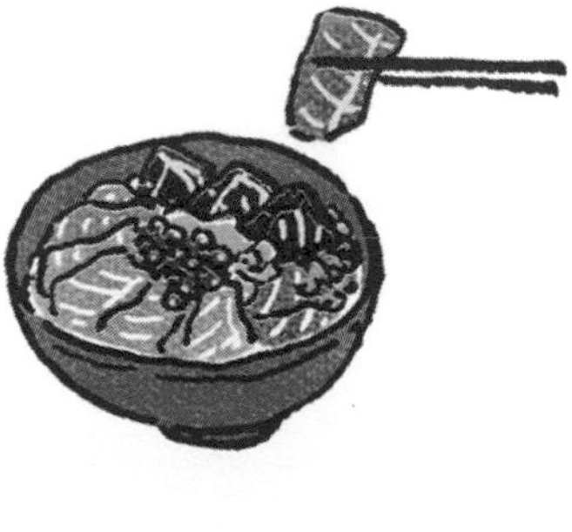

The Story of Rice

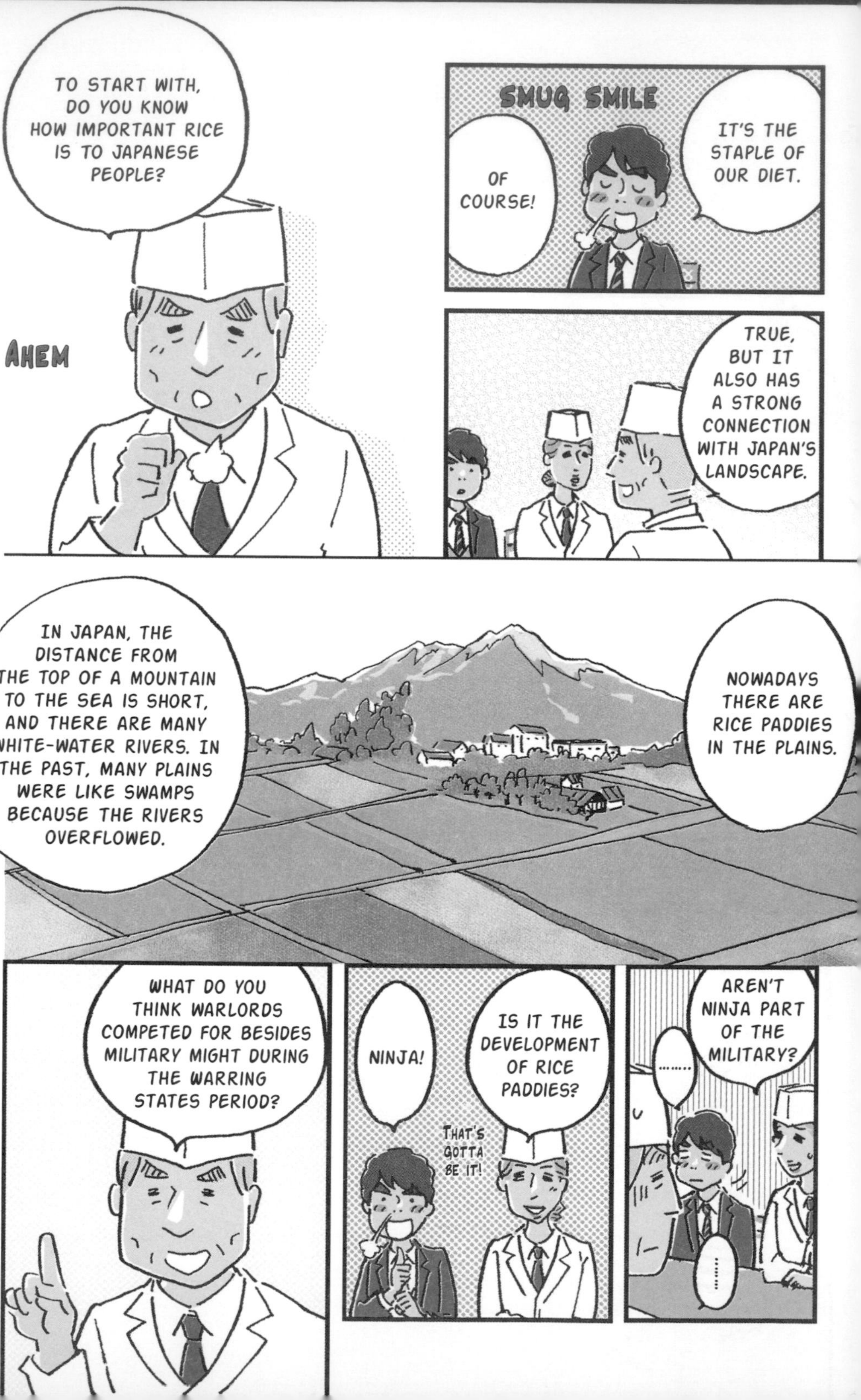
TO START WITH, DO YOU KNOW HOW IMPORTANT RICE IS TO JAPANESE PEOPLE?
AHEM
SMUG SMILE
OF COURSE!
IT'S THE STAPLE OF OUR DIET.
TRUE, BUT IT ALSO HAS A STRONG CONNECTION WITH JAPAN'S LANDSCAPE.
IN JAPAN, THE DISTANCE FROM THE TOP OF A MOUNTAIN TO THE SEA IS SHORT, AND THERE ARE MANY WHITE-WATER RIVERS. IN THE PAST, MANY PLAINS WERE LIKE SWAMPS BECAUSE THE RIVERS OVERFLOWED.
NOWADAYS THERE ARE RICE PADDIES IN THE PLAINS.
WHAT DO YOU THINK WARLORDS COMPETED FOR BESIDES MILITARY MIGHT DURING THE WARRING STATES PERIOD?
NINJA!
IS IT THE DEVELOPMENT OF RICE PADDIES?
THAT'S GOTTA BE IT!
AREN'T NINJA PART OF THE MILITARY?
....
....

Tokugawa Ieyasu

YOU'RE RIGHT EMMA. RICE WAS LIKE MONEY TO PEOPLE BACK THEN.

WOW, TOKYO TOO?

THE AMOUNT OF RICE HARVESTED WAS THE POWER OF THE NATION, SO THE LORDS OF EACH REGION WORKED HARD TO CONTROL FLOODING AND INCREASED THE NUMBER OF RICE PADDIES. MANY OF THE CITIES WE LIVE IN TODAY WERE DEVELOPED BACK THEN.

Flood control of the Tone River

Takeda Shingen

Kato Kiyomasa

Flood control of the Shira River

Flood control of the Kamanashi River

WHEN IEYASU ESTABLISHED THE EDO SHOGUNATE, HE CHANGED THE FLOW OF THE ONCE-WILD TONE RIVER. BY BUILDING CHANNELS THROUGH RICE PADDIES, RICH FARMLAND WAS CREATED. TODAY THAT IS THE KANTO PLAIN, WHERE TOKYO IS LOCATED.

The current Tone River

Before

The Kanto Plain

After

The former Tone River

Oh no!

I can't live here.

It's all swampland

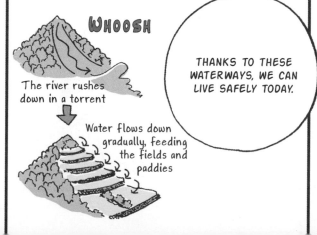

WHOOSH

The river rushes down in a torrent

Water flows down gradually, feeding the fields and paddies

THANKS TO THESE WATERWAYS, WE CAN LIVE SAFELY TODAY.

SO TODAY'S RICE PADDY LANDSCAPE IS THE RESULT OF HARD WORK BY MANY GENERATIONS...

AMAZING...

Rice, the Cornerstone of Japan's Food Culture

The many functions of the rice paddy

Oftentimes people think of rice paddies as part of the natural landscape. In reality, however, they are man-made structures. Past generations invested untold sweat equity to control the flow of water, damming the raging rivers that overflowed when it rained heavily and building reservoirs and irrigation canals to keep the water flowing in and out of rice paddies. The total length of the waterways built throughout Japan to distribute water to rice paddies is 250,000 miles (400,000 kilometers)—enough to circle the earth ten times!

Because steep, rugged mountains cover most of Japan, heavy rainfall can cause rivers to rise rapidly and flood downstream. Rice paddies help prevent flooding because they accumulate water and then slowly return it to rivers or store it as groundwater, regulating the amount of water flowing downstream (Figure 1). This is why paddy fields are called "nature's dams."

A high-yield grain that doesn't require crop rotation

Rice is grown in the same fields every year. This may seem obvious, but from the perspective of world agriculture, it is a very special and privileged situation. In general, when cultivating crops in non-paddy fields, fallowing or crop rotation[1] is necessary to avoid row crop failure,[2] which can occur when the same crop is grown continuously in the same area. In rice paddies, however, water brings new nutrients and washes away toxic substances (Figure 1-2), allowing for continuous cropping.

On the other hand, wheat, the staple food of much of Europe and the United States, cannot be grown continuously. In medieval

---

1 **Crop rotation** is he practice of alternating between different types of crops on the same farmland over a period of time.
2 **Row crop failure** is poor growth caused by growing the same crop in the same field year after year.

Figure 1 The Elements of a Rice Paddy

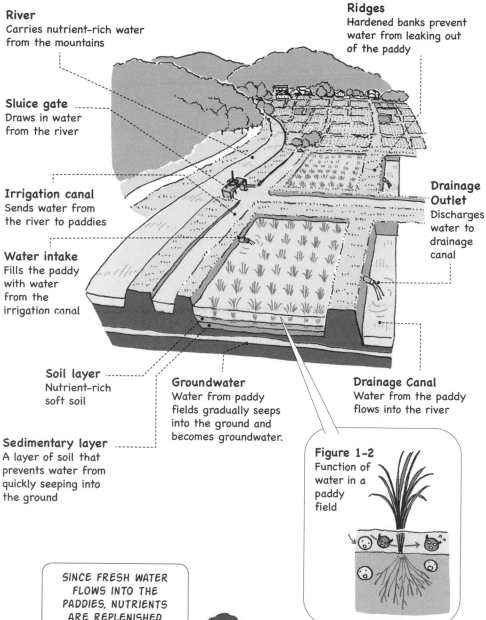

River
Carries nutrient-rich water from the mountains
Ridges
Hardened banks prevent water from leaking out of the paddy
Sluice gate
Draws in water from the river
Irrigation canal
Sends water from the river to paddies
Drainage Outlet
Discharges water to drainage canal
Water intake
Fills the paddy with water from the irrigation canal
Soil layer
Nutrient-rich soft soil
Groundwater
Water from paddy fields gradually seeps into the ground and becomes groundwater.
Drainage Canal
Water from the paddy flows into the river
Sedimentary layer
A layer of soil that prevents water from quickly seeping into the ground

Figure 1-2
Function of water in a paddy field

The water carries nutrients, and if pathogens develop, the water flushes them out.

SINCE FRESH WATER FLOWS INTO THE PADDIES, NUTRIENTS ARE REPLENISHED AND RICE CAN BE GROWN YEAR AFTER YEAR.

Europe, a three-field system of rotation was practiced in which a third of land was planted to grains, a third to legumes, and a third left fallow for livestock grazing. Mixed farming is still practiced in Europe, combining crop cultivation with livestock rearing, and wheat is only grown in the same field once every few years.

Rice is also characterized by a high seed multiplication ratio.[3] In the Muromachi period (1336–1573), the ratios for rice in Japan were between 20 and 30. In the same centuries, the ratios for European wheat were around 3 to 5. Today, with advances in breeding and other factors, the seed multiplication ratio for rice is over 1,000, while for wheat it is about one tenth of that.

Japan's scarce farmland

Let's take a look at the extent of rice paddies in Japan.

Japan's total land area is about 94 million acres (38 million hectares). About 66% of that land is forested, while about 12% is used for agriculture (Figure 2). Rice paddies make up about 54% of agricultural land.

How does that compare to other countries? Farmland makes up about 40% of land area in the U.S., about 50% in France, and about 70% in the United Kingdom. By comparison, the amount of farmland in Japan is very low.[4]

Monsoon Asia, the world's rice basket

Rice cultivation flourishes in Japan because it is part of hot and humid Monsoon Asia. Monsoon Asia is a region stretching from Pakistan south of the Himalayas to India, Southeast Asia, and East Asia (Figure 3) where monsoons (seasonal winds) bring heavy rainfall. The climate of this area is suitable for paddy rice cultivation, and most of the world's rice is produced here. The region covers about 15% of global land area but is home to about 60% of the world's population, indicating that highly productive rice can feed a large number of people. A variety called indica rice accounts for more than 80% of the world's rice production. Japan grows Japonica rice, which makes up about 20% of total production. Table 1 shows the characteristics of each type of rice.

---

3 The seed multiplication ratio is the number of grains harvested from sowing one seed.
4 Statistics from the Ministry of Agriculture, Forestry and Fisheries.

Figure 2 **Land Use in Japan**

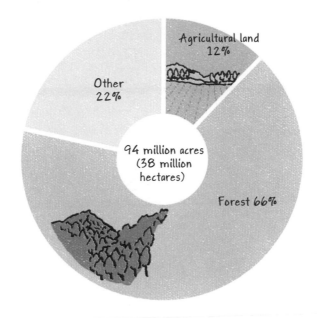

Agricultural land
12%

Other
22%

94 million acres
(38 million
hectares)

Forest 66%

Based on 2017 statistics from the Ministry of
Agriculture, Forestry and Fisheries and Forestry Agency.
The percentages in the figure are approximate.

A HIGH
PERCENTAGE OF
JAPAN IS FORESTED,
BUT ONLY ABOUT
12% IS FARMLAND.

THAT'S MUCH
LESS THAN IN
FRANCE, WHERE
ABOUT HALF THE
LAND IS FARMED.

Table 1 The World's Main Types of Rice

Type	Characteristics and production areas	Uses
Indica Rice 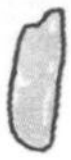	Long grain variety. More than 80% of the world's rice. Grains stay separate when cooked, not sticky. Grown in India, Southeast Asia, southern China, etc.	Boil or cook with other ingredients. Used in curry, fried rice, biryani, etc. Biryani 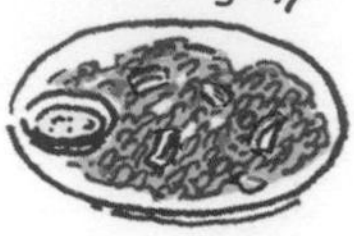
Japonica Rice 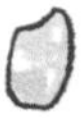	Short grain variety. About 20% of the world's rice. Sticky. Grown in Japan, China, Korea, U.S. West Coast, etc.	Can be boiled or steamed and eaten plain. Plain cooked rice 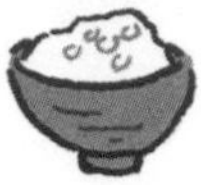
Javanica Rice 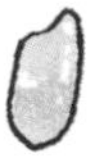	Large-grain variety. Minimal production. Texture between that of the Indica and Japonica varieties. Produced in Indonesia, Italy, Spain, Central and South America, etc.	Used for risotto, paella etc. 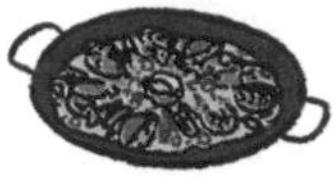 Paella

When rice was money

Rice has played a major role not only as a staple food, but also economically. From the mid 7th century until the Land Tax Reform of 1873,[5] rice was used to pay taxes in Japan. In period dramas, you might hear regional lords referred to as "hyakumangoku no daimyo," meaning that a million *koku* of rice could be harvested in that lord's domain. A koku is a traditional measurement equal to 180 quarts (liters). After Toyotomi Hideyoshi's Taiko-kenchi survey[6] in the late 16th century, the income and status of feudal lords was determined based on *kokudaka*, the amount of brown rice harvested from their land. Rice was the basis for all units of measure in Japan (Figure 5). One traditional unit, the *tan*, is still used to express the area of a field.

5 Land tax reform was implemented by the Meiji government in 1873, and private ownership of land was allowed. Three percent of the land value was paid as tax in gold, instead of rice as was the case previously.

6 The Taiko-kenchi was a survey of the extent and productivity of farmland throughout Japan conducted by Toyotomi Hideyoshi starting in 1582.

Figure 3 Monsoon Asia: Areas Affected by Monsoons

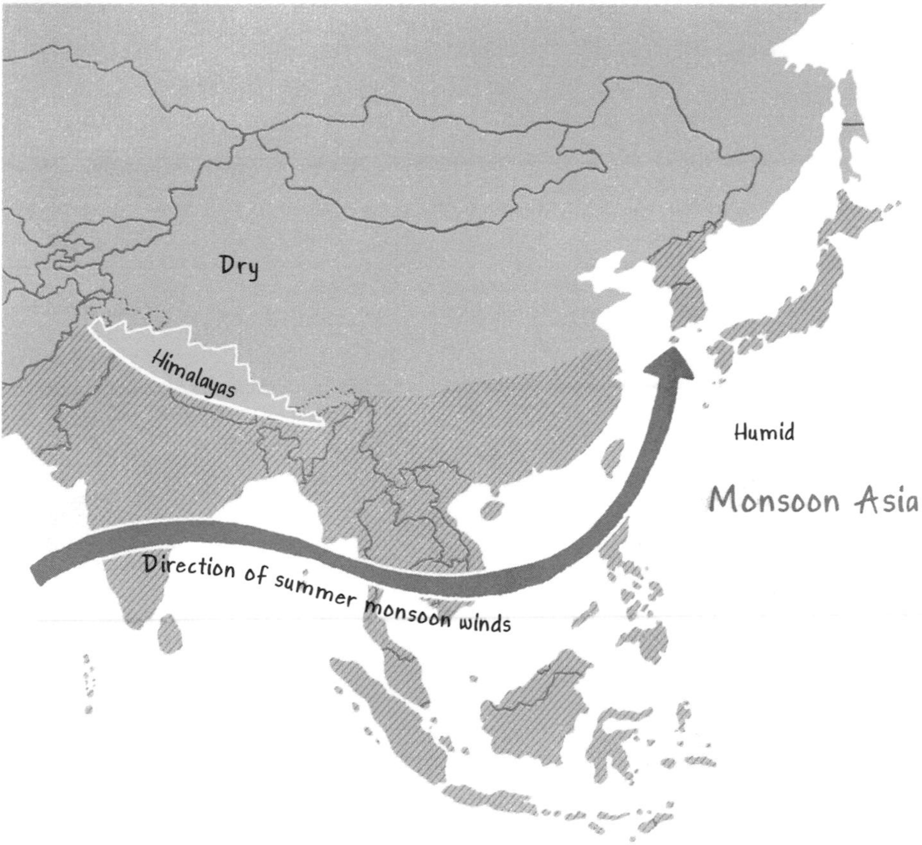
Dry
Himalayas
Humid
Monsoon Asia
Direction of summer monsoon winds

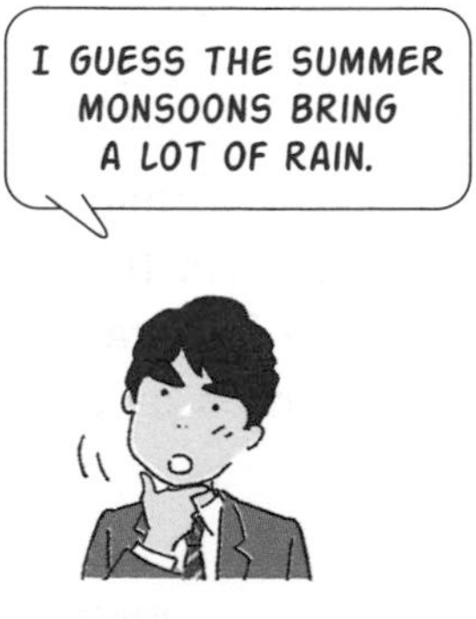
I GUESS THE SUMMER MONSOONS BRING A LOT OF RAIN.

Food culture commonalities in Monsoon Asia

- Rice is the staple
- Fermented soybean products are eaten
- Tea is drunk
- Lacquerware products are used.

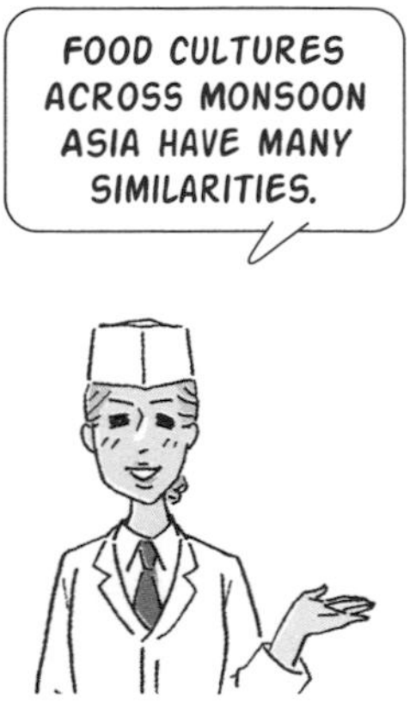
FOOD CULTURES ACROSS MONSOON ASIA HAVE MANY SIMILARITIES.

In the Edo period (1603–1867), samurai were reportedly given 5 cups of uncooked brown rice per day. Rice is rich in carbohydrates, proteins, fats, vitamins and other nutrients. It contains a good balance of essential amino acids, which cannot be produced by the human body. Lysine is the only essential amino acid that rice doesn't contain much of. Soybeans, on the other hand, are rich in lysine. In those days, a daily diet of five cups of rice and miso soup made from soybeans provided the necessary calories and protein.

Figure 4 **Nutritional Content of Rice**

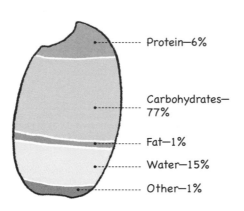

Protein—6%

Carbohydrates—77%

Fat—1%

Water—15%

Other—1%

Cooked rice made from 5 cups of dry rice

RICE IS SO NUTRITIOUS! BUT 10 BOWLS A DAY IS TOO MUCH...

Figure 5

Rice Was the Basic Unit of Measurement in Traditional Japanese Culture

Weight Measurements

<u>1 go</u> = 180 ml (6 oz)

1 sho = 1.8 liters (60 oz)

<u>1 to</u> = 18 liters (600 oz)

1 portion of rice for 1 person

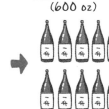

=

=

1 go makes 2 large heaping bowls of cooked rice. That's a lot!

1 large bottle of sake is 1 sho

1 large container of oil is 1 to

Heavy

Area Measurements

<u>3 go</u>

Morning

Noon

Night

= 1 day's worth of rice

<u>1 hyo</u>

1 hyo = 2 tatami mats
The area required to grow 1 day's worth (3 go) of rice

<u>1 tan</u>

31.5 m

31.5 m

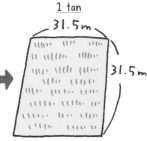

The area needed to grow 1 year's worth (1,080 go) of rice

RICE WAS THE UNIT OF MEASURE? RICE IS AMAZING!

1 koku = 10 to

Ha ha ha

I'm a one million koku lord from Kaga!

1 million koku

A 1 million koku lord, such as the lord of the Kaga clan in current-day Toyama Prefecture, had the financial clout to support 1 million people for 1 year

From status item to staple to sidelined

Before the Meiji era (1868–1912), rice was money, a unit of measure, and a sacred entity that went beyond food. In the Edo period, city dwellers ate white rice, while farmers ate rice mixed with other grains such as millet, except on special occasions. White rice was a symbol of affluence.

Although the Japanese people have grown rice for more than 2,000 years and have long viewed it as a staple food, it was only around 1955, during the period of rapid economic growth after World War II, that the entire nation was able to eat as much rice as they wanted every day. Looking back on the long history of rice, it may be fair to say that the Japanese were a "rice-hungry people" rather than a rice-farming people.[7]

In 1967, the annual rice harvest reached an all-time high of 14.5 million metric tons. Ironically, westernization of the Japanese diet was already causing a shift away from rice. Per capita annual rice consumption peaked at 260 pounds (118 kg) in 1962 and has been declining ever since, falling below half that level by 2016.

Plant breeding for quantity and quality

Since the Meiji era, rice varieties have been repeatedly improved with the primary goal of increasing yield. But as consumption falls, the emphasis has shifted from yield to taste. In 1969, the government changed the law to allow farmers to distribute rice directly to wholesalers rather then selling it to the government, which meant consumers were now able to chose what variety of rice they bought and where it came from. This led to the rise of "brand rice" marketed for specific qualities. In recent years, due to the effects of climate change, prefectures have been working to develop rice that both withstands extreme heat and tastes good.

---

7 The term "rice-hungry people" comes from Tadayo Watanabe, *Where Did Japan's Rice Come From?* (1990, PHP Research Institute).

One reason so many rice brands have emerged over the past few years is the completion of the genome analysis of rice in December 2004. Developing a single rice variety used to take more than ten years, but genome analysis has made it possible to predict how genes work in rice, greatly reducing the time required for development. Research is underway on various types of rice, including very sticky "low-amylose rice," rice that benefits health, and rice suitable for livestock feed.

Figure 6 **Koshihikari Rice and Related Varieties**

MAFF No. 22
Koganeharu
Morinokumasan
Hinohikari
Shonai No. 29
Koshihikari
Haenuki
Akitakomachi
Yamagata No. 70
Ou No. 292
Tsuyahime
Hitomebore
Tohoku No. 164
Hatsuboshi
Kukei 90242A
Nanatsuboshi
MAFF No. 1
Akiho

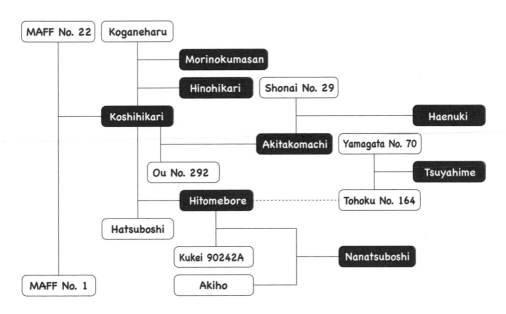

This table has been simplified. "Brand rice" varieties are shown in red boxes.

SO MOST "BRAND RICE" IS PART OF THE KOSHIHIKARI FAMILY...

How rice varieties shape national cuisines

Japanese people pick up rice with chopsticks and carry it to their mouths. This is possible because japonica rice is sticky. The regions where japonica rice is the main type eaten (parts of China, the Korean peninsula, and Japan) coincide with regions where chopsticks are used (see page 48).

Japan's long history of eating sticky, chewy rice has led to a preference for chewy, bouncy and sticky foods. The soft, chewy white bread called shokupan was developed in Japan and marketed starting in the 1990s as "bread that's like freshly cooked rice," with lasting success. Although people are eating less rice, food preferences nurtured over many centuries do not change so easily.

We love sticky, chewy and bouncy foods!
Brazilian cheese bread popular in Japan
Japanese "shokupan" bread
Soft, chewy and bouncy
Bouncy, chewy texture
Tapioca

The Big Picture

Seasoning Food on Your Plate, or in Your Mouth?

Seasoning as you chew

This is a way of eating in which multiple foods are mixed together in the mouth to create a personalized taste.

Japanese people typically put rice in their mouth, chew it a little, and then pick up morsels of more strongly flavored foods with their chopsticks. As they chew, they taste these foods together with the rice—in other words, seasoning the rice in their mouth.

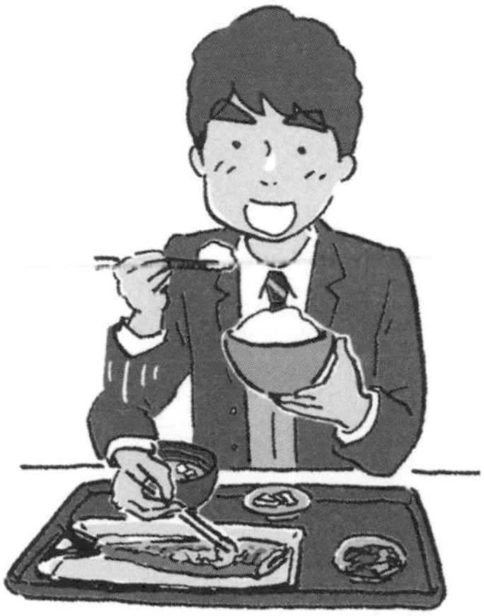

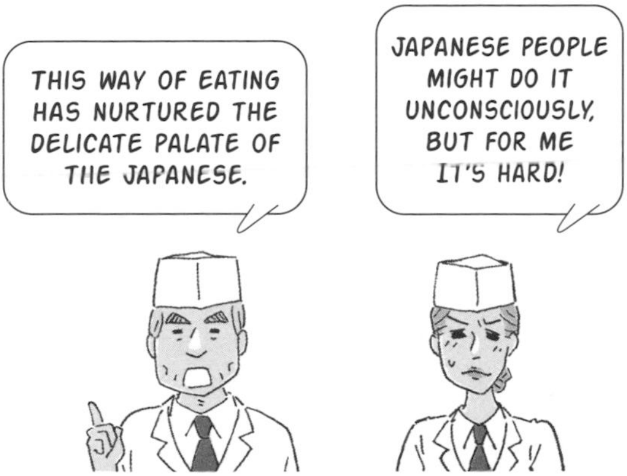
THIS WAY OF EATING HAS NURTURED THE DELICATE PALATE OF THE JAPANESE.
JAPANESE PEOPLE MIGHT DO IT UNCONSCIOUSLY, BUT FOR ME IT'S HARD!

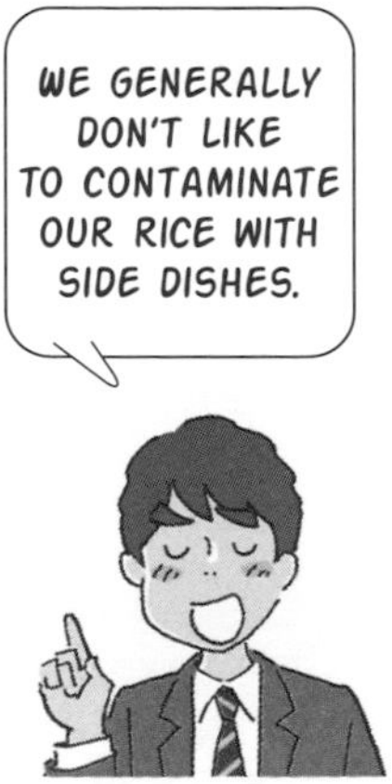
WE GENERALLY DON'T LIKE TO CONTAMINATE OUR RICE WITH SIDE DISHES.

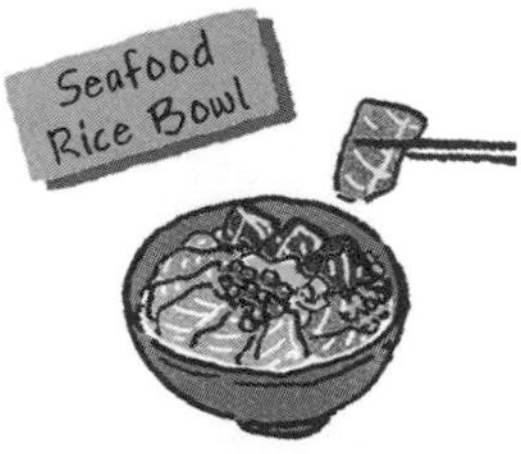
Seafood Rice Bowl

Japanese eat a seafood rice bowl by picking out the ingredients one by one and "seasoning" them in their mouth.

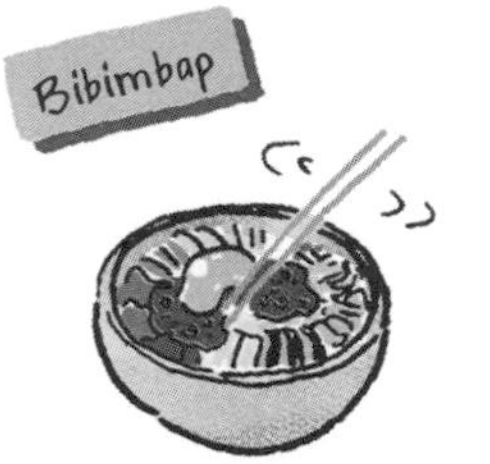
Bibimbap

Koreans eat bibimbap by mixing the ingredients well with the rice to make the taste uniform before eating.

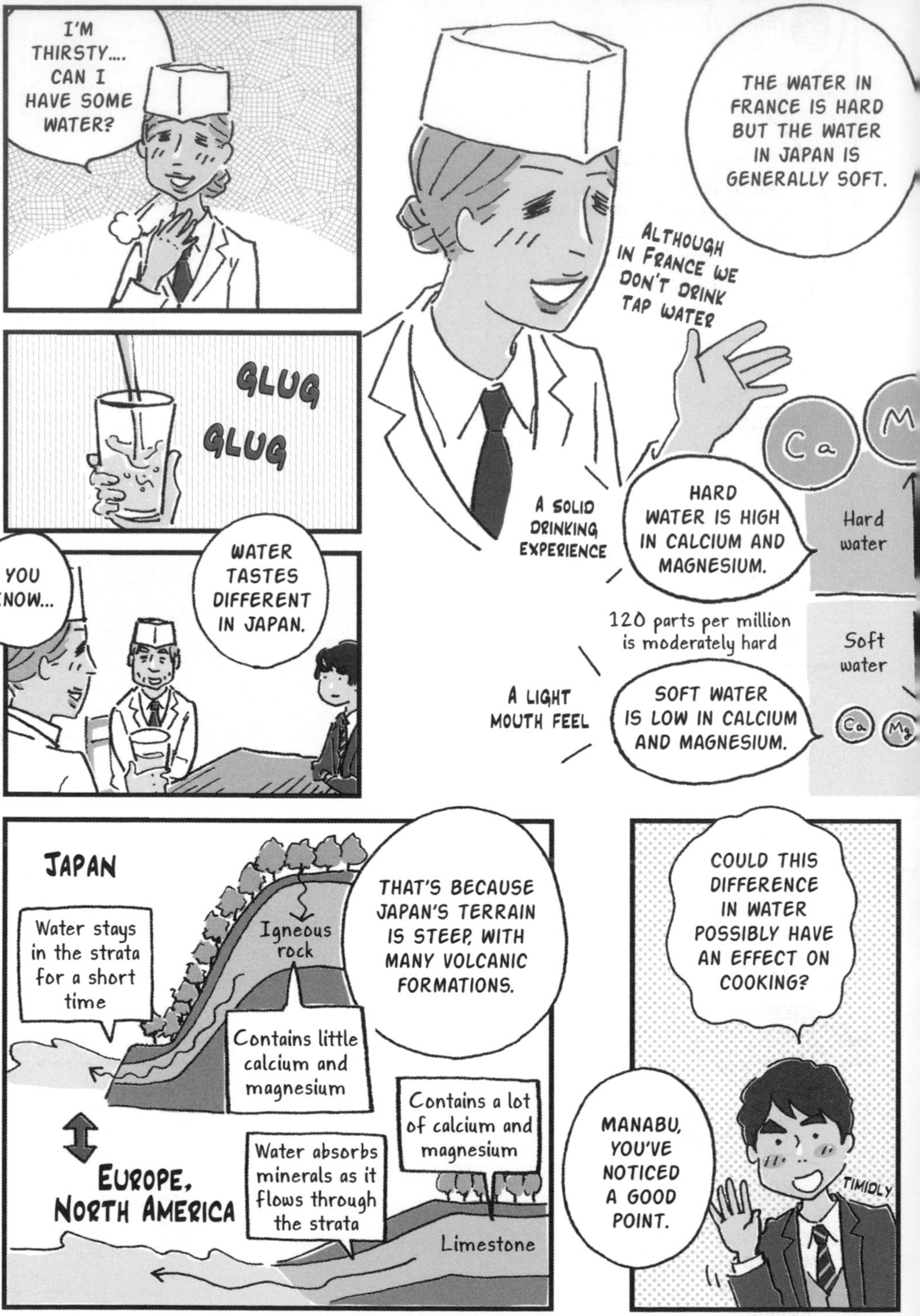
I'M THIRSTY.... CAN I HAVE SOME WATER?
GLUG
GLUG
YOU KNOW...
WATER TASTES DIFFERENT IN JAPAN.
THE WATER IN FRANCE IS HARD BUT THE WATER IN JAPAN IS GENERALLY SOFT.
ALTHOUGH IN FRANCE WE DON'T DRINK TAP WATER
Ca
Hard water
A SOLID DRINKING EXPERIENCE
HARD WATER IS HIGH IN CALCIUM AND MAGNESIUM.
120 parts per million is moderately hard
Soft water
A LIGHT MOUTH FEEL
SOFT WATER IS LOW IN CALCIUM AND MAGNESIUM.
Ca
Mg
JAPAN
Water stays in the strata for a short time
Igneous rock
Contains little calcium and magnesium
THAT'S BECAUSE JAPAN'S TERRAIN IS STEEP, WITH MANY VOLCANIC FORMATIONS.
EUROPE, NORTH AMERICA
Water absorbs minerals as it flows through the strata
Contains a lot of calcium and magnesium
Limestone
COULD THIS DIFFERENCE IN WATER POSSIBLY HAVE AN EFFECT ON COOKING?
MANABU, YOU'VE NOTICED A GOOD POINT.
TIMIDLY

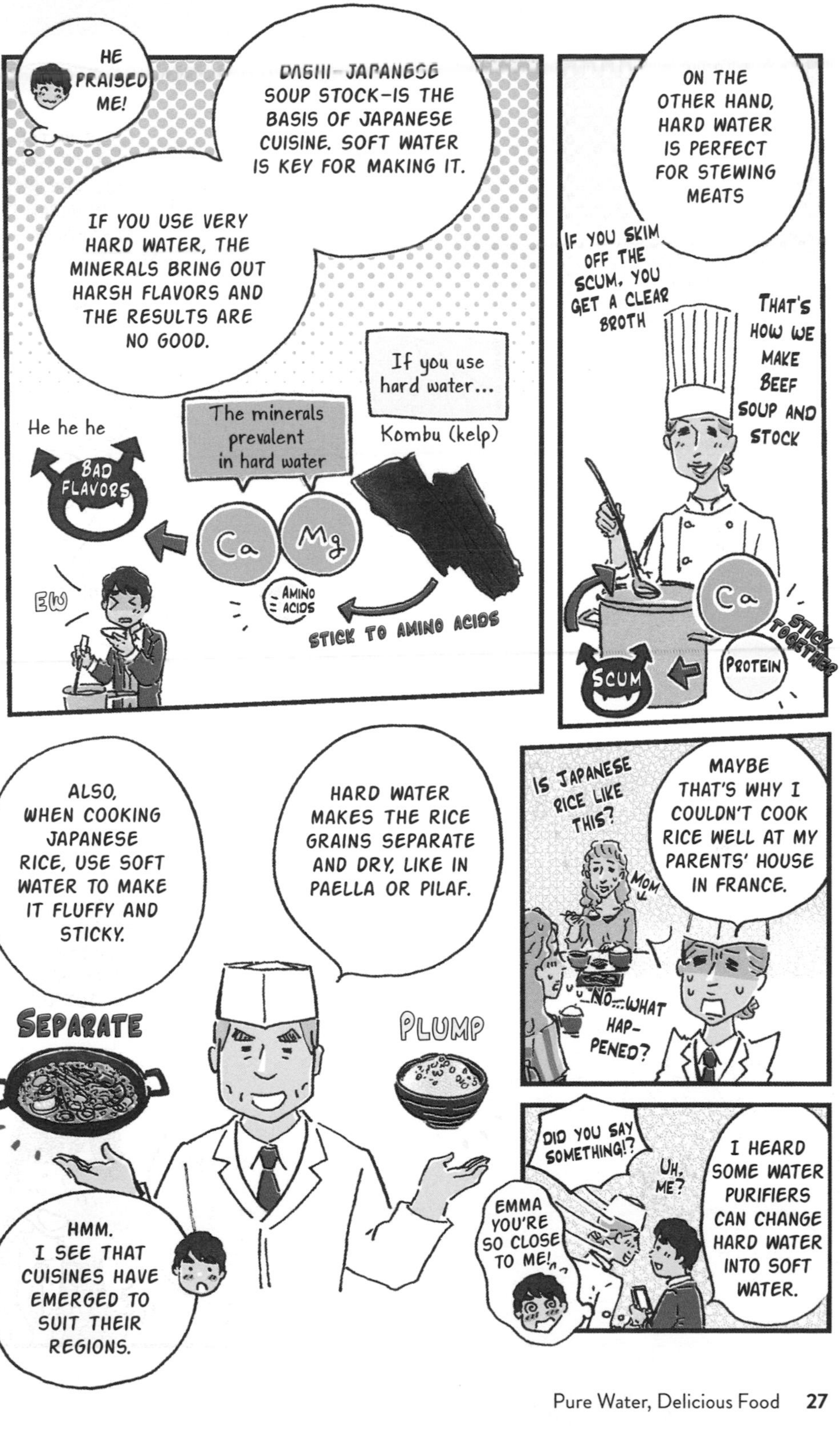
DASHI—JAPANESE SOUP STOCK—IS THE BASIS OF JAPANESE CUISINE. SOFT WATER IS KEY FOR MAKING IT.
HE PRAISED ME!
IF YOU USE VERY HARD WATER, THE MINERALS BRING OUT HARSH FLAVORS AND THE RESULTS ARE NO GOOD.
If you use hard water...
Kombu (kelp)
The minerals prevalent in hard water
Ca
Mg
AMINO ACIDS
STICK TO AMINO ACIDS
BAD FLAVORS
He he he
EW
ON THE OTHER HAND, HARD WATER IS PERFECT FOR STEWING MEATS
IF YOU SKIM OFF THE SCUM, YOU GET A CLEAR BROTH
THAT'S HOW WE MAKE BEEF SOUP AND STOCK
Ca
STICK TOGETHER
PROTEIN
SCUM
ALSO, WHEN COOKING JAPANESE RICE, USE SOFT WATER TO MAKE IT FLUFFY AND STICKY.
HARD WATER MAKES THE RICE GRAINS SEPARATE AND DRY, LIKE IN PAELLA OR PILAF.
SEPARATE
PLUMP
HMM. I SEE THAT CUISINES HAVE EMERGED TO SUIT THEIR REGIONS.
MAYBE THAT'S WHY I COULDN'T COOK RICE WELL AT MY PARENTS' HOUSE IN FRANCE.
IS JAPANESE RICE LIKE THIS?
MOM
NO... WHAT HAPPENED?
I HEARD SOME WATER PURIFIERS CAN CHANGE HARD WATER INTO SOFT WATER.
DID YOU SAY SOMETHING!?
UH, ME?
EMMA YOU'RE SO CLOSE TO ME!

How Abundant Water Impacted Japanese Cuisine

From sushi to soba, pure water matters

Japan receives an average of 68 inches (173 cm) of rain per year, about twice the world average, and enjoys high quality water thanks to the forests that cover about 66% of the country. This abundance of clean water has nurtured Japan's food culture. Dashi, the broth used to flavor so many Japanese foods, is just one of many elements in the cuisine that rely on plentiful pure water.

One distinctive characteristic of Japanese cuisine is that many foods are served raw. In Japan, people have long eaten poultry, seafood and vegetables without cooking them. Thanks to the clean, safe water, most foods could be simply washed with water and served.

The Chinese historian Chen Shou, who came to Japan during the Yayoi period (c. 300 BCE–300 CE), wrote in his book *Wei Zhi Wa-jin Dian* (The Biography of Wei Zhi Wa-jin),[1] "The land of Japan is warm, and people eat raw vegetables both in winter and summer." In China, people ate a dish of thinly sliced raw meat or fish called namasu,[2] but not raw vegetables. Chen Shou was probably surprised to see the Japanese eating raw vegetables.

---

1 The account is part of the third-century chronicle *Sanguozhi* (Records of the Three Kingdoms), and is an important historical document for understanding Japan at that time.
2 Namasu has been eaten in China since around 700 BCE and is mentioned in the *Kojiki* (Records of Ancient Matters), Japan's oldest surviving book.

Because of the slow flow of China's large rivers, the water tends to become muddy, and the country does not enjoy abundant naturally pure water like Japan. Cooked foods have always been the core of Chinese cuisine. Although Japanese cuisine is heavily influenced by Chinese cuisine, one big difference is that in China food is often cooked in hot oil, while in Japan water is more often used.

To make the Japanese dish ohitashi, vegetables are blanched and then cooled in water. To make zarusoba (cold soba noodles), soba is boiled and then soaked in cold water. Such cooking methods are less common in other countries. They arose in Japan because clean water was readily available and people could afford to "waste" it.

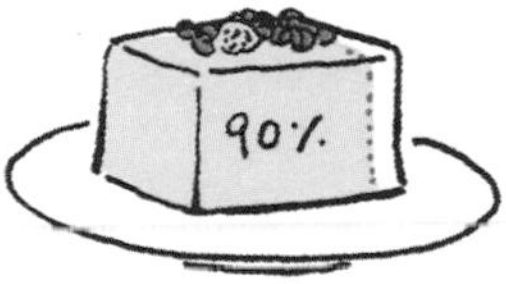
90%

Tofu—90% water

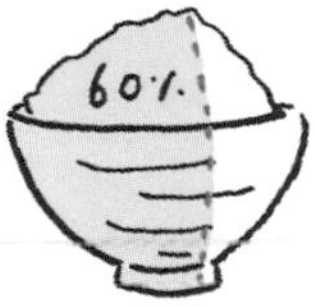
60%

Cooked Rice—60% water

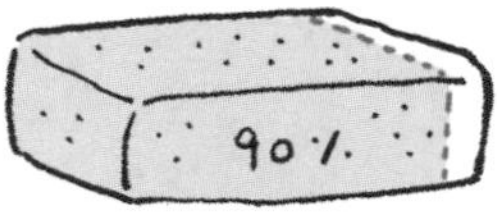
90%

Konnyaku
(devil's tongue jelly)—90% water

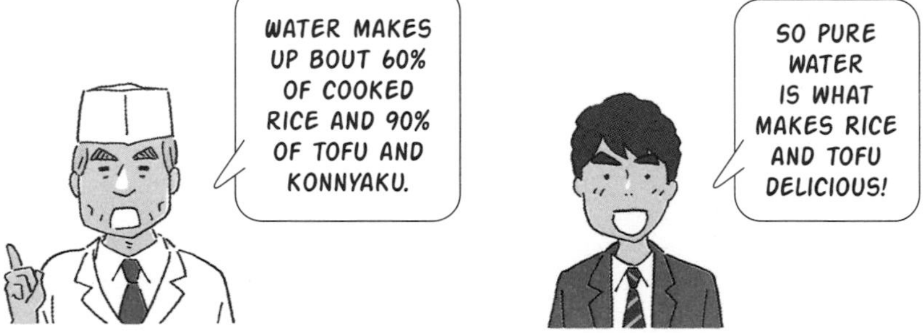
WATER MAKES UP BOUT 60% OF COOKED RICE AND 90% OF TOFU AND KONNYAKU.
SO PURE WATER IS WHAT MAKES RICE AND TOFU DELICIOUS!

The origins of dashi

The first mention of dashi in Japanese literature is found in *Tenzo kyokun* (Instructions for the Cook; see page 117), written by Dogen, a Zen Buddhist monk of the Kamakura period (1185–1333). In this book, which explains the importance of food in Buddhism, there is a story about an old monk Dogen met while he was training in China who used dried shiitake mushrooms to make soup stock. After Dogen introduced Zen Buddhist vegetarian cuisine to Japan, people began to cook with vegetarian dashi.

The oldest known descriptions of a dashi equivalent to what we make today is found in a 16th century cookbook called *Okusadono yori soden no kikigaki* (A Record of Lord Okusa's Instructions).[3] Among them are descriptions of dashi made from katsuobushi (bonito flakes) and "dashi bags" for making stock.

Let's take a closer look at the history of katsuobushi as well as kombu (kelp), both of which are essential ingredients for dashi.

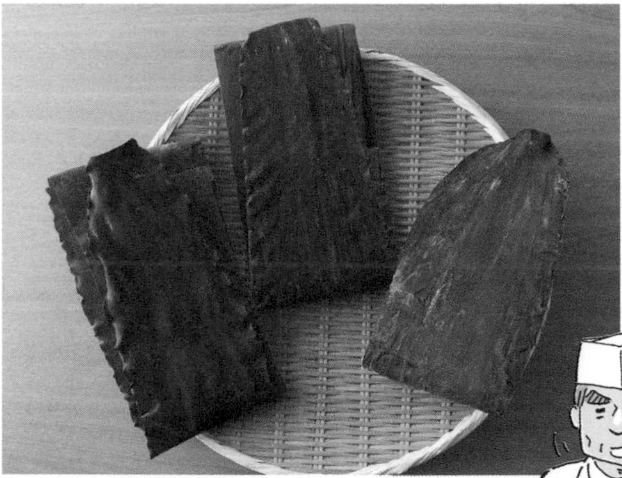

Typical seaweeds used for soup stock. From left to right: Rishiri kombu, makombu, and rausu kombu. Makombu is also called yamadashi kombu, meaning wild kelp.

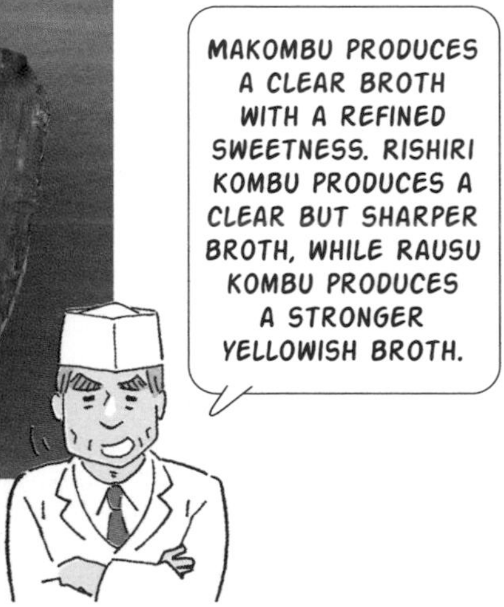
MAKOMBU PRODUCES A CLEAR BROTH WITH A REFINED SWEETNESS. RISHIRI KOMBU PRODUCES A CLEAR BUT SHARPER BROTH, WHILE RAUSU KOMBU PRODUCES A STRONGER YELLOWISH BROTH.

3 A cookbook of the Okusa school of Japanese cuisine written in the late Muromachi period (1336–1573).

Figure 1 The Kombu Road and Kitamaebune Ships

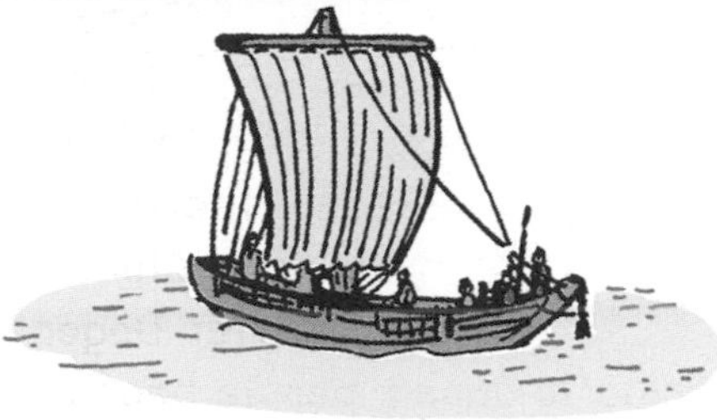

From the middle of the Edo period to the early 1900s, trading vessels called kitamaebune sailed between Ezo (northeastern Japan), the Seto Inland Sea, and Osaka. On the outbound voyage from Osaka, they carried sugar, salt, and sake from Kansai and the Seto Inland Sea, medicines from the Hokuriku region, and rice from the Tohoku region. On the return voyage, they carried herring and kombu from Ezo.

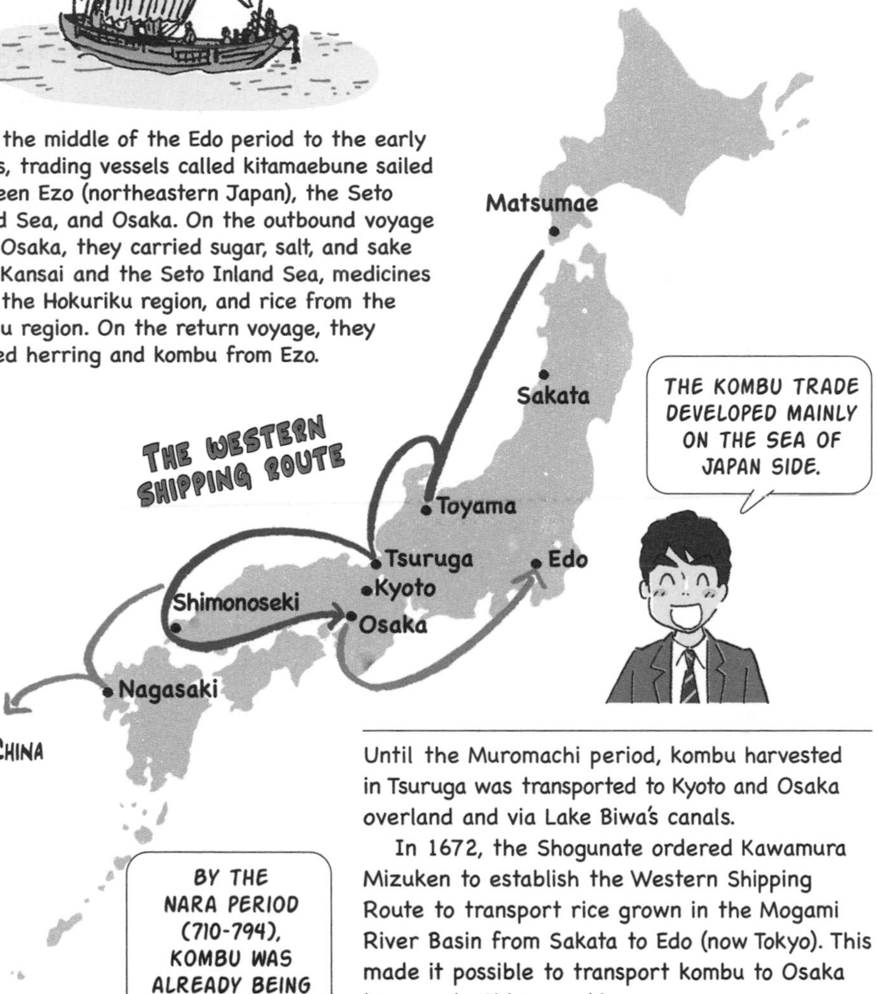
Matsumae
Sakata
THE KOMBU TRADE DEVELOPED MAINLY ON THE SEA OF JAPAN SIDE.
THE WESTERN SHIPPING ROUTE
Toyama
Tsuruga
Edo
Kyoto
Shimonoseki
Osaka
Nagasaki
TO CHINA

Until the Muromachi period, kombu harvested in Tsuruga was transported to Kyoto and Osaka overland and via Lake Biwa's canals.

In 1672, the Shogunate ordered Kawamura Mizuken to establish the Western Shipping Route to transport rice grown in the Mogami River Basin from Sakata to Edo (now Tokyo). This made it possible to transport kombu to Osaka by sea via Shimonoseki.

Around the 1700s, the Kombu Road was completed, connecting Ezo to Osaka via the Hokuriku region on the Sea of Japan side. Kombu was transported on this route on kitamaebune ships. Between Osaka and Edo, it was transported on higakikaisen and tarukaisen ships. From there it was then transported to Nagasaki and exported to China.

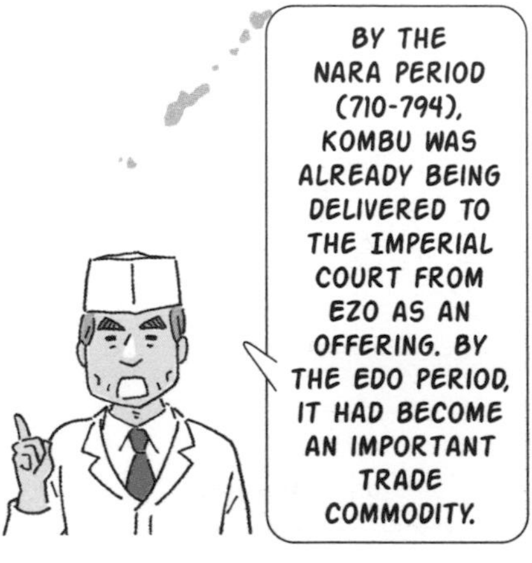
BY THE NARA PERIOD (710-794), KOMBU WAS ALREADY BEING DELIVERED TO THE IMPERIAL COURT FROM EZO AS AN OFFERING. BY THE EDO PERIOD, IT HAD BECOME AN IMPORTANT TRADE COMMODITY.

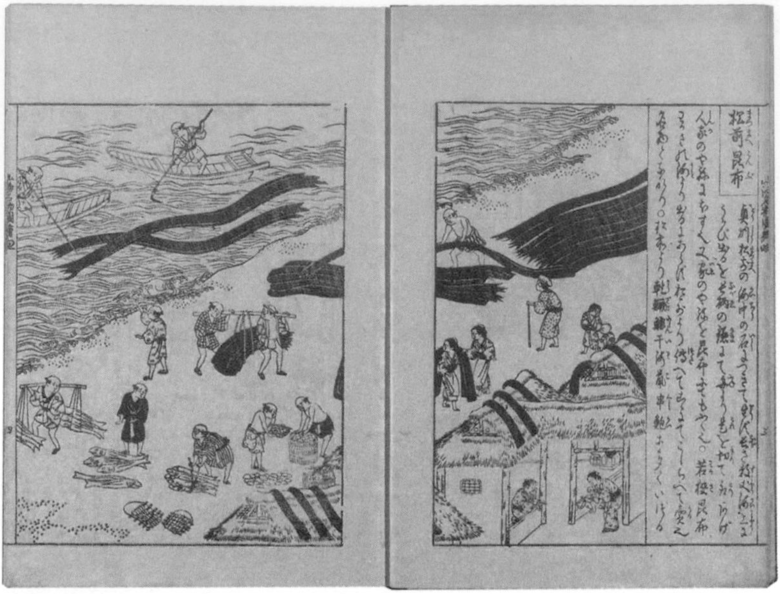
松前昆布

Nihon sankai meisan zue (Japan Mountain and Sea Products) (Digital Collections, National Diet Library)

Published in 1799, this book illustrates fishing methods and the production of specialty products in various regions of Japan. This spread depicts kombu harvested in Matsumae, Hokkaido, being dried on beaches and roofs.

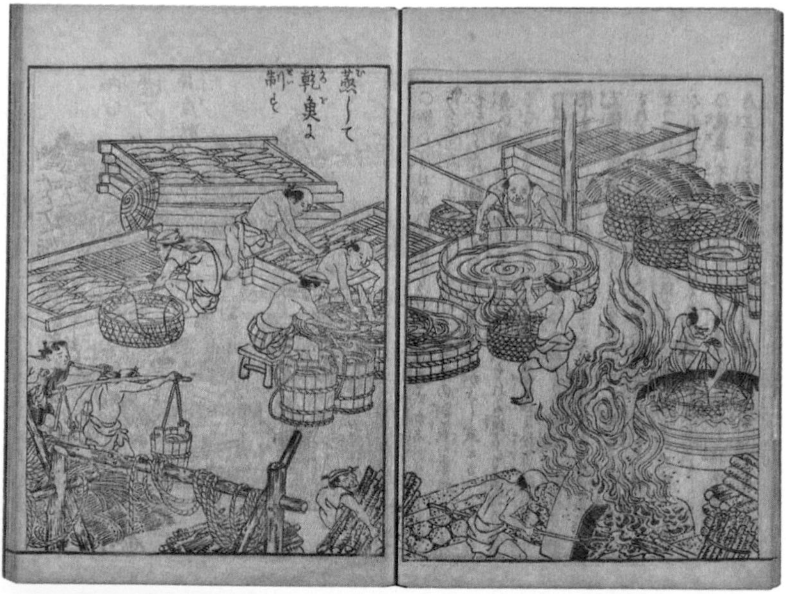
蒸して

Nihon sankai meisan zue (Japan Mountain and Sea Products) (Digital Collections, National Diet Library)

This illustration shows katsuobushi being made. Pieces of bonito are placed in baskets and boiled in huge pots (right). After cooling in water, small bones are removed (center) before the fish is lined up on racks.

The Kombu Road

The oldest written reference to kombu is in the *Shoku Nihongi* (Chronicles of Japan, Continued), compiled in the early Heian period (794–1185). A passage written in 715 describes an offering of kombu to the Imperial Court by Emishi chiefs from the far north.

Until the Muromachi period, kombu harvested in the Ezo region (today's Hokkaido) was unloaded at Tsuruga on the Sea of Japan coast and transported to Kyoto and Osaka overland and on Lake Biwa's canals. In the Edo period the Western Shipping Route was established, carrying goods including kombu to Osaka via the Seto Inland Sea and Shimonosaki (Figure 1). This transportation route is called the Kombu Road and is said to be one of the reasons kombu dashi is mainly used in the Kansai region around Osaka while katsuobushi dashi is mainly used in the Kanto region around Tokyo. The best quality kombu was transported from Ezo to Osaka and sold there, while the unsold kombu was carried on to Edo. For this reason, kombu dashi was not as well developed in Kanto as in Kansai.

Another reason kombu was mainly used in Kansai and katsuobushi in Kanto is the difference in water quality between the two regions. The water in Kansai is soft and suitable for making kombu dashi, while the water in Kanto is slightly harder due to the Kanto Loam layer of volcanic ash, which makes it more difficult for the umami components of kombu to dissolve out. As a result, strongly flavored katsuobushi stock became the mainstay in Kanto.

The history of katsuobushi

In the *Ryonoshuge*, a commentary on the Yoro Code enacted in 757, "katauo" and "nikatauo"—considered to be predecessors to katsuobushi—are listed among the taxes to be paid on products from various regions. Katauo is dried bonito and nikatauo is dried bonito that has been boiled before drying. Katsuo no irori, an extract made by boiling down the broth of nikatauo, is also listed.

The 1489 cookbook *Shijo-ryu hochogaki* (The Shijo School Kitchen Knife Book) uses the words "hana katsuo," meaning finely shaved katsuobushi, which indicates that hard katsuobushi was already being shaved into thin strips by the late Muromachi period.

In the mid-Edo period, a major technological innovation in the katsuobushi manufacturing process took place. Until then, boiled bonito was dried in the sun and using fire, but Jintaro Kadoya, a fisherman from Inanoura, Kishu (current day Inan, Wakayama Prefecture) developed the smoked-dry method, in which bonito is smoked to remove the moisture. The result was a very popular product called Kumano-bushi, similar to today's arabushi type of katsuobushi. Jintaro taught this process to artisans in the Tosa domain, and the quality of katsuobushi from Tosa improved dramatically.

Around 1700, one of Jintaro's children developed a method of mold inoculation. Traditional katsuobushi from Tosa was prone to mold

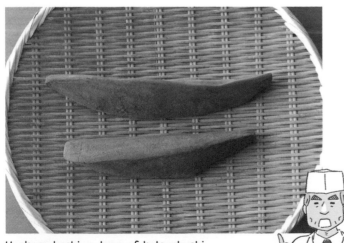

KATSUOBUSHI FROM THE DORSAL SIDE IS LESS FATTY AND HAS A REFINED TASTE. KATSUOBUSHI FROM THE BELLY SIDE HAS MORE FAT, GIVING IT A RICHER FLAVOR.

Honkare-bushi, a type of katsuobushi, inoculated with mold. Above is the obushi, made from dorsal flesh. Below is the mebushi, from the belly side.

growth, so he prevented the growth of malignant mold by applying benign mold to the surface of the katsuobushi—in other words, controlling mold with mold. Katsuobushi made in this way was called "improved Tosa-bushi" and became a major product in Osaka, a katsuobushi distribution center.

In those days, mold sometimes grew on arabushi (smoked katsuobushi) during transport from Osaka to Edo. However, as this mold was repeatedly removed, people noticed that the flavor improved, and the mold application process advanced. In the early Meiji period (1868–1912), a type of katsuobushi with three mold applications was developed in the Izu region. Between 1907 and 1917, honkare-bushi with four to six mold applications was created.

Incidentally, the 1668 cookbook *Ryouri anbaishu* (Culinary Seasoning) describes a dashi combining kombu and katsuobushi, indicating that this type of stock was already in use at that time.

Figure 2 **How Katsuobushi is Made**

Fillet the raw fish
The bonito is filleted
Put into baskets
The fillets are arranged neatly in baskets for simmering
Simmer
Cooked in hot water at 170°F -208°F (75–98°C) for 60–90 minutes
De-bone
The skins, scales and bones are removed
Smoke and dry
The fish is smoked repeatedly to dry
Ara-bushi
Shape
The fish is dried for half a day and cut to shape
Hadaka-bushi
Apply mold
Mold is applied to the surface and the fish is aged
Hongare-bushi
AS THE MOLD GROWS, IT ABSORBS MOISTURE AND DRIES OUT THE FISH. THE MOLD BREAKS DOWN THE FAT AND GIVES THE FISH ITS AROMA.

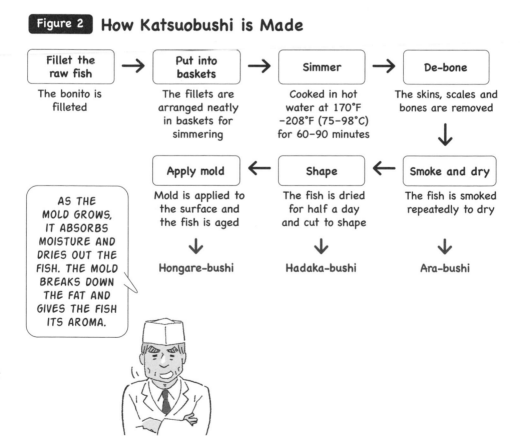

Dashi versus other broths

Table 1 shows typical fond and bouillon, which correspond to dashi in French cuisine, and the typical tang stocks in Chinese cuisine. In French and Chinese cuisine, stock is made by simmering ingredients for hours to bring out the best in them.

Japanese dashi, on the other hand, uses dried ingredients such as kelp and katsuobushi, extracting their essence in a very short time. The reason the flavors can be extracted so quickly is that much time is put into maturing the dry ingredients, giving them complex components not present in raw materials. Another feature of dashi is that it contains no fat or oil.

One unique way dashi is used is to bring out the flavor of vegetables and other foods by transferring or infusing the dashi flavor into them.

Table 1 Typical French and Chinese Soup Stocks

French cuisine		
Fond The stock used to make sauce	White fond	Fond de volaille (chicken stock) Fond de poisson (fish stock), etc.
	Brown fond	Fond de veau (veal meat, bones and savory vegetables are grilled, browned and braised) Fond de gibier (game is grilled and braised)

Bouillon
The broths that form the base of soups such as consommé and potage. Made by simmering beef, chicken, vegetables, etc.

Chinese cuisine	
Hong tang Animal stock	Chii tang (made from chicken meat or bones) Mao tang (made by adding pork or pork bones to chicken stock) Ching tang (Chicken stock with minced meat added and clarified) Bai tang (Mao tang ingredients with pork fat, pig's feet, and chicken legs added and simmered to produce a creamy white stock) etc.
Suu tang Vegetable stock	Shan ru tang (made with dried shiitake mushrooms) Tou yaa tang (made with bean sprouts) etc.

The Big Picture

Creating Flavor Takes Time

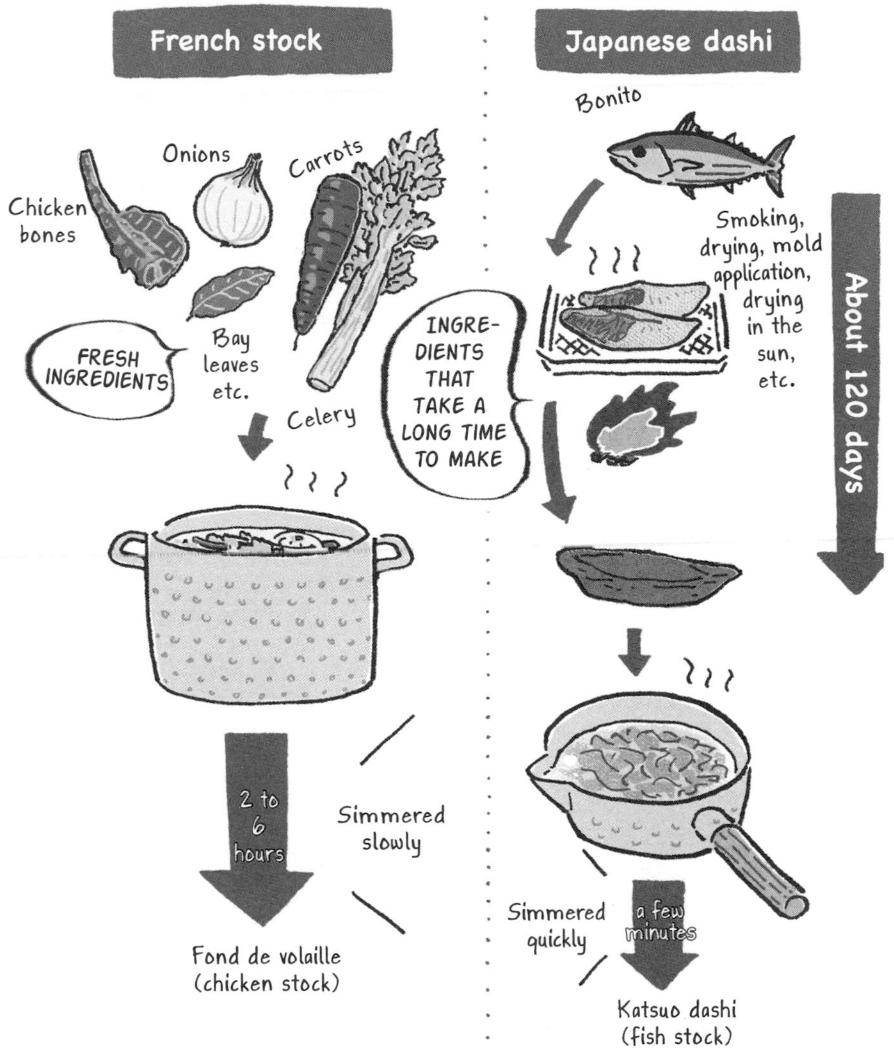
French stock
Chicken bones
Onions
Carrots
Bay leaves etc.
Celery
FRESH INGREDIENTS
2 to 6 hours
Simmered slowly
Fond de volaille (chicken stock)
Japanese dashi
Bonito
Smoking, drying, mold application, drying in the sun, etc.
About 120 days
INGREDIENTS THAT TAKE A LONG TIME TO MAKE
Simmered quickly
a few minutes
Katsuo dashi (fish stock)

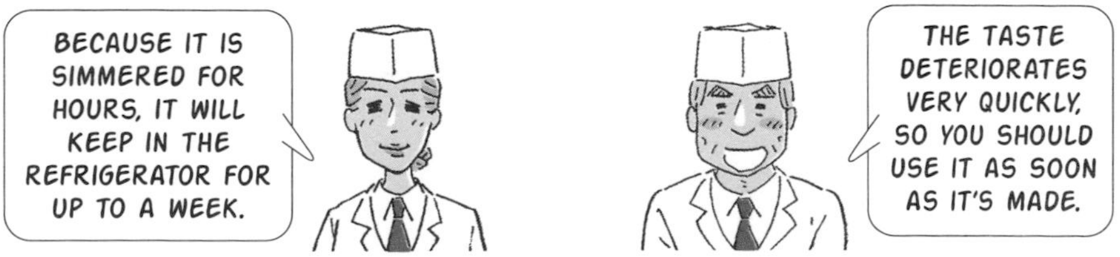
BECAUSE IT IS SIMMERED FOR HOURS, IT WILL KEEP IN THE REFRIGERATOR FOR UP TO A WEEK.
THE TASTE DETERIORATES VERY QUICKLY, SO YOU SHOULD USE IT AS SOON AS IT'S MADE.

Japan's Wooden Tableware

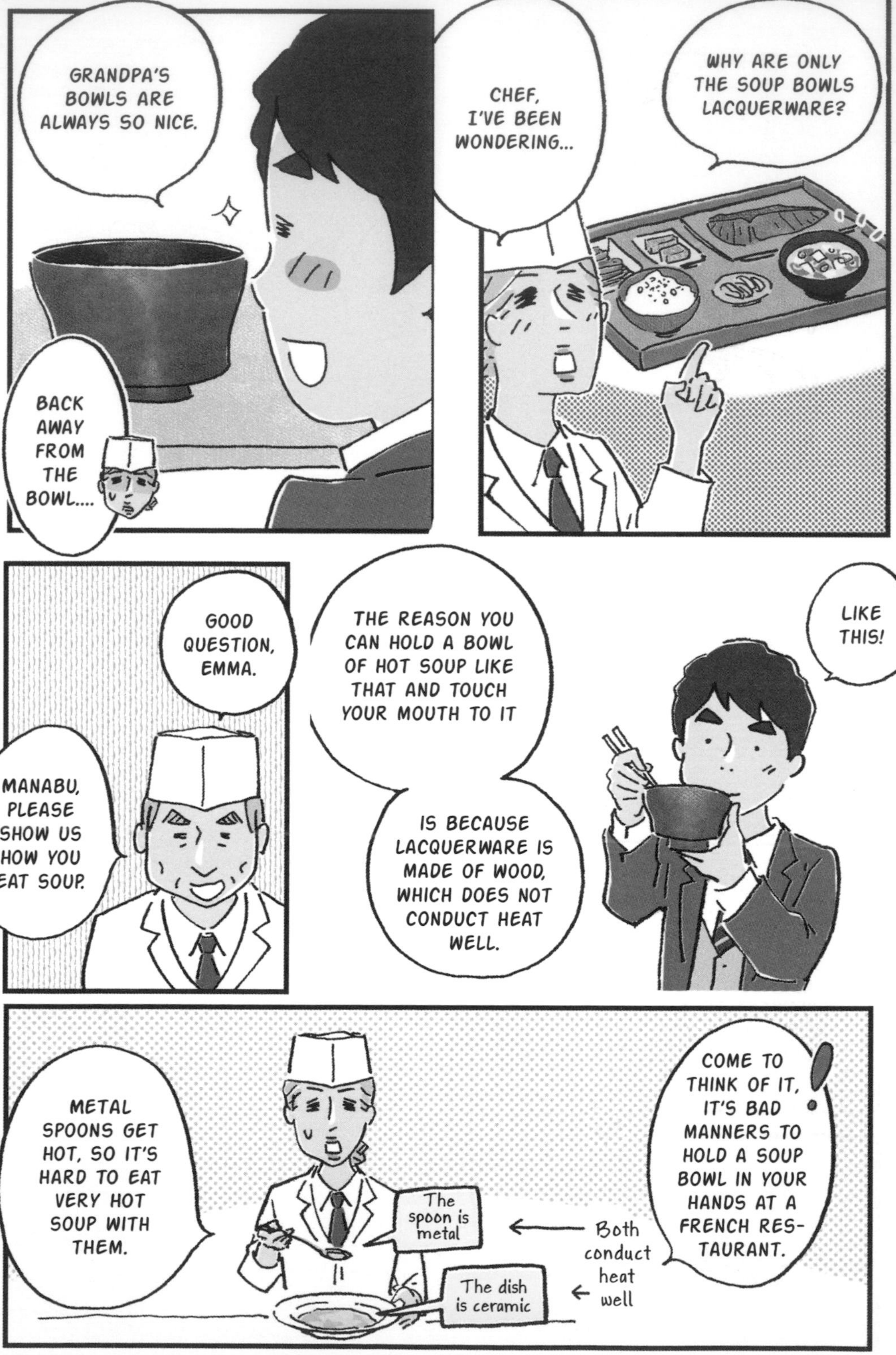
GRANDPA'S BOWLS ARE ALWAYS SO NICE.
BACK AWAY FROM THE BOWL....
CHEF, I'VE BEEN WONDERING...
WHY ARE ONLY THE SOUP BOWLS LACQUERWARE?
GOOD QUESTION, EMMA.
MANABU, PLEASE SHOW US HOW YOU EAT SOUP.
LIKE THIS!
THE REASON YOU CAN HOLD A BOWL OF HOT SOUP LIKE THAT AND TOUCH YOUR MOUTH TO IT
IS BECAUSE LACQUERWARE IS MADE OF WOOD, WHICH DOES NOT CONDUCT HEAT WELL.
COME TO THINK OF IT, IT'S BAD MANNERS TO HOLD A SOUP BOWL IN YOUR HANDS AT A FRENCH RES-TAURANT.
METAL SPOONS GET HOT, SO IT'S HARD TO EAT VERY HOT SOUP WITH THEM.
The spoon is metal
The dish is ceramic
Both conduct heat well

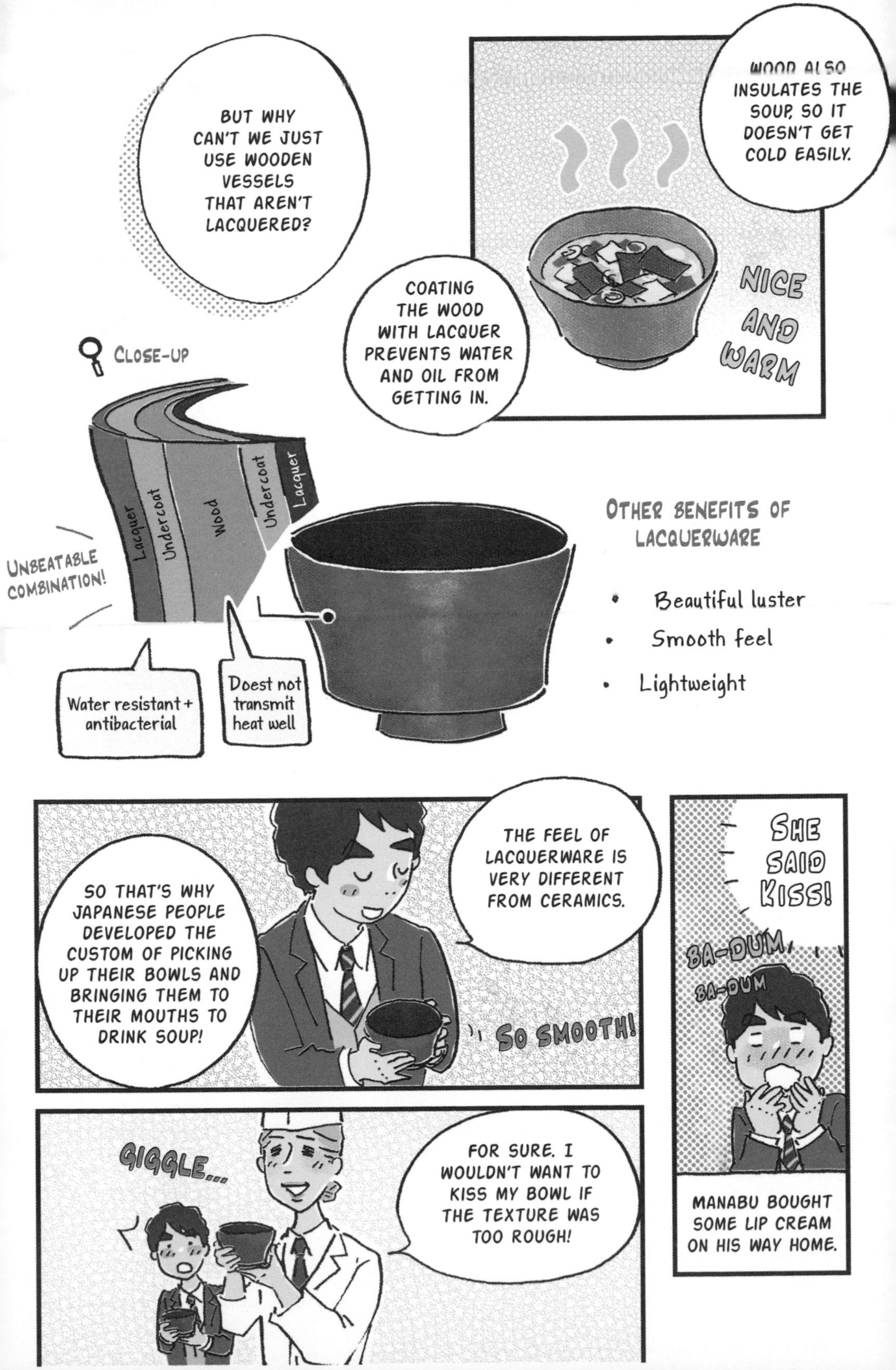

BUT WHY CAN'T WE JUST USE WOODEN VESSELS THAT AREN'T LACQUERED?
COATING THE WOOD WITH LACQUER PREVENTS WATER AND OIL FROM GETTING IN.
WOOD ALSO INSULATES THE SOUP, SO IT DOESN'T GET COLD EASILY.
NICE AND WARM
CLOSE-UP
Lacquer
Undercoat
Wood
Undercoat
Lacquer
UNBEATABLE COMBINATION!
Water resistant + antibacterial
Doest not transmit heat well
OTHER BENEFITS OF LACQUERWARE
• Beautiful luster
• Smooth feel
• Lightweight
SO THAT'S WHY JAPANESE PEOPLE DEVELOPED THE CUSTOM OF PICKING UP THEIR BOWLS AND BRINGING THEM TO THEIR MOUTHS TO DRINK SOUP!
THE FEEL OF LACQUERWARE IS VERY DIFFERENT FROM CERAMICS.
SO SMOOTH!
GIGGLE...
FOR SURE. I WOULDN'T WANT TO KISS MY BOWL IF THE TEXTURE WAS TOO ROUGH!
SHE SAID KISS!
BA-DUM
BA-DUM
MANABU BOUGHT SOME LIP CREAM ON HIS WAY HOME.

The Origins of Lacquerware

Who—or what—discovered lacquer?

The reason Japanese tableware did not develop from earthenware to pottery to porcelain is that most of the country is forested, making wood and lacquerware readily available. This is probably one explanation for the uniquely Japanese way of eating, which is to bring the bowl to the mouth and eat with the mouth touching the bowl.

The natural coating that makes Japanese wooden bowls comfortable to eat from is called *urushi*, meaning lacquer. Urushi lacquer is a natural coating refined from the sap of the urushi, or lacquer, tree.[1] Surprisingly, even with modern science and technology, no synthetic paint has surpassed urushi lacquer. Let's start by tracing the history of lacquerware. Pages 46 and 47 show the process by which it is made, from harvesting sap to making vessels.

Who first discovered urushi lacquer? One theory says it was wasps. It has been observed that paper wasps living near lacquer trees harden the base of their nests with the tree's sap. Perhaps our ancestors saw this and initially began using urushi lacquer as an adhesive.

---

1 *Toxicodendron vernicifluum.* In this book we call the lacquer produced from this tree urushi lacquer, and the tree itself the lacquer tree.

Scientific dating has shown that a lacquer burial accessory excavated from the Kakinoshima B site in the city of Hakodate, Hokkaido, is approximately 9,000 years old, confirming that Japanese people have been using urushi lacquer since the early Jomon period.

The people's dishware

The Asuka (552–645) and Nara (710–794) periods saw the arrival of Buddhism in Japan, and lacquer techniques advanced with the production of Buddhist statues and ritual utensils. As for tableware of the Nara period, some black lacquer bowls and plates survive in Shosoin Repository, the treasury of Todaiji Temple in Nara, but it is not known whether lacquerware was widely used.

During much of the Heian period (794–1185) urushi lacquerware was a luxury item used by the nobility. By the 12th century, however, it had spread to the general population.

URUSHI LACQUER IS ALSO USED AS AN ADHESIVE IN KINTSUGI.

WASPS USE URUSHI LACQUER TO ATTACH THE BASE OF THEIR HIVE TO A TREE BRANCH!

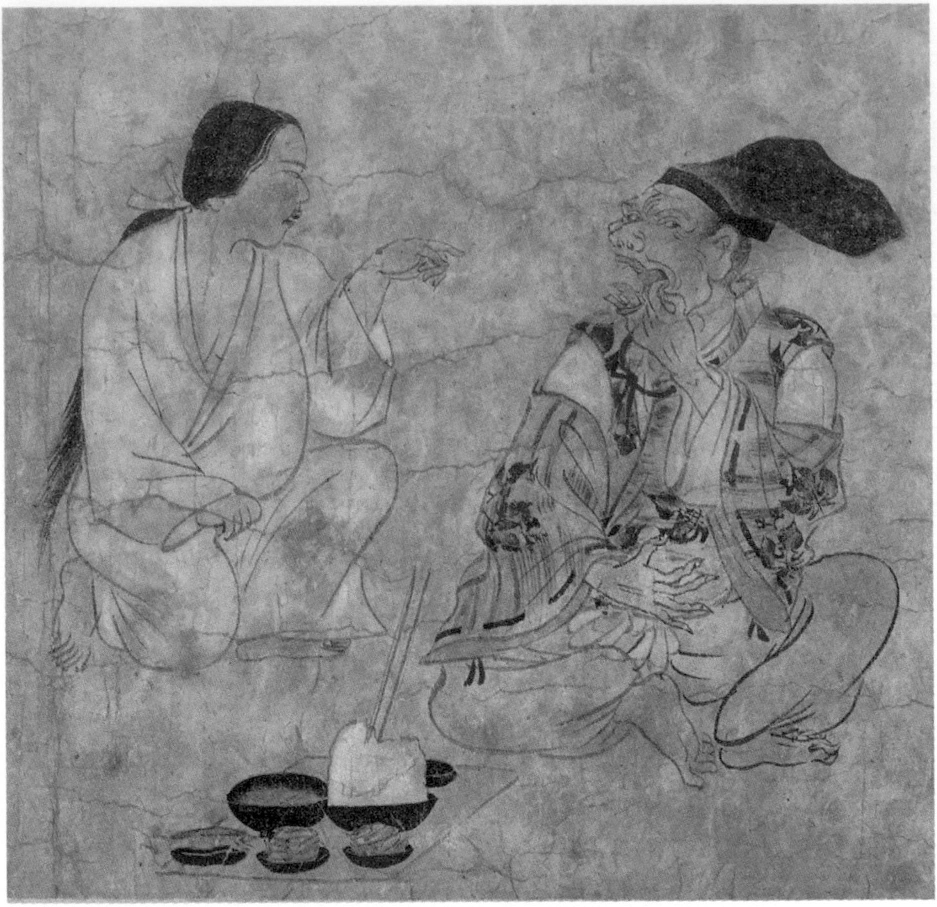

Yamai no soshi/Shiso noro no otoko (The Man with Pyorrhea from Diseases and Deformities) (Kyoto National Museum collection)

This picture scroll from the 12th century depicts various illness. The lower left of this image shows a rice bowl, soup bowl, and several small dishes on a wooden tray. The rice and soup bowls appear to be black lacquer with a vermilion pattern.

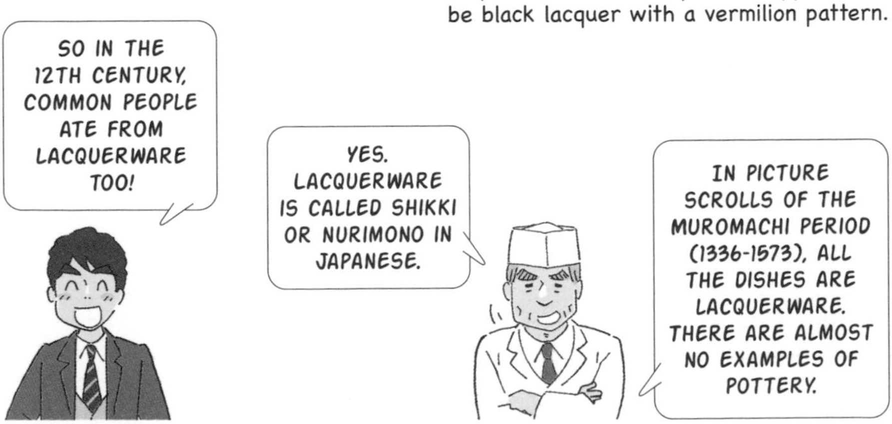
SO IN THE 12TH CENTURY, COMMON PEOPLE ATE FROM LACQUERWARE TOO!
YES. LACQUERWARE IS CALLED SHIKKI OR NURIMONO IN JAPANESE.
IN PICTURE SCROLLS OF THE MUROMACHI PERIOD (1336-1573), ALL THE DISHES ARE LACQUERWARE. THERE ARE ALMOST NO EXAMPLES OF POTTERY.

In a picture depicting a meal from the 12th century scroll *Yamai no soshi* (Diseases and Deformities) (see page 42), a black lacquered rice bowl, soup bowl and several small plates sit on an oshiki wooden tray.[2] Recently excavated ruins from the Kamakura period (1185–1333) have yielded a large number of lacquered bowls and small plates that were presumably used by low-ranking samurai.

During the Edo period (1603–1867), the urushi lacquerware industry was established with the protection and encouragement of each han or region. In addition to traditional crafts such as lacquered weapons, production of lacquerware for daily use flourished. Each clan was encouraged to plant lacquer trees, and a system was established for the integrated production of lacquerware, from collecting sap to making the base, applying the lacquer, and decorating it. Most of today's lacquerware production areas were established during the Edo period.

From the late Heian Period to the late Edo Period, urushi lacquerware was the main type of tableware, at least for rice and soup bowls. When porcelain became popular in the mid-Edo period, it was first used to make plates and bowls for foods other than rice and soup. When porcelain began to be mass-produced in the Meiji period (1868–1912), porcelain rice bowls also became widespread. However, soup bowls continued to be made of urushi lacquerware. This is because lacquerware allowed diners to bring bowls of hot soup to their mouth and place their lips against the rim.

A global love affair with "japan"

Urushi lacquerware was once known as "japan," and was much admired in Europe. Jesuit missionaries and Spanish and Portuguese merchants who came to Japan in the late 16th and early 17th centuries were fascinated by the beauty of maki-e[3] and ordered various church utensils, Western-style chests and decorative boxes to be made for sale in Europe. The crafts made in this way for export are called Nanban lacquerware.

---

2 An oshiki is a thin square tray with a rim around the edge.
3 Makie is a method of decorating urushi lacquerware. A picture or design is drawn on the lacquered surface with a brush dipped in lacquer, and gold, silver, or colored powder is sprinkled on the surface before the lacquer dries. When the powder is brushed away, some remain stuck to the lacquer and the picture or design emerges.

Japan's shrinking lacquerware industry

The context surrounding lacquer production changed drastically in the Meiji Era. Lacquer-tree groves were no longer protected by domains, so they were soon replaced by mulberry and tea plantations, sending the production of urushi lacquer plunging. The industry that had established itself under the self-sufficient economy of the Edo period was no longer viable.

In 1907, a Belgian-American named Leo Hendrik Baekeland invented Bakelite,[4] the world's first synthetic plastic, and succeeded in its industrialization. In Japan, production of Bakelite began in 1911, and it was used as a substitute for lacquerware.

After World War II, as the chemical industry developed, synthetic lacquerware was mass-produced using synthetic resins[5] for the base and surface coatings. In 1949, the Industrial Standardization Law (now the Industrial Standardization Act, commonly known as the JIS Law) allowed products made of synthetic resin coating on a synthetic resin base to be classified as lacquerware. As a result,

JET BLACK WAS A COVETED COLOR IN EUROPE DURING THE MIDDLE AGES, WHEN BLACK PAINT WAS NOT AVAILABLE. MARIE ANTOINETTE WAS A COLLECTOR OF LACQUERWARE.

Changing terminology

In Europe and the U.S., lacquerware was called "japan" in the past, but the term is not used today. You can use the term "Japanese lacquer" or "Japanese urushi lacquer" to distinguish it from lacquer made in other parts of the world.

---

4 **Bakelite** is the registered trademark name for a phenolic resin, a thermosetting resin that becomes hard when heated and will not return to its original state. Most plastics in circulation today are thermoplastic resins that soften when heated.

5 **Synthetic resins** are resins that are mass-produced artificially from petroleum oil, as opposed to natural resins such as pine needles and urushi lacquer. Also called plastic.

synthetic lacquerware and traditional urushi lacquerware were mixed together on the market, making it difficult for consumers to tell the difference.

In 1970, concern arose when formalin was detected in synthetic lacquerware made with urea resin,[6] and in 1972 the Household Goods Quality Labeling Law was revised to require producers to label the type of base material and coating they used. Under the current law, only items whose surface coating is exclusively natural urushi lacquer can be labeled as shikki or urushi lacquerware.

Currently, only 3% of the natural lacquer used in Japan is produced domestically,[7] with most of the balance produced in China. In 2015, the Agency for Cultural Affairs issued a notice requiring the restoration of national treasures and important cultural properties to use domestic lacquer whenever possible. The need to increase urushi lacquer production has led to efforts to revive the urushi lacquer industry in Iwate and other prefectures.

Urushi Lacquer and Chemistry

Urushi lacquer is alive

The main components of lacquer are urushiol, a resinous oil, water, gum, and enzymes (laccase). While synthetic resin paints are at their best when first applied, natural lacquer becomes more lustrous with use. This is because the enzymes in the lacquer film remain live, hardening the lacquer even after the item is fully made.

Urushi lacquer is sustainable

While synthetic resin paints require large amounts of heat during the drying process and consume petroleum resources, urushi lacquer is environmentally friendly.

Colorful urushi lacquer

The discovery of a new metal called titanium in the 20th century led to the development of synthetic pigments made from titanium oxide powder that produce white, blue, pink, and other colors that were difficult to obtain in the past.

Urushi lacquer for glass

Urushi lacquer has been applied to all kinds of substrates, including bamboo, paper, cloth, ceramics and metal, but it has been difficult to apply to glass. Recently, however, the development of ultra-fine nano-lacquer has made this possible.

---

6 Urea resin is a thermosetting resin produced by the reaction of urea and formalin.
7 Forestry and Forest Products Agency data for the year 2016 (press release, 2017).

From collecting sap to making a bowl

Urushi lacquer is made from the sap of the lacquer tree. This section introduces the main steps in the process of producing lacquerware.

On page 47, for the sake of clarity, we say that the urushi lacquer "dries," but in reality, the urushi lacquer hardens rather than dries. To be more precise, the enzyme laccase in urushi lacquer takes in oxygen from the moisture in the air, causing a chemical reaction that hardens the resin (urushiol) in the lacquer. A humid environment of between 70°F and 85°F (20–30°C) and 70% to 85% humidity is required for the lacquer to harden. Strange, isn't it? Once hardened, lacquer is extremely tough, resistant to acids, alkalis, and chemicals, and has excellent water resistance and antiseptic properties.

Lacquer tree. Photo shows the tree after lacquer has been harvested. The harvest takes place 15 years after planting the saplings.

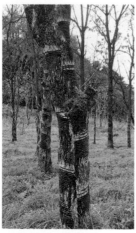

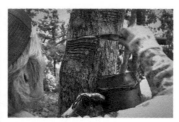

The lacquer gathering process involves scratching the trunks and collecting the oozing liquid, which is done between June and October. Afterwards the trees are cut down.

The urushi lacquer is then refined.

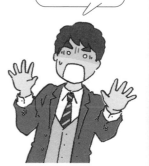

LESS THAN A CUP (200ML) OF LACQUER CAN BE OBTAINED PER TREE!

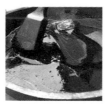

The main steps in making lacquerware (honkataji method)

Making the Wood Base

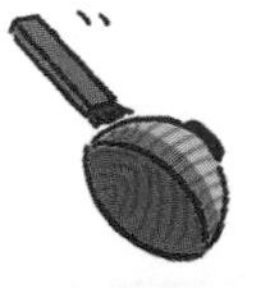

Hardening the wood

Harden and polish the wood

Raw lacquer is rubbed over the entire wooden surface to harden it. After drying the lacquer in a device that maintains a temperature of 70°F to 85°F (20–30°C) and a humidity of 70% to 85%, the surface is polished with sandpaper.

Reinforcement, smoothing, and polishing

The bowl is reinforced by applying a cloth soaked in raw lacquer to the edges and bottom of the bowl. The cloth is then covered with a mixture of baked diatomaceous earth and raw lacquer to smooth any bumps. After drying, the object is polished with a whetstone.

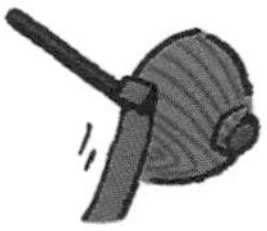

Reinforcing

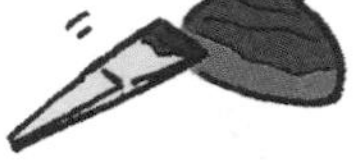

Reinforcing

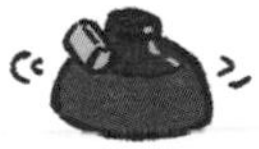

Polishing

Basecoat and polishing

A mixture of powdered earth and raw lacquer is applied as a basecoat, dried, and then polished with a whetstone. This is repeated about three times. Finer particles of powdered earth are used in each successive step.

Grit application and wet polishing

"Rust lacquer," a mixture of grit (baked clay powder) and raw lacquer, is applied. After drying, the object is polished with a whetstone while soaking in water to smooth the surface.

Lacquering

Undercoat

The object is coated with refined black lacquer, dried, and gently wet-polished using charcoal.

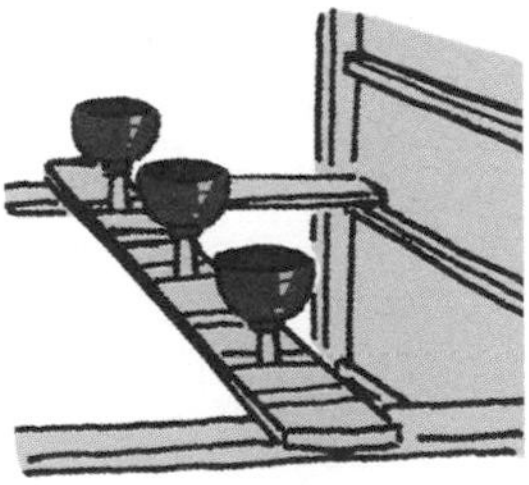

The drying device

Middle coat

Another coat of refined black lacquer is applied over the undercoat, dried, and wet-polished using charcoal.

Top coat

The finishing lacquer (clear, black, vermilion, etc.) is filtered repeatedly through washi (Japanese paper). The finishing lacquer is applied and dried. Plain lacquerware is complete at this stage.

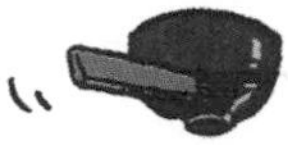

Applying the top coat

Decoration

Decorations such as maki-e or gold inlay are applied.

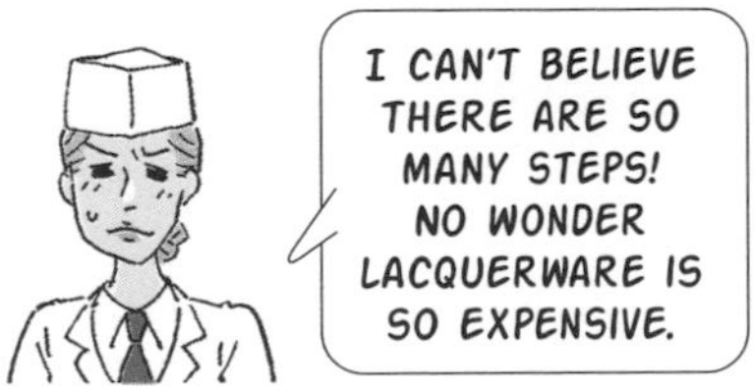
I CAN'T BELIEVE THERE ARE SO MANY STEPS! NO WONDER LACQUERWARE IS SO EXPENSIVE.

How chopsticks are used in China, Korea and Japan

Along with soup bowls, the other type of lacquered tableware used daily in Japan is chopsticks. Let's compare the use of chopsticks and other eating utensils in China, Korea and Japan.

In China, people typically sit in chairs around a dining table and use chopsticks to take food from a plate on the table. The basic rule is to eat with chopsticks or a porcelain spoon, leaving the plate on the table. Korea, like Japan, has a long history of sitting on the floor and eating at a table, but table manners are quite different. It is considered impolite to lift the bowl or put your mouth on it, and food is eaten with a spoon or chopsticks, leaving the bowl on the table.

Of all the countries where people eat with chopsticks, Japan is the only one where no other type of utensil is used. The custom of having your own rice bowl, soup bowl and chopsticks that you use at every meal is also unique to Japan and Korea.

A comparison of chopstick use

China

Korea

Chopsticks are made of ivory, wood, or bamboo, have a cylindrical tip, and are not thin. They are long (about 11 in/ 27 cm) so it is easy to take food from a platter. There are no strict rules about where to place the utensils.

Chopsticks are usually made of metal, are thin, and are about 8 inches (20 cm) long. The spoon is the main utensil, with the chopsticks used only to pick up foods other than rice. Chopsticks and spoons are placed side by side, with the spoon closer to the diner because it is used more frequently.

Japan

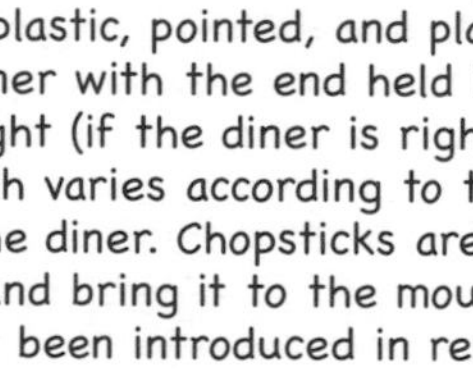

The chopsticks are made of lacquerware, wood or plastic, pointed, and placed in front of the diner with the end held in the hand to the right (if the diner is right handed). The length varies according to the age and size of the diner. Chopsticks are used to pick up food and bring it to the mouth. Spoons have only been introduced in recent decades.

ONLY IN JAPAN DO CHILDREN, MEN AND WOMEN HAVE CHOPSTICKS OF DIFFERENT LENGTHS.

The Big Picture

How the World Eats

Major regions: Europe, South and North America, Russia, etc.
Major religion: Christianity
Major foods: bread, meat

Major regions: Southeast Asia, South Asia, West Asia, Africa, Oceania, etc.
Major religions: Hinduism, Islam
Major foods: indica rice, starchy root vegetables, fruits, etc.

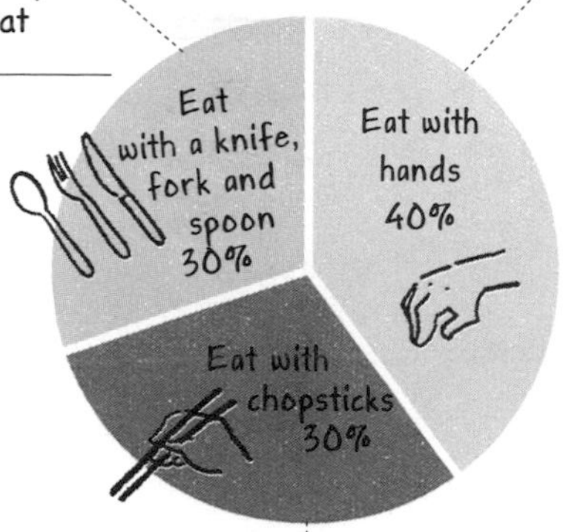
Eat with a knife, fork and spoon 30%
Eat with hands 40%
Eat with chopsticks 30%

Main regions: Japan, China, Korea, Taiwan, Vietnam, etc.
Main religions: Buddhism, Confucianism
Main foods: japonica rice, noodles

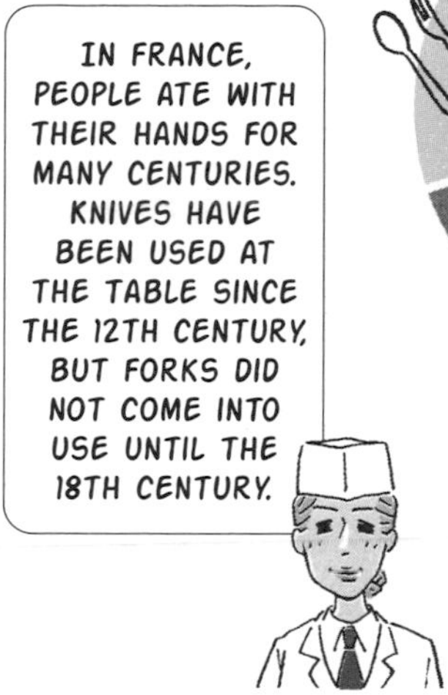
IN FRANCE, PEOPLE ATE WITH THEIR HANDS FOR MANY CENTURIES. KNIVES HAVE BEEN USED AT THE TABLE SINCE THE 12TH CENTURY, BUT FORKS DID NOT COME INTO USE UNTIL THE 18TH CENTURY.

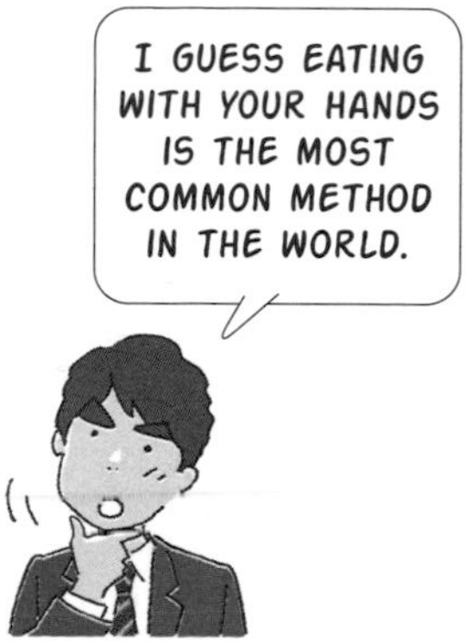
I GUESS EATING WITH YOUR HANDS IS THE MOST COMMON METHOD IN THE WORLD.

Eating with your hands

In Hinduism and Islam, using utensils to eat is considered unclean; eating with your hands is seen as the cleanest way to eat. In Hinduism, the left hand is considered unclean. The right hand is used to bring food to the mouth while the left hand is used for serving.

However, as smartphones rapidly gain popularity in India, more and more people are eating with spoons to avoid getting food on their phones.

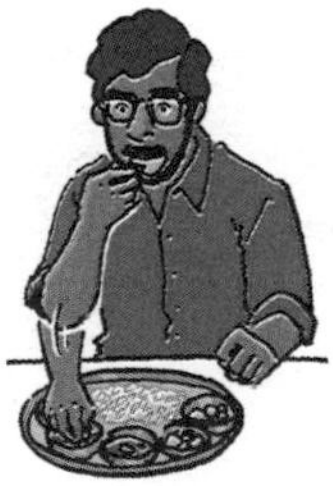

People used to eat using three fingers of their right hand.

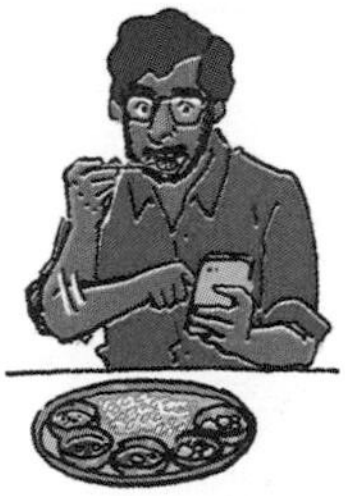

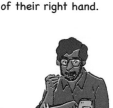

Now they've started eating with spoons to avoid getting their smartphones dirty.

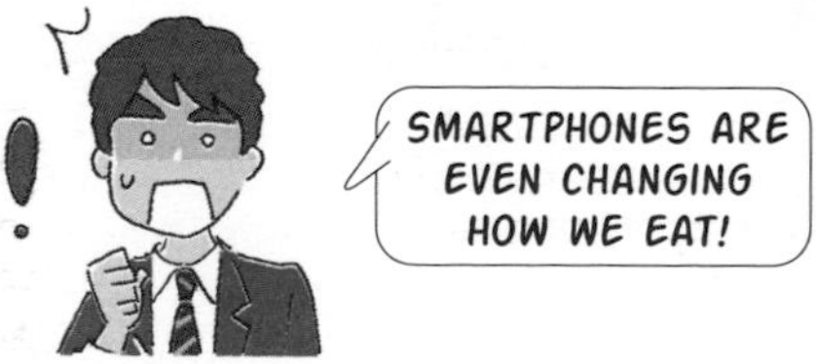
SMARTPHONES ARE EVEN CHANGING HOW WE EAT!

Seafood on All Sides

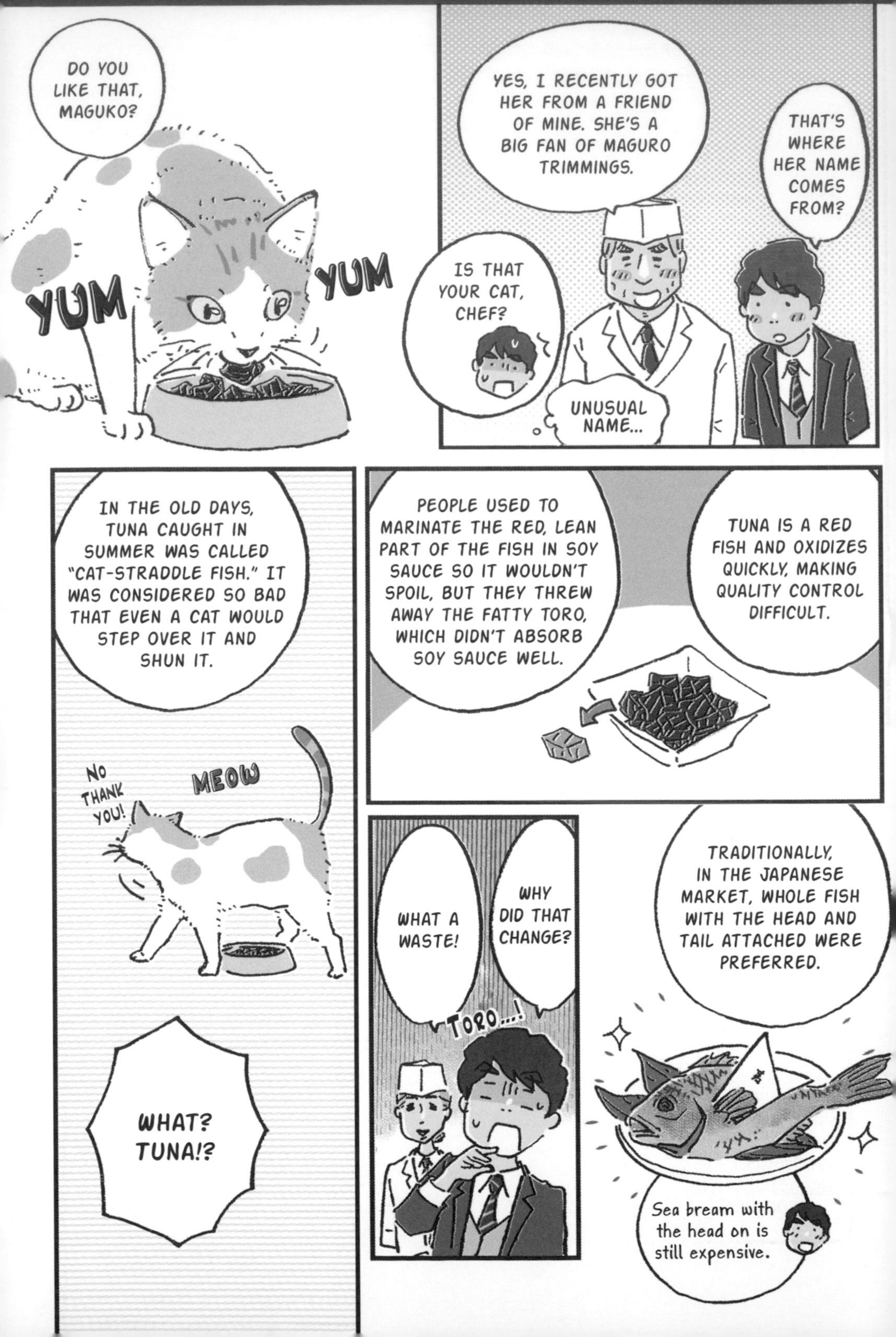

DO YOU LIKE THAT, MAGUKO?
YUM
YUM
IS THAT YOUR CAT, CHEF?
YES, I RECENTLY GOT HER FROM A FRIEND OF MINE. SHE'S A BIG FAN OF MAGURO TRIMMINGS.
THAT'S WHERE HER NAME COMES FROM?
UNUSUAL NAME...
IN THE OLD DAYS, TUNA CAUGHT IN SUMMER WAS CALLED "CAT-STRADDLE FISH." IT WAS CONSIDERED SO BAD THAT EVEN A CAT WOULD STEP OVER IT AND SHUN IT.
NO THANK YOU!
MEOW
WHAT? TUNA!?
PEOPLE USED TO MARINATE THE RED, LEAN PART OF THE FISH IN SOY SAUCE SO IT WOULDN'T SPOIL, BUT THEY THREW AWAY THE FATTY TORO, WHICH DIDN'T ABSORB SOY SAUCE WELL.
TUNA IS A RED FISH AND OXIDIZES QUICKLY, MAKING QUALITY CONTROL DIFFICULT.
WHAT A WASTE!
WHY DID THAT CHANGE?
TORO...!
TRADITIONALLY, IN THE JAPANESE MARKET, WHOLE FISH WITH THE HEAD AND TAIL ATTACHED WERE PREFERRED.
Sea bream with the head on is still expensive.

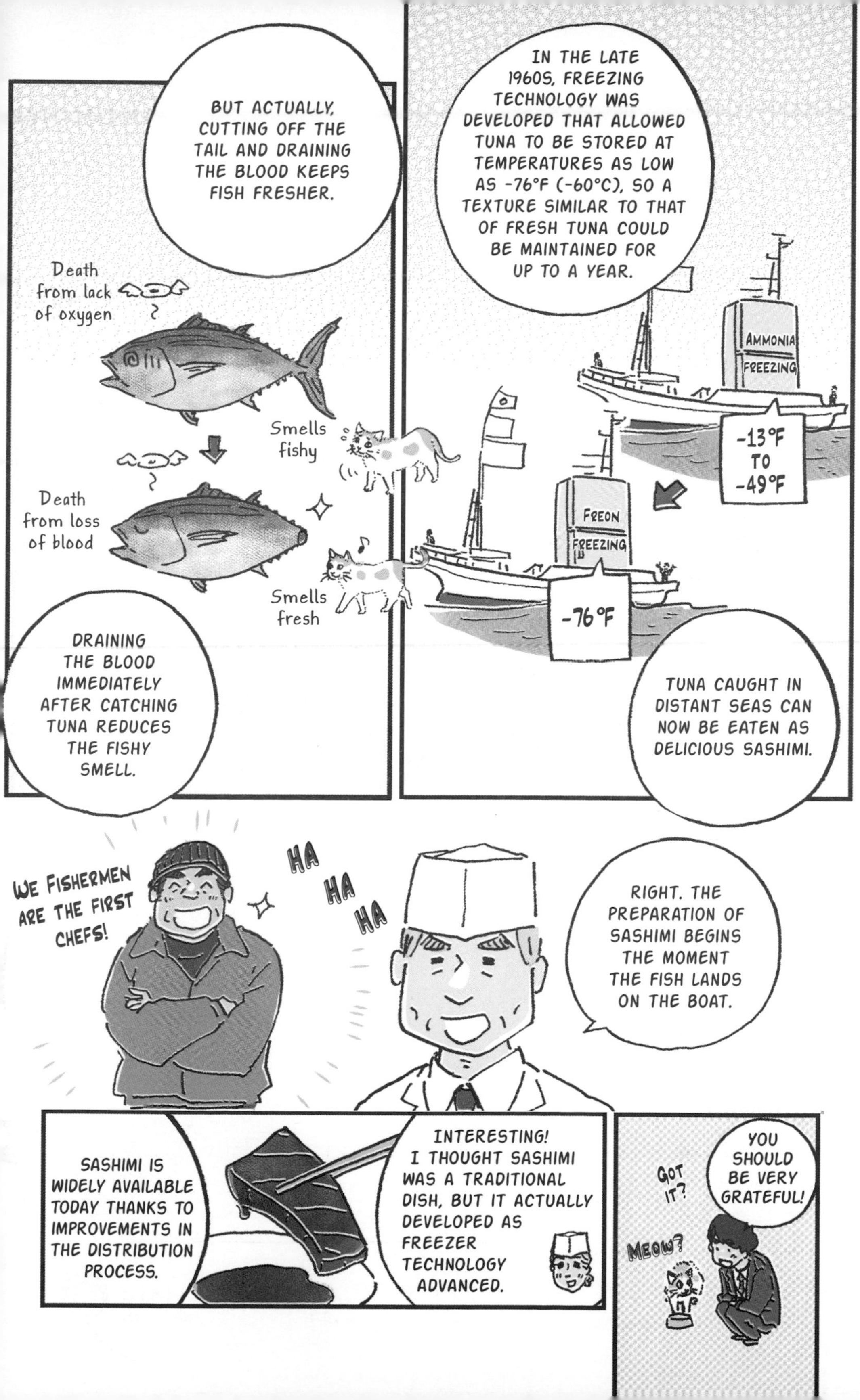
BUT ACTUALLY, CUTTING OFF THE TAIL AND DRAINING THE BLOOD KEEPS FISH FRESHER.
Death from lack of oxygen
Smells fishy
Death from loss of blood
Smells fresh
DRAINING THE BLOOD IMMEDIATELY AFTER CATCHING TUNA REDUCES THE FISHY SMELL.
IN THE LATE 1960S, FREEZING TECHNOLOGY WAS DEVELOPED THAT ALLOWED TUNA TO BE STORED AT TEMPERATURES AS LOW AS -76°F (-60°C), SO A TEXTURE SIMILAR TO THAT OF FRESH TUNA COULD BE MAINTAINED FOR UP TO A YEAR.
AMMONIA FREEZING
-13°F TO -49°F
FREON FREEZING
-76°F
TUNA CAUGHT IN DISTANT SEAS CAN NOW BE EATEN AS DELICIOUS SASHIMI.
WE FISHERMEN ARE THE FIRST CHEFS!
HA HA HA
RIGHT. THE PREPARATION OF SASHIMI BEGINS THE MOMENT THE FISH LANDS ON THE BOAT.
SASHIMI IS WIDELY AVAILABLE TODAY THANKS TO IMPROVEMENTS IN THE DISTRIBUTION PROCESS.
INTERESTING! I THOUGHT SASHIMI WAS A TRADITIONAL DISH, BUT IT ACTUALLY DEVELOPED AS FREEZER TECHNOLOGY ADVANCED.
YOU SHOULD BE VERY GRATEFUL!
GOT IT?
MEOW?

An Island Country Awash in Fish

Japan's abundant coastal waters

Even before the development of freezer technology, Japanese people ate raw fish seasoned with vinegar and in other preparations. The *Manyoshu* (Collection of Ten Thousand Leaves), compiled in the 8th century, contains the following poem:

> I long for sea bream with wild garlic in hishio and vinegar.
> Don't give me water hyacinth soup.

Hishio is the original form of soy sauce (see page 92). The poem's author is saying they want to eat sea bream with a sauce of garlicky miso-vinegar, not clear soup with water hyacinth. In the Nara period (710–794), a dish called namasu[1] was made by thinly slicing raw fish and dressing it with soy sauce and vinegar. This dish is said to be a predecessor of sashimi, and as the above poem shows, people in those days seem to have liked it. They were able to eat this dish because there was an abundance of fish in the seas around Japan that could be eaten raw.

Four ocean currents around the Japanese archipelago significantly impact fish migration and fishing grounds (see Figure 1).

---

1 **Namasu** is a dish of thinly sliced raw meat or fish that has been eaten in China since around 700 BCE and is mentioned in the *Kojiki* (Records of Ancient Matters), Japan's oldest surviving book.

Figure 1 Ocean Currents Around Japan

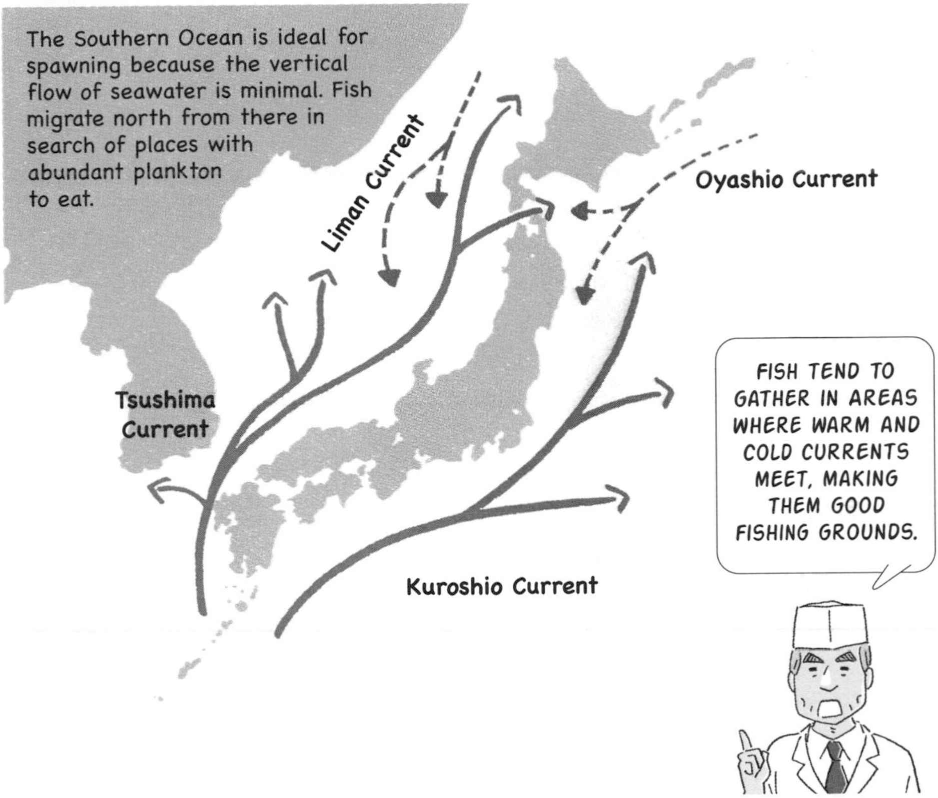

The Southern Ocean is ideal for spawning because the vertical flow of seawater is minimal. Fish migrate north from there in search of places with abundant plankton to eat.
Liman Current
Oyashio Current
Tsushima Current
Kuroshio Current
FISH TEND TO GATHER IN AREAS WHERE WARM AND COLD CURRENTS MEET, MAKING THEM GOOD FISHING GROUNDS.

Figure 2 Movement of Seawater in the Oyashio Current

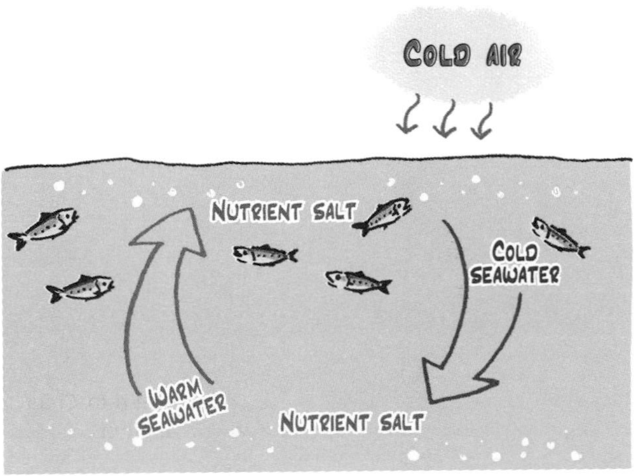

COLD AIR
NUTRIENT SALT
COLD SEAWATER
WARM SEAWATER
NUTRIENT SALT

Cold seawater in the Oyashio Current causes seawater to cycle vertically, bringing nutrient salts on the seafloor upward. This increases the amount of plankton and attracts fish.

The Kuroshio Current (also called the Black or Japan Current) is blue-black when seen from the sky. It is a large current with a speed of about 6.5 feet (2 m) per second and a width of 60 miles (100 km), carrying enormous amounts of heat from the equator. By contrast, the Oyashio (also called the Kurile Current) is a weak current, but it runs deep and is said to have a flow volume comparable to that of the Kuroshio Current. The name Oyashio means "parent current" and comes from the fact that it is rich in plankton, which is food for fish, making it like a parent raising a large number of fish. The Sanriku Coast, where the Kuroshio and Oyashio currents collide, is one of the world's three largest fishing grounds.

The northwestern Pacific Ocean around Japan is the world's most productive fishery, producing 22.75 million metric tons annually, or 25% of the world's seafood production.[2] Surrounded on all sides by the sea, Japan ranks 62nd globally in terms of area, but 6th in terms of the length of its intricate coastlines and exclusive economic

Figure 3 The Marine Food Chain

Plant plankton
Animal plankton
Fish that eat plankton
Fish that eat small fish
Nutrient salt
Bacteria etc.
Shells and remains

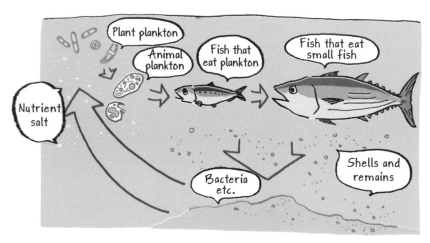

Animal plankton eats plant plankton, small fish such as sardines eat plant and animal plankton, and larger fish such as tuna eat small fish. When plankton and fish die, they are decomposed by bacteria into nutrients.

2 Fisheries Agency 2016 statistics.

zones.[3] These waters are home to approximately 3,700 species,[4] or 25% of the world's 15,000 saltwater fish species. The rich ecosystems created by the collision of cold and warm currents, as well as the abundance and variety of fish, are key characteristics of Japan's fisheries.

As the world's catch grows, Japan's shrinks

Japan used to have the world's largest fishing industry, but now it is in decline. Graphs 1 and 2 show that while global fishery production is increasing, Japan's annual production has decreased by about one-third since its peak in 1984. Today, about half the fish eaten in Japan is imported.

There are several possible reasons for the decline in Japanese fishery production. Contributing factors may include the drastic reduction in the extent of Japan's broadleaf forests, which provide nutrients to the sea; changes in the marine environment caused by global warming; and the fact that foreign fishing vessels are now actively fishing in the high seas, resulting in fewer fish migrating to the waters around Japan. However, the biggest cause is believed to be overfishing.

Advanced fishing countries such as Norway and Iceland were among the first to address fisheries resource management. In the 1970s, these countries established the maximum amount of fish that could be caught for each species based on scientific evidence (the TAC system[5]), and each fisherman was assigned an individual quota (IQ[6]) to ensure that fish were not caught before they were large enough. As a result, fishing in these countries has become a highly profitable and coveted profession, with a stable supply of large, mature fish and high catches.

---

3 Exclusive economic zones are waters established under the United Nations Convention on the Law of the Sea where one country has the exclusive right to fishery resources up to 200 nautical miles (370 km) from the shoreline.
4 Fisheries Agency 2016 statistics.
5 TAC is short for Total Allowable Catch. These systems are intended to protect fisheries resources by determining how much can sustainably be harvested.
6 IQ is a system for allocating the catch established by the TAC to individual fishermen or vessels.

Graph 1 Global Fishing and Aquaculture Production Trends

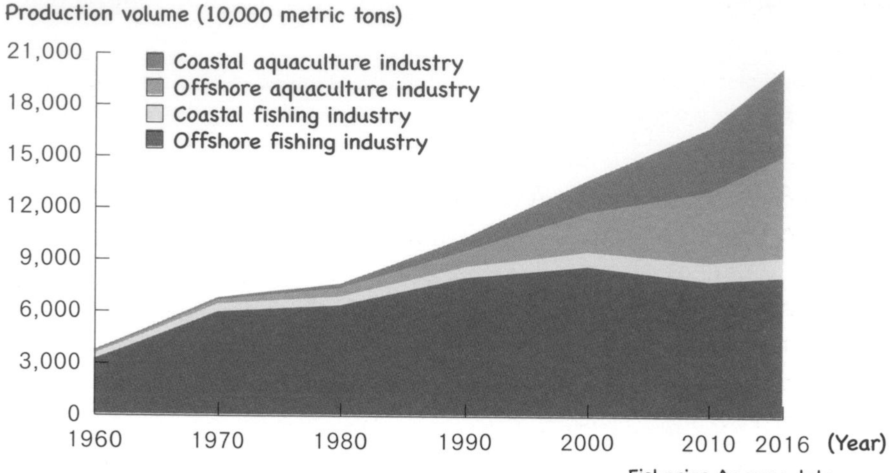
Production volume (10,000 metric tons)
21,000
18,000
15,000
12,000
9,000
6,000
3,000
0
Coastal aquaculture industry
Offshore aquaculture industry
Coastal fishing industry
Offshore fishing industry
1960
1970
1980
1990
2000
2010
2016
(Year)

Fisheries Agency data

Graph 2 Japan Fishing and Aquaculture Production Trends

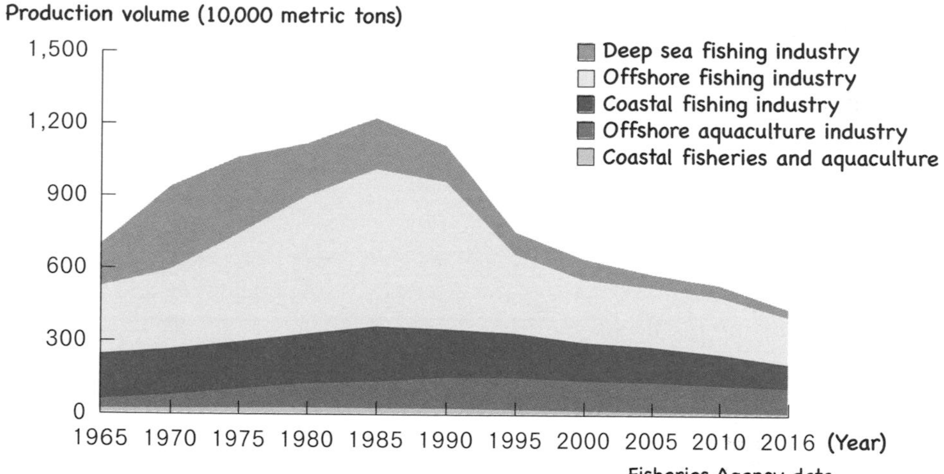
Production volume (10,000 metric tons)
1,500
1,200
900
600
300
0
Deep sea fishing industry
Offshore fishing industry
Coastal fishing industry
Offshore aquaculture industry
Coastal fisheries and aquaculture
1965
1970
1975
1980
1985
1990
1995
2000
2005
2010
2016
(Year)

Fisheries Agency data

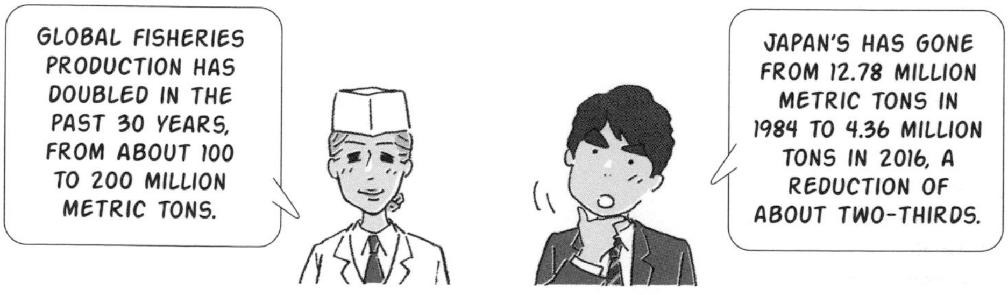
GLOBAL FISHERIES PRODUCTION HAS DOUBLED IN THE PAST 30 YEARS, FROM ABOUT 100 TO 200 MILLION METRIC TONS.
JAPAN'S HAS GONE FROM 12.78 MILLION METRIC TONS IN 1984 TO 4.36 MILLION TONS IN 2016, A REDUCTION OF ABOUT TWO-THIRDS.

Japan also established catch limits in 1996, but the number of target species was low[7] and the upper limits were lax. In addition, because catch quotas are allocated on a prefectural or fishery cooperative basis and not on an individual fisherman or vessel basis, there is a tendency for fishermen to catch even immature fish on a "first-come, first-served" basis in an attempt to out-harvest other fishermen. As a result, overfishing has not been prevented and the price of fish has fallen due to high catches, resulting in a situation where income cannot rise.

In response to this situation, the Fisheries Law was revised for the first time in 70 years in 2018, introducing a system for allocating catch limits to individual fishermen. Now that Japan is moving toward stronger resource management, there is hope that its fisheries can be sustainably operated.

The long road to sustainable aquaculture

Although a dietary shift away from fish consumption is occurring in Japan, worldwide, fish consumption continues to grow due to health consciousness and the worldwide Japanese food boom. Graph 1 shows that global fishery production has grown by a factor of approximately 1.6 over the past 20 years in response to this growth in consumption. The increase has been supported by growing aquaculture production. Global fish farming has more than tripled in the last 20 years, and since 2013 has accounted for more than 50% of total fishery production. In Japan too, a similar shift from catching to raising fish will be needed in order to increase marine resources.

---

7 As of September 2020, limits had been established for 8 species: horse mackerel, mackerel, blue mackerel, Japanese pilchard, walleye pollock, Pacific saury, snow crab, and bluefin tuna.

Fish stocking is a common type of aquaculture in Japan. In fish stocking systems, the fish are raised from eggs in a hatchery and released when they are mature enough to defend themselves against predators. About 40 species, including snapper, flatfish and flounder, are stocked throughout Japan.

In other systems, fish are raised to harvest in captivity. One well-known example in Japan is called Kindai Maguro. In 2002, the Fisheries Laboratory at Kinki University succeeded in creating a full-cycle aquaculture system for bluefin tuna. In full-cycle aquaculture, fish are artificially hatched, raised to maturity, and used to produce more eggs which are then artificially hatched again, allowing for sustainable fish production without relying on wild-harvested eggs or fry. In contrast, most farmed tuna in Japan use wild-caught juveniles raised to adulthood in tanks before being sold. Most imported farmed tuna is "fattened," meaning adult fish are caught at sea, raised for a period of time to add fat, and then sold.

Figure 4 Tuna Stocking, Farming and Fattening

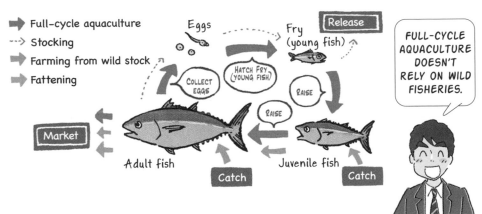

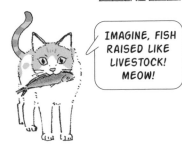

Full-cycle aquaculture
Stocking
Farming from wild stock
Fattening
Eggs
Fry
(young fish)
Release
Collect eggs
Hatch fry (young fish)
Raise
Raise
Market
Adult fish
Juvenile fish
Catch
Catch

FULL-CYCLE AQUACULTURE DOESN'T RELY ON WILD FISHERIES.

Full-cycle aquaculture: Fish are raised to adulthood and their eggs harvested for the next generation of farmed fish.

Stocking: Fry are raised from eggs and released in the wild.

Farmed from wild stock: Wild juvenile fish are caught, grown to adulthood and sold.

Fattening: Adult fish are caught, fattened, and sold.

IMAGINE, FISH RAISED LIKE LIVESTOCK! MEOW!

The biggest challenge in aquaculture is feed. Using small wild-caught fish as feed is not a sustainable production method and is expensive. Various efforts are underway to increase the value of farmed fish, including the use of fish scraps from processing in feed, the development of plant-based feed, and the addition of citrus fruits to feed to reduce discoloration and fishy smells.

The story of fish paste

One method people in Japan developed to preserve the abundant fish harvest was to make fish-paste products such as kamaboko, chikuwa, and hanpen. When fish meat is pulverized with 2% to 3% its weight in salt, it becomes a sticky paste called surimi. Various products can be made by boiling, steaming, or deep frying surimi. In the Heian period (794–1185), surimi was rolled around bamboo sticks and grilled. This is thought to be the origin of today's kamaboko.

Frozen surimi revolutionized kamaboko, which was once a luxury item. It was developed in 1959 by the Hokkaido Fisheries Experiment Station (now the Central Fisheries Experiment Station of the Hokkaido National Research Institute) as part of its research into

A scene from *Kinsei shokunin zukushi ekotoba* (Craftsmen at Their Work) (Digital Collections, National Diet Library)

This 19th century picture scroll depicts people of various occupations living in Edo (see page 136).

THIS PAINTING VIVIDLY DEPICTS THE MAKING OF HANPEN FISH CAKES.

ways to use pollock, which spoils easily. Frozen surimi is made by soaking fish flesh in water, dehydrating it, mixing in sugar, phosphate, and other ingredients, and finally freezing it. This technology enables long-term preservation of fish without the loss of elasticity, a necessary quality in fish paste products, during freezing and thawing. From 1965 on, high-quality frozen surimi was produced by offshore processing vessels, and its use rapidly expanded.

Frozen surimi does not require the same processing as raw fish and can be stored for a long time. It is now produced and used in many countries, and surimi has become a common word around the world.

Fish paste products
Kamaboko
Chikuwa
Satsuma-age
Charcuterie
Ham
Bacon
Sausages
FISH IN JAPAN, MEAT IN FRANCE. BOTH LOOK DELICIOUS, MEOW!
JAPANESE FISH PASTE PRODUCTS REMIND ME OF FRENCH CHARCUTERIE.
CHARCUTERIE?
CHARCUTERIE REFERS TO PROCESSED MEAT PRODUCTS.

The Big Picture

Imitation Crab, an International Favorite

A brief chronology of imitation crab sticks

1972
Sugiyo launches the world's first crab-flavored fish paste product, Kaniashi (Crab Legs).

1977
Decrease in Japan's crab catch due to establishment of 200-nautical-mile fishing zone.

1980
United Airlines adopts the product for in-flight meals. Export to the U.S. goes into full swing.

1980s
Popularized in Europe under the name "surimi."

Present
Lithuania is the world's largest producer of imitation crab sticks (80,000 metric tons compared to Japan's 60,000 metric tons)
French consumption of imitation crab sticks is comparable to that of Japan (about 50,000 metric tons per year).

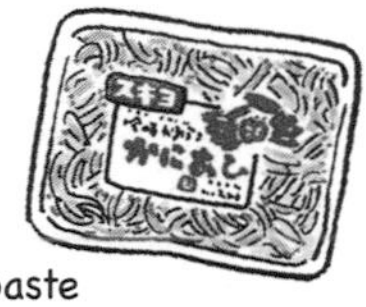

The world's first crab-flavored fish paste product, Kaniashi (Crab Legs), was launched in 1972.

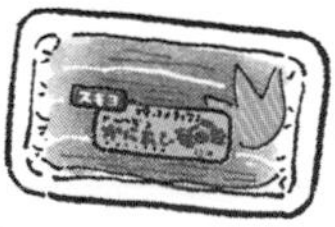

Golden Kaniashi was launched in 1975. The shape changed from flakes to crab legs.

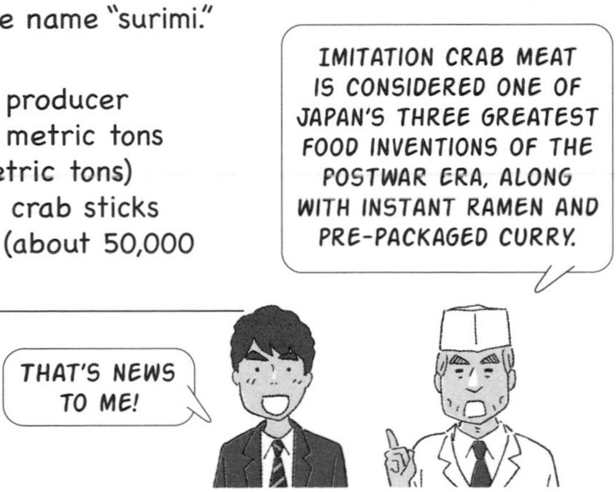
IMITATION CRAB MEAT IS CONSIDERED ONE OF JAPAN'S THREE GREATEST FOOD INVENTIONS OF THE POSTWAR ERA, ALONG WITH INSTANT RAMEN AND PRE-PACKAGED CURRY.
THAT'S NEWS TO ME!

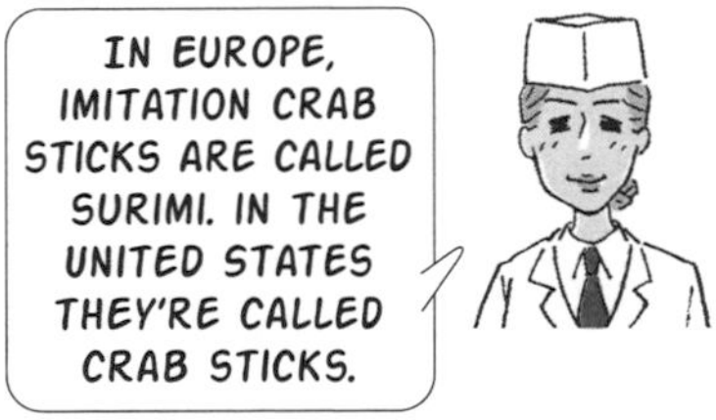
IN EUROPE, IMITATION CRAB STICKS ARE CALLED SURIMI. IN THE UNITED STATES THEY'RE CALLED CRAB STICKS.

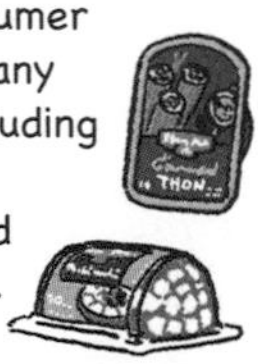

France is a major consumer of surimi. There are many different products, including rolled surimi, surimi wrapped in cheese, and shrimp-flavored surimi.

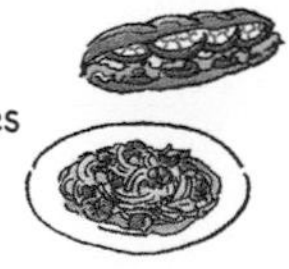

Surimi is used in baguette sandwiches and pasta.

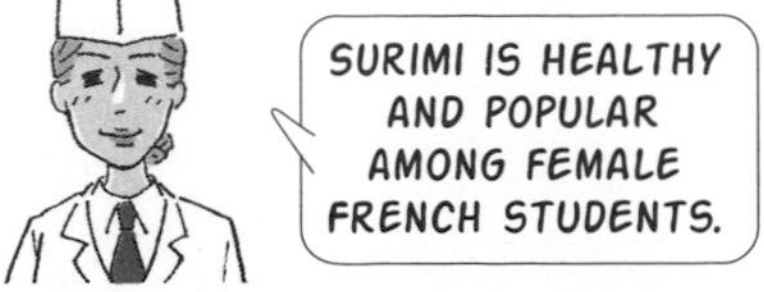
SURIMI IS HEALTHY AND POPULAR AMONG FEMALE FRENCH STUDENTS.

Why is imitation crab popular around the world?

1. Cheap compared to real crab meat
2. No bones, no fishy smell, pre-cooked and convenient
3. Can be used in a variety of ways to meet the needs of each country's food culture
4. High protein, low fat, healthy
5. Easy to manufacture once the machines are installed
6. The main ingredient is Alaskan pollack. Other fish species can be substituted, and there is little concern about depletion of stocks.

Food for the Gods

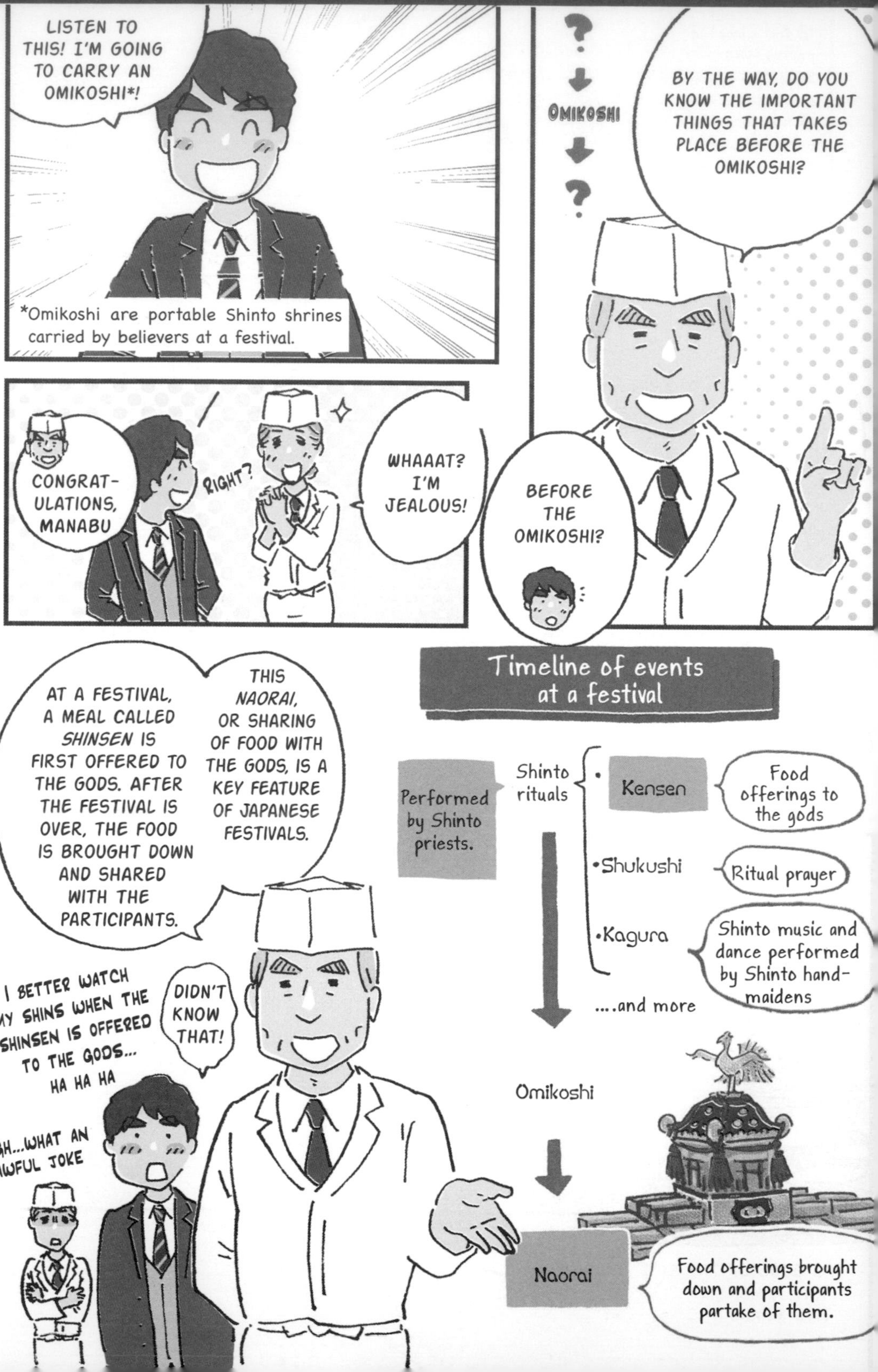

LISTEN TO THIS! I'M GOING TO CARRY AN OMIKOSHI*!
*Omikoshi are portable Shinto shrines carried by believers at a festival.
CONGRAT-ULATIONS, MANABU
RIGHT?
WHAAAT? I'M JEALOUS!
?
OMIKOSHI
?
BY THE WAY, DO YOU KNOW THE IMPORTANT THINGS THAT TAKES PLACE BEFORE THE OMIKOSHI?
BEFORE THE OMIKOSHI?
AT A FESTIVAL, A MEAL CALLED SHINSEN IS FIRST OFFERED TO THE GODS. AFTER THE FESTIVAL IS OVER, THE FOOD IS BROUGHT DOWN AND SHARED WITH THE PARTICIPANTS.
THIS NAORAI, OR SHARING OF FOOD WITH THE GODS, IS A KEY FEATURE OF JAPANESE FESTIVALS.
DIDN'T KNOW THAT!
I BETTER WATCH MY SHINS WHEN THE SHINSEN IS OFFERED TO THE GODS... HA HA HA
UGH...WHAT AN AWFUL JOKE
Timeline of events at a festival
Performed by Shinto priests.
Shinto rituals
• Kensen
Food offerings to the gods
•Shukushi
Ritual prayer
•Kagura
Shinto music and dance performed by Shinto hand-maidens
....and more
Omikoshi
Naorai
Food offerings brought down and participants partake of them.

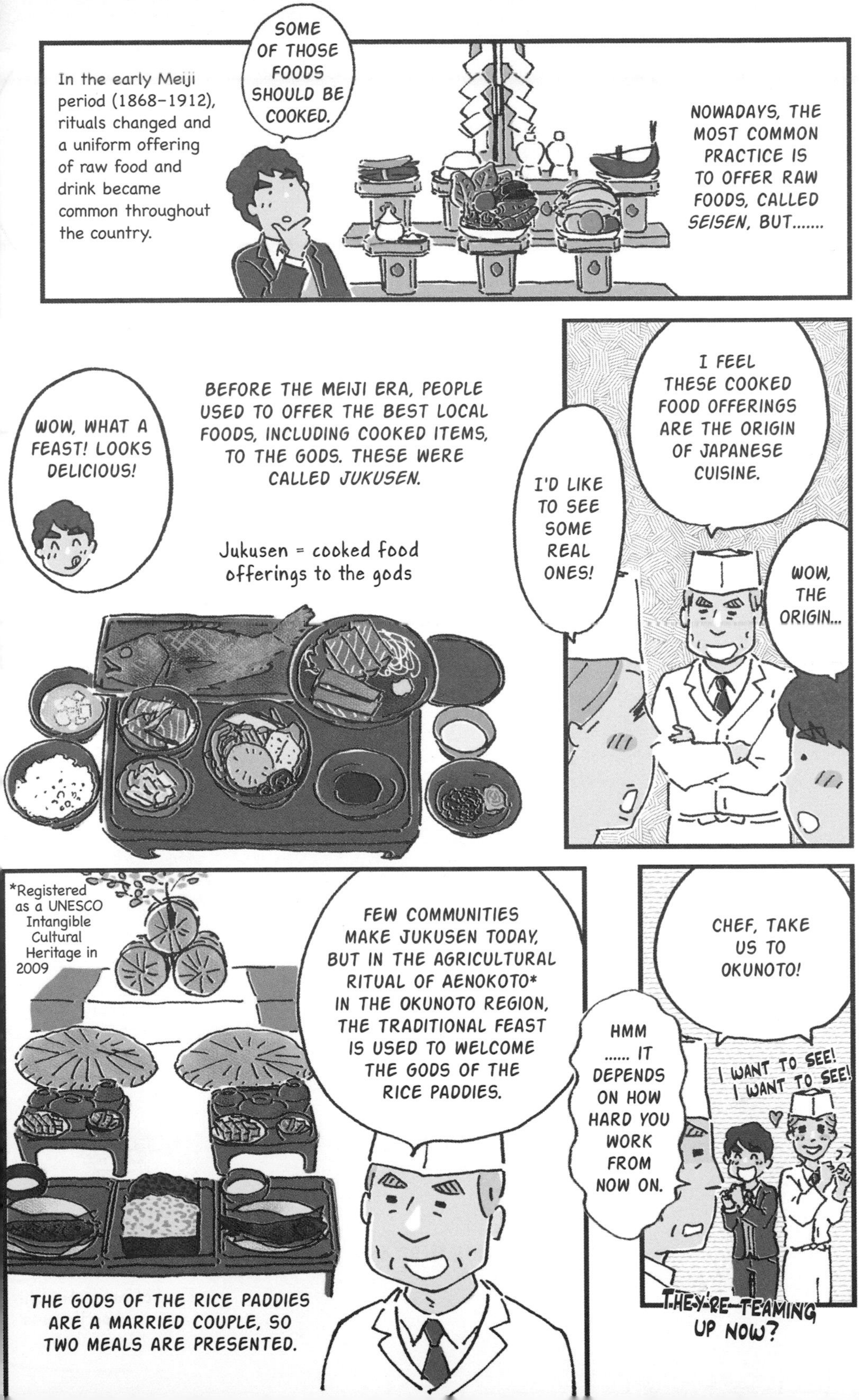
In the early Meiji period (1868–1912), rituals changed and a uniform offering of raw food and drink became common throughout the country.
SOME OF THOSE FOODS SHOULD BE COOKED.
NOWADAYS, THE MOST COMMON PRACTICE IS TO OFFER RAW FOODS, CALLED SEISEN, BUT.......
WOW, WHAT A FEAST! LOOKS DELICIOUS!
BEFORE THE MEIJI ERA, PEOPLE USED TO OFFER THE BEST LOCAL FOODS, INCLUDING COOKED ITEMS, TO THE GODS. THESE WERE CALLED JUKUSEN.
Jukusen = cooked food offerings to the gods
I FEEL THESE COOKED FOOD OFFERINGS ARE THE ORIGIN OF JAPANESE CUISINE.
WOW, THE ORIGIN...
I'D LIKE TO SEE SOME REAL ONES!
*Registered as a UNESCO Intangible Cultural Heritage in 2009
FEW COMMUNITIES MAKE JUKUSEN TODAY, BUT IN THE AGRICULTURAL RITUAL OF AENOKOTO* IN THE OKUNOTO REGION, THE TRADITIONAL FEAST IS USED TO WELCOME THE GODS OF THE RICE PADDIES.
THE GODS OF THE RICE PADDIES ARE A MARRIED COUPLE, SO TWO MEALS ARE PRESENTED.
CHEF, TAKE US TO OKUNOTO!
HMM ...... IT DEPENDS ON HOW HARD YOU WORK FROM NOW ON.
I WANT TO SEE! I WANT TO SEE!
THEY'RE TEAMING UP NOW?

A Cuisine Rooted in Sharing with the Gods

The origins of Japanese New Year's foods

Mere survival was once much harder than it is today, and famines occurred often. Ancient people prayed to the gods to protect them from disasters, illness and other calamities. They thanked the gods for the abundance of nature's bounty, offered meals to the gods, and joined in these meals themselves. Offering food to the gods and partaking of it together with them must have felt quite natural.

These practices may seem far removed from modern life. However, vestiges remain in the New Year's custom of offering round mochi (rice cakes) to the gods and eating New Year's feast food and ozoni soup with mochi. New Year's Day was originally a time to welcome the god of grain called Toshigami-sama.[1]

The round mochi are both an offering to Toshigami-sama and the deity's *yorishiro*[2] during the New Year's holiday. Since ancient times, people have believed that rice grains contain the spiritual power of rice. As a condensed form of rice grains, mochi was regarded as containing a concentrated amount of the sacred power of rice.

---

1 The Toshigami is a deity who visits households during the New Year, believed to be the spirit of grain who brings a good rice harvest or the spirit of ancestors.
2 Yorishiro are objects to which a divine spirit is attracted or which they possess. In Japan, people have long believed that gods and spirits inhabit all things.

The five seasonal festivals

Nowadays, the word *osechi* refers to special foods eaten during the New Year's holiday. In the past, however, seasonal foods were also offered to the gods at five seasonal festivals called Gosekku. The following five days of the year made up the Gosekku: Jinjitsu on the 7th day of the New Year (Nanakusa-no-Sekku); Joshi on March 3 (Momo-no-Sekku), Tango on May 5 (Shobu-no-Sekku); Shichiseki on July 7th (Tanabata-no-Sekku); and Choyo on September 9 (Kiku-No-Sekku). These were established as national holidays in the Edo period (1603–1867).

The origin of the Gosekku is a mixture of ancient Chinese customs, traditional Japanese court ceremonies, and agricultural rituals to pray for a good harvest. The traditional Gosekku differ from today's Gosseku in some respects.

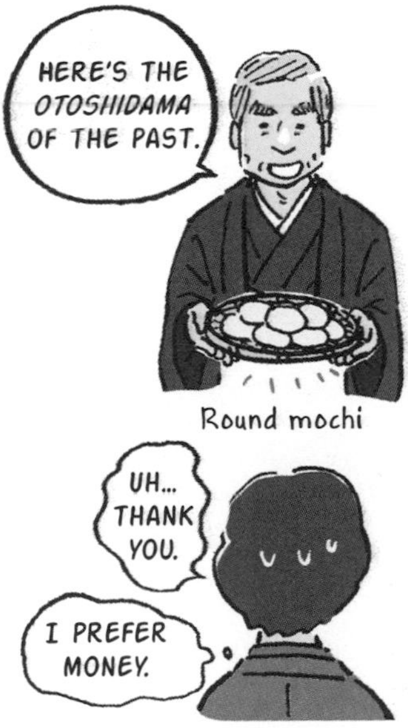
HERE'S THE *OTOSHIDAMA* OF THE PAST.
Round mochi
UH... THANK YOU.
I PREFER MONEY.

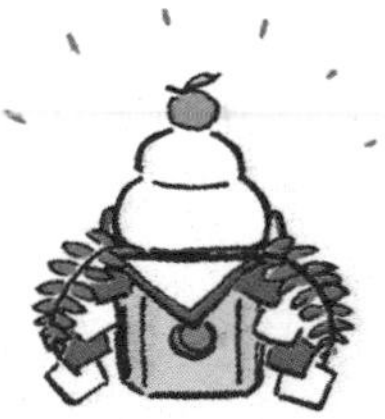

It is said that Toshigami-sama is attracted to the round New Year's mochi. The god's spirit was divided between the mochi served in ozoni soup and the *otoshidama* gifts given by adults to children on New Year's Day. Today money is given, but in the past the sacred mochi was broken up and given as *otoshidama*.

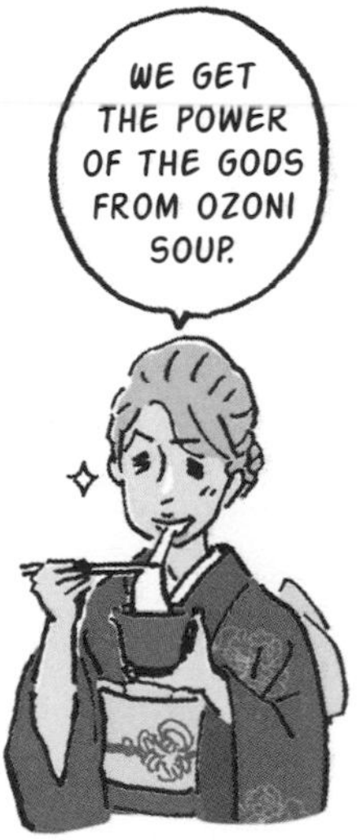
WE GET THE POWER OF THE GODS FROM OZONI SOUP.

Food and Agricultural Rituals for the Gosekku, or Five Seasonal Festivals

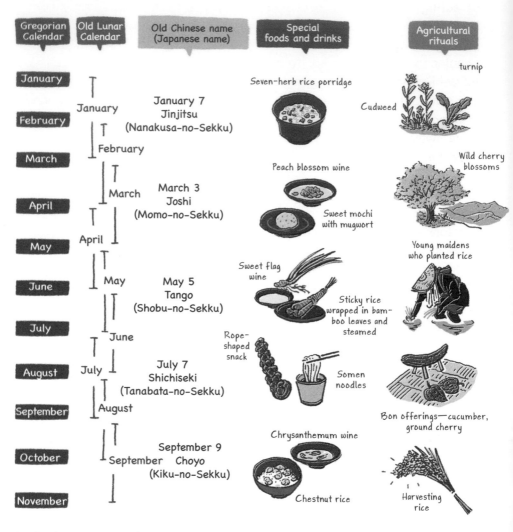

Gregorian Calendar	Old Lunar Calendar	Old Chinese name (Japanese name)	Special foods and drinks	Agricultural rituals
January	January	January 7 Jinjitsu (Nanakusa-no-Sekku)	Seven-herb rice porridge	turnip / Cudweed
February	February			
March	March	March 3 Joshi (Momo-no-Sekku)	Peach blossom wine / Sweet mochi with mugwort	Wild cherry blossoms
April	April			
May	May	May 5 Tango (Shobu-no-Sekku)	Sweet flag wine / Sticky rice wrapped in bamboo leaves and steamed	Young maidens who planted rice
June	June			
July	July	July 7 Shichiseki (Tanabata-no-Sekku)	Rope-shaped snack / Somen noodles	
August	August			Bon offerings—cucumber, ground cherry
September	September	September 9 Choyo (Kiku-no-Sekku)	Chrysanthemum wine / Chestnut rice	Harvesting rice
October				
November				

In the lunar calendar (see footnote on page 68), Risshun marks the beginning of the new year, a few months later than in the Gregorian calendar. Since the first day of each month in the lunar calendar is determined by the waxing and waning of the moon, the difference between the lunar calendar and the Gregorian calendar varies from year to year. The red line in the diagram above shows the maximum extent to which each month of the lunar calendar corresponds to that of the Gregorian.

THE GOSEKKU WERE ORIGINALLY HELD ACCORDING TO THE LUNAR CALENDAR, SO THEY ARE OUT OF SYNC WITH THE CURRENT SEASONS.

The custom of eating nanakusagayu, a rice gruel with seven herbs,[3] on Jinjitsu (January 7) is said to be a blending of the Chinese custom of eating hot soup with seven kinds of young vegetables to pray for good health and the ancient Japanese custom of *wakanazumi*,[4] or picking young spring greens. Starting around the 1800s it became popular in farming villages to loudly sing a song called "Nanakusa-bayashi" when chopping up the seven herbs for the rice gruel. Part of the song goes, "Before the birds of the land of China come to the land of Japan, chop the seven herbs."[5] The song expressed the need to both drive away birds that destroyed crops and pray to the gods for a good harvest.

The origin of the Girls' Festival on March 3 is said to combine an ancient Chinese custom of going to a body of water to ward off bad luck and a Japanese custom of making dolls and having them carry bad luck on their backs as they float down a river. On Joshi (Momo-no-Sekku), people drank peach blossom wine and ate green rice cakes with mugwort kneaded into them. Peaches were thought to ward off evil spirits and bring longevity, while mugwort was believed to ward off bad luck.

This illustrated storybook from the late Edo period depicts a mother protecting her child from a "bird from China" while chopping the seven herbs on the night of the sixth day of the New Year. The bird was feared as a destroyer or crops, and was also thought in Chinese legend to bring bad luck to young children.

A page from *Gosekku osana koshaku* (Children's Stories About the Five Seasonal Festivals) (National Diet Library Digital Collections)

THE SONG WAS LIKE A SPELL TO WARD OFF BAD HARVESTS!

3 The porridge was made with the following seven wild plants: Japanese parsley, shepherd's purse, cudweed, chickweed, Japanese nipplewort, turnip and daikon.
4 It was customary to pick young wild greens in the meadows on the first day of the rat in the New Year. A poem by 9th century Emperor Koko (see page 80) in the *Hyakunin Isshu* refers to this custom: "For you, I go out to the fields in spring to pick young greens, while snow falls on my sleeves."
5 The lyrics vary slightly from region to region. The words given here are from Fukushima Prefecture.

March 3 in the lunar calendar[6] corresponds to April in the Gregorian calendar, and was the time before rice planting began. On March 3,[7] villagers would pack a feast in stacked lunchboxes and climb a nearby mountain to eat and drink together. It was believed that the gods of the mountain descended to the village and became the gods of the rice paddies, so people would go up to the mountain to welcome the gods at the beginning of the farming season and share a meal with them. This event was held throughout the country and was called *yama-asobi* (mountain celebration). In regions near the sea, similar activities were held on the beach and were called *iso-asobi* (shore celebration). Today's cherry blossom viewing parties and clam harvesting outings are said to bear traces of *yama-asobi* and *iso-asobi*.

The origin of Children's Day on May 5 is an ancient Chinese tradition. In China on May 5, people drank sweetflag wine, which is believed to ward off bad luck, and ate chimaki (zongzi in Chinese; dumplings wrapped in bamboo leaves) to ward off bad luck.

Scenes of soaking in a sweetflag bath on Children's Day.

Gosekku no uchi satsuki (The Five Festivals: The Fifth Month) by Utagawa Kunisada (National Diet Library Digital Collection)

---

6 The lunar calendar was used before December 31, 1872, when it was replaced by the current Gregorian calendar. The first day of the month was the day of the new moon. The phases of the moon have a cycle of about 29.5 days, so a "leap month" took place about once every three years to regulate the calendar.

7 The most common day for *yama-asobi* was March 3 in warmer regions and April 8 in colder regions.

In Japan these days, Children's Day (Tango-no-Sekku) is more of a day for boys, but originally it was a women's festival. May in the lunar calendar is the month of rice planting. In the old days rice planting was women's work. Rice planting was considered a Shinto ritual to pray to the gods for a bountiful harvest, and the young women who planted the rice were called *saotome*. They played the role of *miko*, sacred maidens who welcomed the gods of the rice paddies. *Saotome* purified themselves by staying inside their houses with sweetflag and mugwort hung from the eaves from the evening of May 4 to May 5, then planted the rice paddies. After concluding the ritual purification, the *saotome* planted seedlings in the rice paddies wearing festive clothing consisting of navy blue unlined kimonos, red sashes, navy blue hand coverings, and sedge hats called *sugegasa*. Tango-no-Sekku is said to have changed to a men's festival during the Heian period (794–1185), when the court began to hold a horseback archery event called Umayumi on this day in addition to performing traditional Chinese rituals. During the Kamakura period (1185–1333), the festivities became even more male-centered, in part because the word for sweetflag was pronounced the same as the word meaning "to respect military affairs."

Tanabata, the Star Festival on July 7, is a mixture of several Japanese and Chinese events. One of the origins is a Chinese festival called Kikkoden, during which people pray for the improvement of sewing and artistic skills. The Tanabata legend of the deities Hikoboshi and Orihime meeting in the heavens is also derived from a Chinese legend.

In Japan, Tanabata was part of the Bon festival during which the spirits of ancestors were welcomed back. Today the Bon Festival falls in August, but in the lunar calendar it was in July. July 7 was the day to prepare a *shoryodana*[8] or "spirit shelf" to welcome the ancestors. July 7 is also known as Hozuki-no-Sekku, the ground cherry festival. In the past, the root of the ground cherry plant was used to induce abortions. If a woman became pregnant during this time of year, she would be three or four months pregnant—often the

---

8 The *shoryodana*, or *bondana*, is a special shelf built for the Bon Festival. In the center of the shelf a tablet is placed to welcome the spirits, and various offerings are made.

most difficult time of a pregnancy—just around the rice harvest. To avoid this, she would take the ground cherry root.

Tanabata was also a harvest festival for wheat and summer vegetables, so somen noodles made from wheat, melons, and fruits were eaten. The custom of eating somen noodles is said to originate in the ancient Chinese custom of eating a wheat-flour snack called sakubei[9] on July 7 to pray for good health. The custom was introduced to Japan, and eventually changed to somen noodles.

The Choyo-no-Sekku festival on September 9 originated in the ancient Chinese custom of drinking chrysanthemum wine to ward off evil spirits, which spread to Japan. In the year 685, during the reign of Emperor Tenmu, a banquet to view the chrysanthemums was held at the imperial palace on this day. September 9 in the lunar calendar falls in October in the Gregorian calendar, which is the time of the rice harvest in farming villages, and people celebrated the harvest by drinking chrysanthemum wine and eating rice with chestnuts. Even today, autumn festivals in northern Kyushu and other areas are still called Kunchi. The name is said to derive from O-Ku-Nichi, a harvest festival held on Choyo-no-Sekku.

A reverence for odd numbers

Did you notice that all of the Gosekku months and days consist of pairs of odd numbers such as 3 and 3 or 5 and 5, except for January 7, Jinjitsu? The reason for this lies in the ancient Chinese philosophy of yin and yang.[10] In yin-yang philosophy, odd numbers are auspicious yang numbers, but when two odd numbers overlap, as on 3/3 and 5/5, they turn to yin, and offerings had to be made to the gods to ward off evil spirits. It is also because of the yin-yang philosophy that odd numbers are valued in Japanese cooking. Page

---

9 Sakubei is a type of savory snack introduced from China during the Nara period (710–794). Made by kneading flour and twisting it into a long rope that is then deep-fried. It is also called muginawa, or wheat rope.

10 According to yin-yang philosophy, all things in the world are composed of yin, the passive female principle of the universe, and yang, the active male principle. Yin and yang complement and harmonize with each other for the creation and development of all things.

76 introduces the yin-yang of kitchen knives, and page 165 discusses the yin-yang of tableware.

Why meat eating was forbidden

For many centuries before the Meiji era, meat was not widely eaten in Japan. To understand why, we need to consider Japanese religious beliefs. The Japanese have, since ancient times, viewed all things as inhabited by gods and spirits. In addition, they have held a unique conception of "uncleanness" as a state of impurity caused by death, childbirth, and other events. The basic concept of Shinto is that uncleanness makes us unhappy and needs to be cleansed through purification and exorcism. This belief explains the past avoidance of meat.

Before the Nara period (710–794), meat eating was common in Japan. This changed in 675, when Emperor Tenmu issued a decree banning meat consumption. However, since the prohibition only

A page from *Funbonko* (Sketches) (Collection of Kurimori Memorial Library, Odate, Akita Prefecture)

THE JAPANESE WERE NOT IN THE HABIT OF EATING LIVESTOCK, BUT THEY DID EAT THE MEAT OF DEER, BOAR, AND BIRDS THEY HUNTED.

This Edo-era travel sketchbook by Sugae Masumi depicts a deer head and a skewered rabbit observed on a visit to Suwa Taisha Shrine during a festival to pray for a bountiful harvest in 1784. In the past, 75 deer heads were presented as offerings at the festival. It is evident that many farmers hunted at the time.

applied to the five domesticated animals (cows, horses, dogs, monkeys and chickens) and was limited to the farming season from April to September, the main purpose of the prohibition is thought to have been the encouragement of rice cultivation. In the 12th century, the Buddhist teaching that killing is a sin melded with the Shinto concept of uncleanness, and people began to avoid eating animal flesh because it was considered unclean. The trend toward avoiding meat gradually increased, peaking in the 17th century.

Incidentally, many Japanese people are reluctant to use chopsticks that other people have used, even if they've been washed. This reluctance is rooted in a sense of "uncleanness" unrelated to physical dirt or germs that can be removed by washing. This sensibility has led to the Japanese custom of each person having their own chopsticks and bowls that they use at each meal.

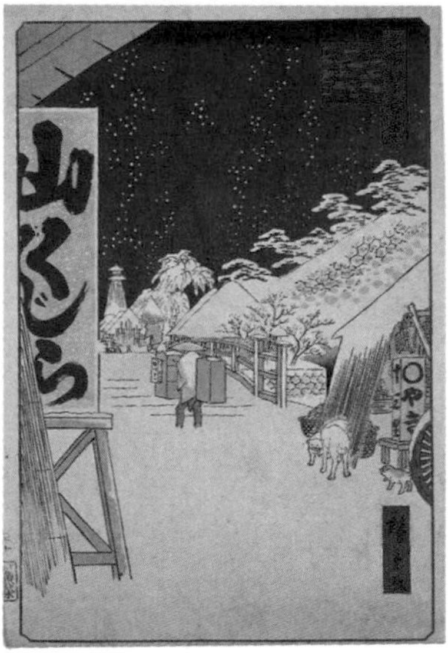
山くじら

Meisho Edo hyakkei/Bikunihashi yukinaka (Bikuni Bridge in Snow, from One Hundred Famous Views of Edo) by Utagawa Hiroshige (National Diet Library Digital Collections)

In the 19th century, restaurants serving meat began to open, and people frequented them in the name of "medicinal eating" to nourish their bodies. Because of the prevailing antipathy toward eating meat, people did not call the food served at these restaurants "meat," but instead called wild boar "mountain whale," venison "maple leaf" and horse meat "cherry blossom."

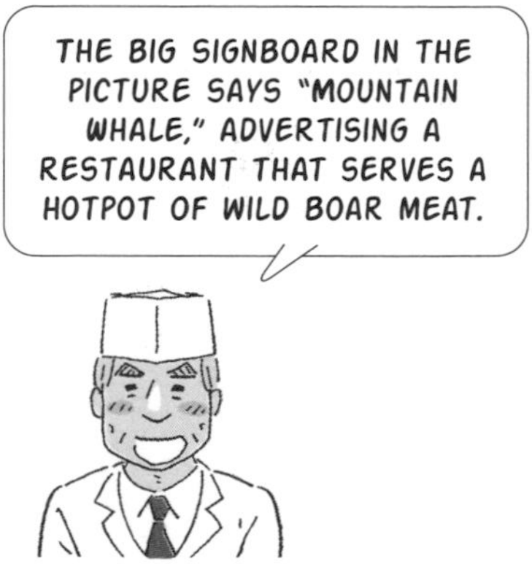
THE BIG SIGNBOARD IN THE PICTURE SAYS "MOUNTAIN WHALE," ADVERTISING A RESTAURANT THAT SERVES A HOTPOT OF WILD BOAR MEAT.

The Big Picture

Religious Food Prohibitions

Islam

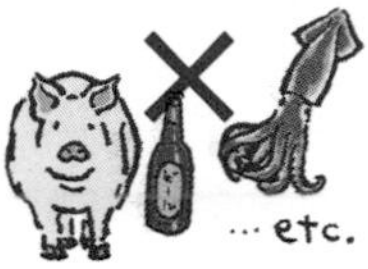
...etc.

Foods permitted by religious law are called "halal" and those that are forbidden are called "haram."

Foods to avoid

Pork, alcohol, blood, meat that has not been subjected to proper religious treatment, eggs, squid, octopus, shellfish, fermented foods such as pickled vegetables, etc.

Judaism

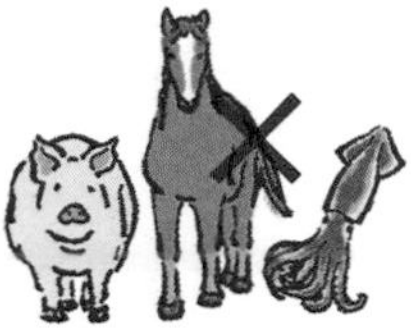

There are dietary rules, and the foods that are acceptable to eat are called "kosher."

Foods to avoid

Pork, blood, squid, octopus, shrimp, crab, sea urchin, shellfish, beef, horse meat, meat that has not been properly processed according to religious standards, dairy and meat combinations, etc.

Hinduism

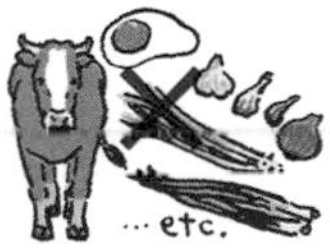
...etc.

Cows are objects of worship, so beef in particular is avoided.

Foods to avoid

Meat, beef, pork, seafood, eggs, raw food, the five pungent roots (garlic, chives, leeks, onions, scallions)

Christianity

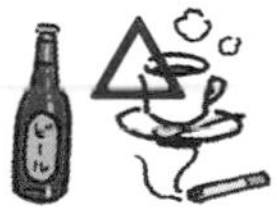

There are few prohibitions in general, except in some sects.

Foods to avoid

Some sects prohibit alcohol, caffeine, tobacco; some prohibit all meat

Buddhism

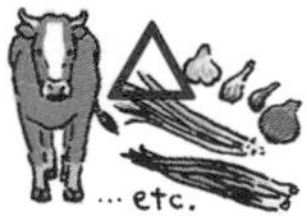
...etc.

Some monks and strict believers observe food prohibitions.

Foods to avoid

Some sects prohibit all meat, some prohibit beef, and some prohibit the five pungent roots

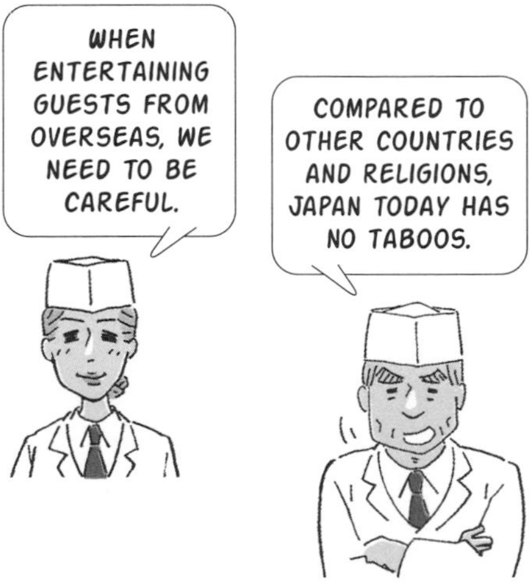
WHEN ENTERTAINING GUESTS FROM OVERSEAS, WE NEED TO BE CAREFUL.
COMPARED TO OTHER COUNTRIES AND RELIGIONS, JAPAN TODAY HAS NO TABOOS.

This graphic is based on the *Manual for Foreign Visitors with Diverse Food Cultures and Food Habits* (Tourism Business Division, Ministry of Land, Infrastructure, Transport and Tourism)

The Importance of Cutting

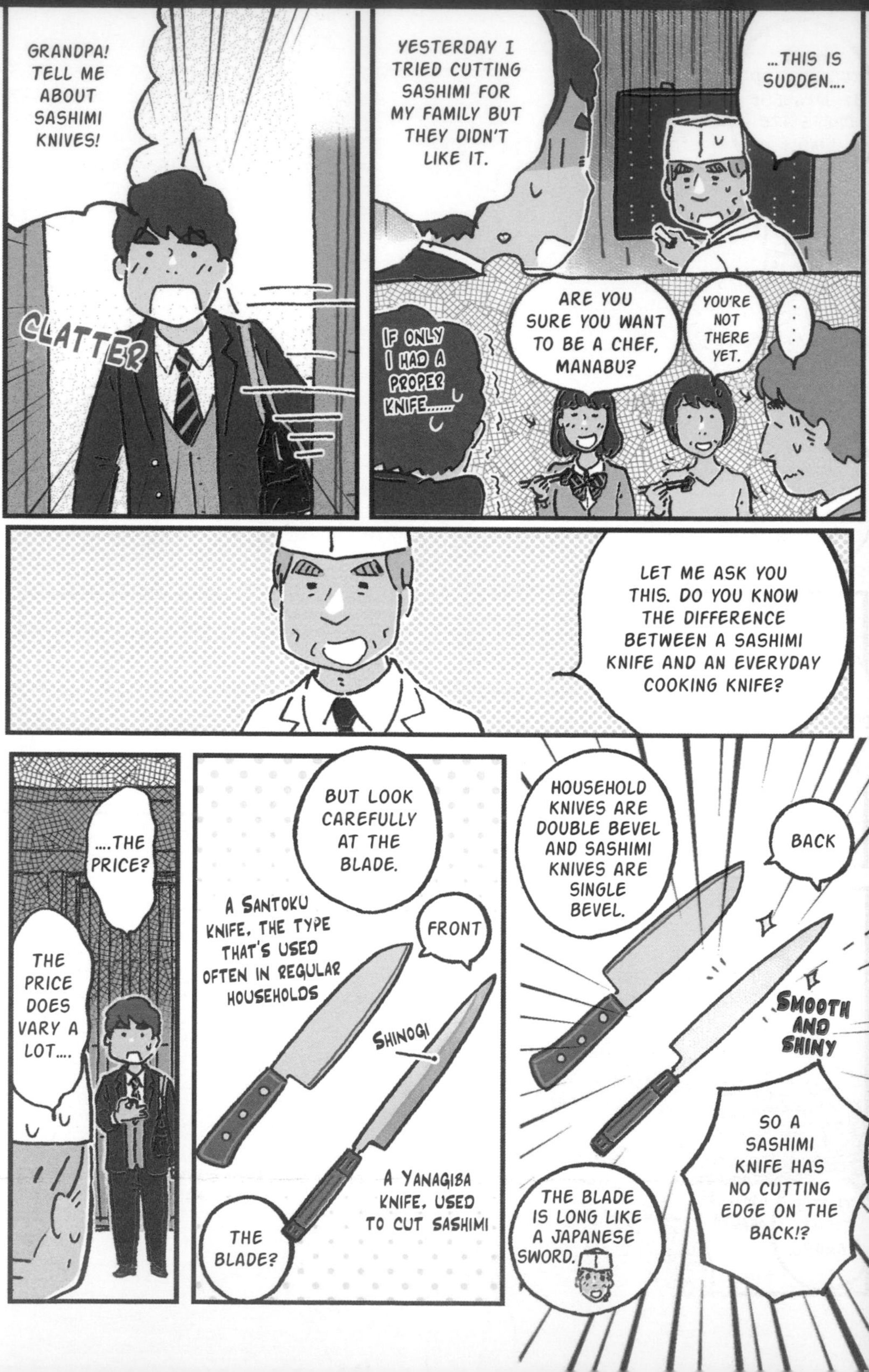
GRANDPA! TELL ME ABOUT SASHIMI KNIVES!
CLATTER
YESTERDAY I TRIED CUTTING SASHIMI FOR MY FAMILY BUT THEY DIDN'T LIKE IT.
...THIS IS SUDDEN....
IF ONLY I HAD A PROPER KNIFE......
ARE YOU SURE YOU WANT TO BE A CHEF, MANABU?
YOU'RE NOT THERE YET.
· · ·
LET ME ASK YOU THIS. DO YOU KNOW THE DIFFERENCE BETWEEN A SASHIMI KNIFE AND AN EVERYDAY COOKING KNIFE?
....THE PRICE?
THE PRICE DOES VARY A LOT....
BUT LOOK CAREFULLY AT THE BLADE.
THE BLADE?
A SANTOKU KNIFE, THE TYPE THAT'S USED OFTEN IN REGULAR HOUSEHOLDS
FRONT
SHINOGI
A YANAGIBA KNIFE, USED TO CUT SASHIMI
HOUSEHOLD KNIVES ARE DOUBLE BEVEL AND SASHIMI KNIVES ARE SINGLE BEVEL.
BACK
SMOOTH AND SHINY
SO A SASHIMI KNIFE HAS NO CUTTING EDGE ON THE BACK!?
THE BLADE IS LONG LIKE A JAPANESE SWORD.

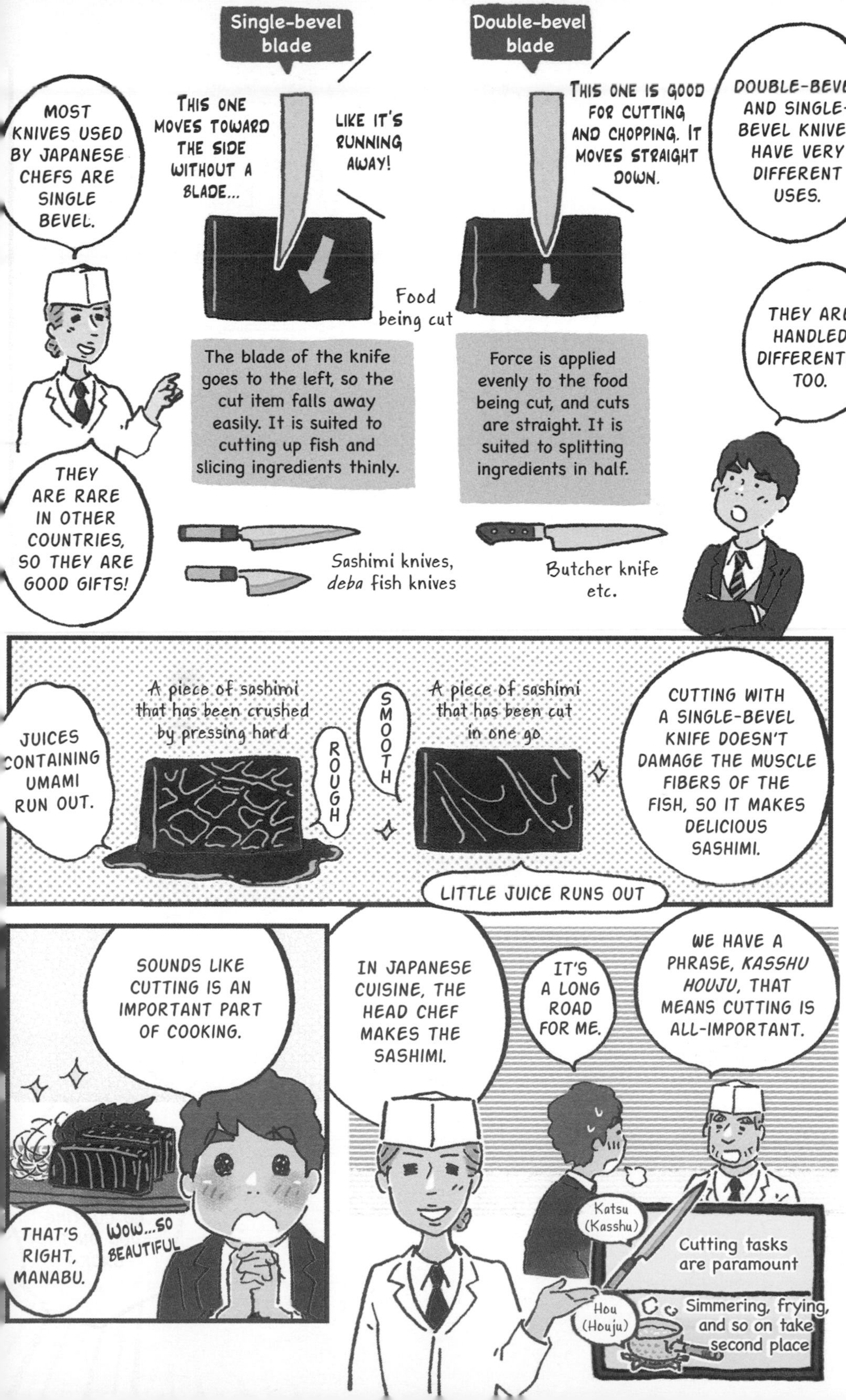
MOST KNIVES USED BY JAPANESE CHEFS ARE SINGLE BEVEL.
Single-bevel blade
THIS ONE MOVES TOWARD THE SIDE WITHOUT A BLADE...
LIKE IT'S RUNNING AWAY!
The blade of the knife goes to the left, so the cut item falls away easily. It is suited to cutting up fish and slicing ingredients thinly.
Food being cut
Double-bevel blade
THIS ONE IS GOOD FOR CUTTING AND CHOPPING. IT MOVES STRAIGHT DOWN.
Force is applied evenly to the food being cut, and cuts are straight. It is suited to splitting ingredients in half.
DOUBLE-BEVEL AND SINGLE-BEVEL KNIVES HAVE VERY DIFFERENT USES.
THEY ARE HANDLED DIFFERENTLY TOO.
THEY ARE RARE IN OTHER COUNTRIES, SO THEY ARE GOOD GIFTS!
Sashimi knives, *deba* fish knives
Butcher knife etc.
JUICES CONTAINING UMAMI RUN OUT.
A piece of sashimi that has been crushed by pressing hard
ROUGH
SMOOTH
A piece of sashimi that has been cut in one go
CUTTING WITH A SINGLE-BEVEL KNIFE DOESN'T DAMAGE THE MUSCLE FIBERS OF THE FISH, SO IT MAKES DELICIOUS SASHIMI.
LITTLE JUICE RUNS OUT
SOUNDS LIKE CUTTING IS AN IMPORTANT PART OF COOKING.
WOW...SO BEAUTIFUL
THAT'S RIGHT, MANABU.
IN JAPANESE CUISINE, THE HEAD CHEF MAKES THE SASHIMI.
IT'S A LONG ROAD FOR ME.
WE HAVE A PHRASE, *KASSHU HOUJU*, THAT MEANS CUTTING IS ALL-IMPORTANT.
Katsu (Kasshu)
Cutting tasks are paramount
Hou (Houju)
Simmering, frying, and so on take second place

In Japanese Cuisine, Cutting Takes Priority

The yin and yang of knives

"It's part of a chef's training to go on a journey with a single knife stuck in his bleached cotton belt." So go the lyrics of the Japanese song "Hozenji Yokocho," a big hit circa 1960. A kitchen knife once had the same meaning for Japanese chefs as a sword for a samurai. Why were knives so valued?

No one knows when kitchen knives were first made in Japan, but the oldest surviving kitchen knife is from the 8th century and is held by the Shosoin Repository in Nara. It looks like a Japanese sword, but it is single bevel, whereas Japanese swords are double bevel. It is highly likely that knife-making technology came from China, but

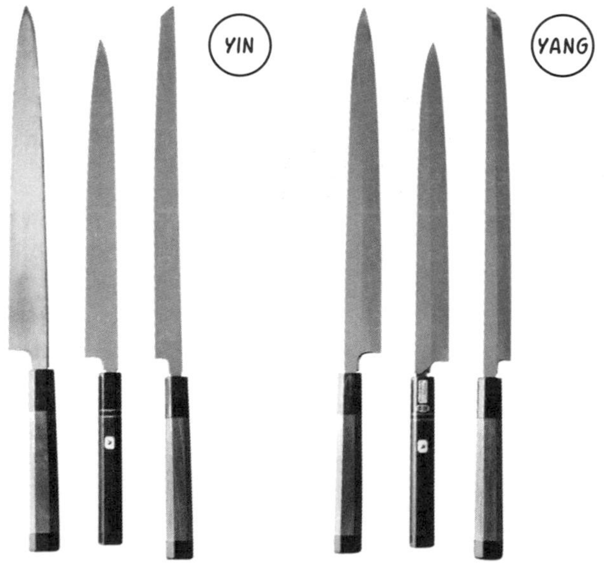
YIN
YANG

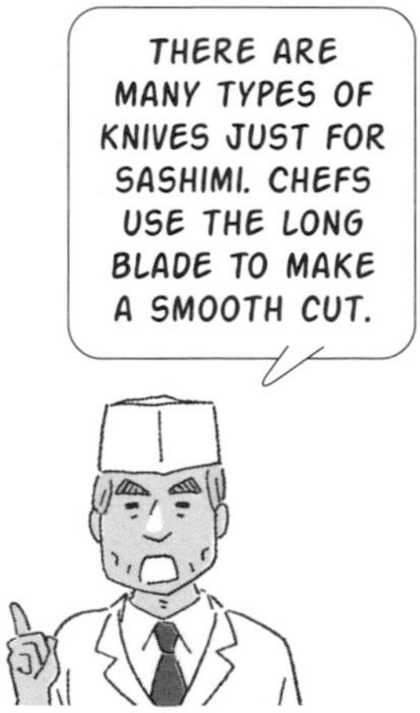
THERE ARE MANY TYPES OF KNIVES JUST FOR SASHIMI. CHEFS USE THE LONG BLADE TO MAKE A SMOOTH CUT.

From left to right: Sashimi (yanagiba) knife, blowfish knife, and takobiki knife (a Kanto-style sashimi knife). The photos on the right show the beveled yang side, while those on the left show the unbeveled yin side.

Chinese knives have been double bevel since ancient times, so single-bevel blades are likely an innovation of the Japanese.

The yin-yang philosophy mentioned on page 70 also extends to knives, applying in particular to those that are single bevel. The side with the blade is viewed as yang and the side without the blade is yin. When peeling round ingredients such as daikon radish with

Figure 1 **The Yin and Yang of Knives**

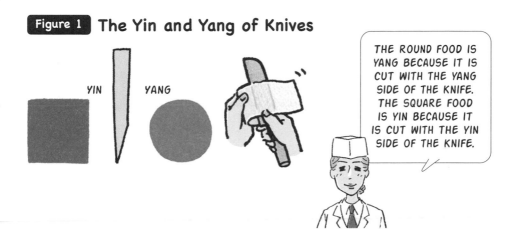

YIN
YANG
THE ROUND FOOD IS YANG BECAUSE IT IS CUT WITH THE YANG SIDE OF THE KNIFE. THE SQUARE FOOD IS YIN BECAUSE IT IS CUT WITH THE YIN SIDE OF THE KNIFE.

Figure 2 **Cross Sections of Laminated Knives Made of Soft Iron and Steel**

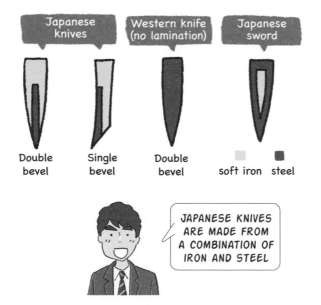

Japanese knives
Western knife (no lamination)
Japanese sword
Double bevel
Single bevel
Double bevel
soft iron
steel
JAPANESE KNIVES ARE MADE FROM A COMBINATION OF IRON AND STEEL

a knife, the yang side of the knife touches the food being peeled, making it, too, yang. Conversely, when cutting a square ingredient, the yin side of the knife touches the food being cut, making it yin (Figure 1). The nature of ingredients change depending on whether they touch the yang or yin side of the knife. By using yin and yang, the chef is able to express harmony.

How eating sashimi led to the single-bevel knife

The development of single-bevel knives in Japan can be attributed to the fact that sashimi was considered the ultimate feast in Japanese cuisine. This is probably due to Japan's abundance of clean water and fish that can be eaten raw, as well as the historical avoidance of meat.

Most Western knives have blades made entirely of stainless steel, with blades too hard to cut soft fish thinly and cleanly. On the other hand, Japanese knives, like Japanese swords, are made by joining steel and soft iron (Figure 2). Combining the hardness of steel with the flexibility of soft iron not only makes it possible to cut fish and soft meat, but also to sense subtle textures when cutting, making it easy to work with great delicacy.

With sashimi, texture more than taste or aroma is the key to deliciousness. When cutting meat a beautiful cross section is not necessary, but in the case of sashimi, a cleanly cut cross section creates a smooth texture on the tongue, which directly affects the taste. Examining a slice of sashimi cut with a well-sharpened sashimi knife under an electron microscope reveals no cellular damage. The ability to cut without destroying cells means that the flavor of the food is preserved, and Japanese knives with excellent sharpness are now used by many international chefs.

Japan's knife ceremony, the original display cooking

Chefs in Japanese restaurants are called *itamae*. The term, which originated in the mid Edo period, means "in front of the cutting board." Before that, a chef was called a *hochonin*, or "knife man" (or "knife master"). Let's take a look at the history of this term. There are many theories about the origin of the Japanese word for knife, *hocho*. Today the word is written 包丁, but originally it was written 庖丁. 庖 in Chinese means kitchen, and 丁 means a person who works in a kitchen, so one theory claims *hocho* meant chef. Another theory traces the word's roots to a legendary chef in classic Chinese literature[1] called Hocho, who used a kitchen knife to dismantle a cow with great skill.

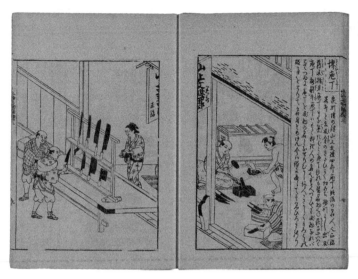

Nihon sankai meibutsu zue (Famous Products of Land and Sea in Japan) (Digital Collections, National Diet Library)

A spread in this illustrated guide to products from various regions of Japan during the mid-Edo period depicts a kitchen knife shop in Sakai, Osaka with a variety of knives displayed in front of the store.

IN THE PEACEFUL EDO PERIOD, THE DEMAND FOR SWORDS DECREASED, AND LOCAL SWORDSMITHS BEGAN TO MAKE KITCHEN KNIVES.

---

1 The story is mentioned in both the *Zhuangzi*, dating to the 3rd or 4th century BCE, and the *Lushii chunqiu*, from the 2nd century BCE.

A traditional practice called the knife ceremony also relates to the concept of chef as "knife man." The knife ceremony is performed by sitting in front of a large cutting board wearing an *eboshi* silk hat and two-piece *hitatare* outfit, both worn since Heian times, holding a kitchen knife in the right hand and an implement called a *manabashi* in the left, without touching the food (see photo below left). Today, the knife ceremony is often held during the dedication of shrines, but its origins lie in a ceremony to purify food presented to the emperor. Since death has been considered unclean in Japan since ancient times (see page 71), when the emperor ate fish or birds, the carcass had to be purified to turn it into food. The knife ceremony accomplished this purification, and was also a ceremony of gratitude for the gift of life.

The knife ceremony is said to have originated in the 9th century when, at the order of Emperor Koko (830–887), the court noble Fujiwara no Yamakage devised a system for cutting and arranging carp, which was then incorporated into court ceremonies. Later, the

An Ikama-style knife ceremony (see page 122).

A kitchen knife (right) and *manabashi* (left) used in the knife ceremony.

term *hocho suru*, "to do the knife," came to be used to describe a person's skill with a kitchen knife in public, and the person doing it was called a *hochonin*, or knife man.

By the 12th century, the knife ceremony, which had been a court ceremony, became a social ritual for entertaining guests. Court nobles would entertain their guests by having the master of the house perform the knife ceremony, after which the family chef would cook the fish and fowl that he had purified. In the Muromachi period (1336–1573), the ceremony became popular among the samurai class, and soon professional knife men began performing the ceremony in place of the head of household. The knife men who served court nobles and samurai established several schools of practice, passing on their secrets and becoming leaders in the development of Japanese food culture (see pages 122 to 125).

At the time, most knife men came from the upper classes and were not the same as the chefs we know today. The knife men only cut fish and fowl with their knives; the actual cooking was done

Shuhanron emaki (Illustrated Debate Over Wine and Rice) (National Diet Library Digital Collections)

In this scene from a picture scroll from the late Muromachi period (see page 124), a samurai-like figure holds a knife in his right hand and a long *manabashi* in his left, cutting up fish and fowl.

THE OLD CUTTING BOARDS HAD LEGS BECAUSE KNIFE MEN COOKED SITTING DOWN

by people of lower status.[2] The knife men knew how to use a knife and proper etiquette, but did not pay much attention to the art of cooking or the pursuit of flavor. This history helps explain why cutting is accorded higher status in Japanese cuisine than grilling, frying and other forms of heating food (see page 83).

By the way, watching the masterful knife work of the chef is a pleasure you can enjoy at an itamae kappo restaurant, where the chefs cook multicourse Japanese meals in front of diners. The teppanyaki restaurants that became successful in the U.S. after World War II gained popularity by putting on a show of grilling steaks. In the West, open kitchens on full view to diners is a recent trend. In Japan, the tradition of displaying the cutting process dates back centuries to the days of the knife ceremony.

BRILLIANT KNIFE WORK IS LIKE A SHOW!

LOOKS DELICIOUS, MEOW!

PUTTING ON A SHOW OF GRILLING STEAKS FOR DINERS MIGHT HAVE ROOTS IN THE KNIFE CEREMONY.

---

2 By the end of the Edo period, chefs began to imitate knife men, and class distinctions fell apart.

Kitchen Hierarchies in France and Japan

Kitchen organization in a Japanese restaurant

A hierarchical organization based on the principle that cutting is all-important (see page 75).

What's *kasshu houju*?

The concept that preparing foods to serve raw, like sashimi, takes precedence over cooking foods using heat.

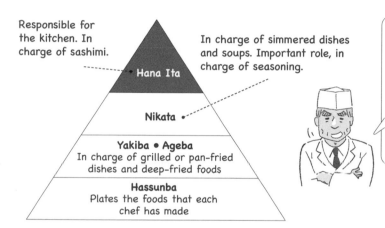

Responsible for the kitchen. In charge of sashimi.

In charge of simmered dishes and soups. Important role, in charge of seasoning.

Hana Ita

Nikata

Yakiba • Ageba
In charge of grilled or pan-fried dishes and deep-fried foods

Hassunba
Plates the foods that each chef has made

THE HANA ITA (FLOWER OF THE CUTTING BOARD) IS SOMETIMES CALLED THE ITA CHO (HEAD OF THE BOARD) OR THE TACHI ITA (STANDING AT THE BOARD).

Kitchen organization in a French restaurant

Division of labor, with each division headed by a *chef de partie*.

THE HEAD CHEF IS THE CHIEF EXECUTIVE OF THE ENTIRE KITCHEN.

Chef de Cuisine
(head chef)

Sous Chef de Cuisine
(sub head chef)

| **Saucier** (sauces) | **Rotissier** (cooking with direct heat) | **Poissonnier** (fish dishes) | **Patissier** (sweets) |

Larger kitchens are subdivided into other categories such as fried foods, appetizers, soups, and cold dishes.

THIS SYSTEM WAS CREATED BY AUGUSTE ESCOFFIER, THE GREAT CHEF OF THE LATE 19TH CENTURY.

Fermenting for Flavor

HI MAGUKO!

MEOW

I WISH I HAD A CUTE CAT LIKE YOU!

STEWED FISH FOR DINNER? HUH...

YOU CAN'T HAVE CATS AT YOUR HOUSE SINCE YOUR MOM HAS ALLERGIES, RIGHT?

YEAH. AND DAD DOESN'T LIKE DOGS.

THEN WHY DON'T YOU TRY GROWING ASPERGILLUS ORYZAE, KOJI MOLD?

KOJI IS A MICROORGANISM USED TO MAKE FERMENTED FOODS LIKE SAKE, MISO AND SOY SAUCE, RIGHT?

BUT YOU CAN'T SEE KOJI AND IT'S NOT CUTE...

GRUMBLE GRUMBLE

sake

RIGHT. FERMENTATION DESCRIBES THE FUNCTION OF MICROORGANISMS THAT ARE BENEFICIAL TO HUMANS.

Fermentation

Putrefaction

...BUT WHEN THE SAME MICROBIAL ACTION IS NOT GOOD FOR US, WE CALL IT PUTREFACTION OR ROT.

KOJI MOLD WAS ORIGINALLY A WILD FUNGUS CALLED ASPERGILLUS FLAVUS, WHICH CAN BE EXTREMELY POISONOUS.

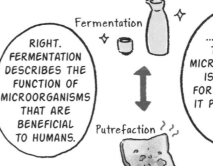

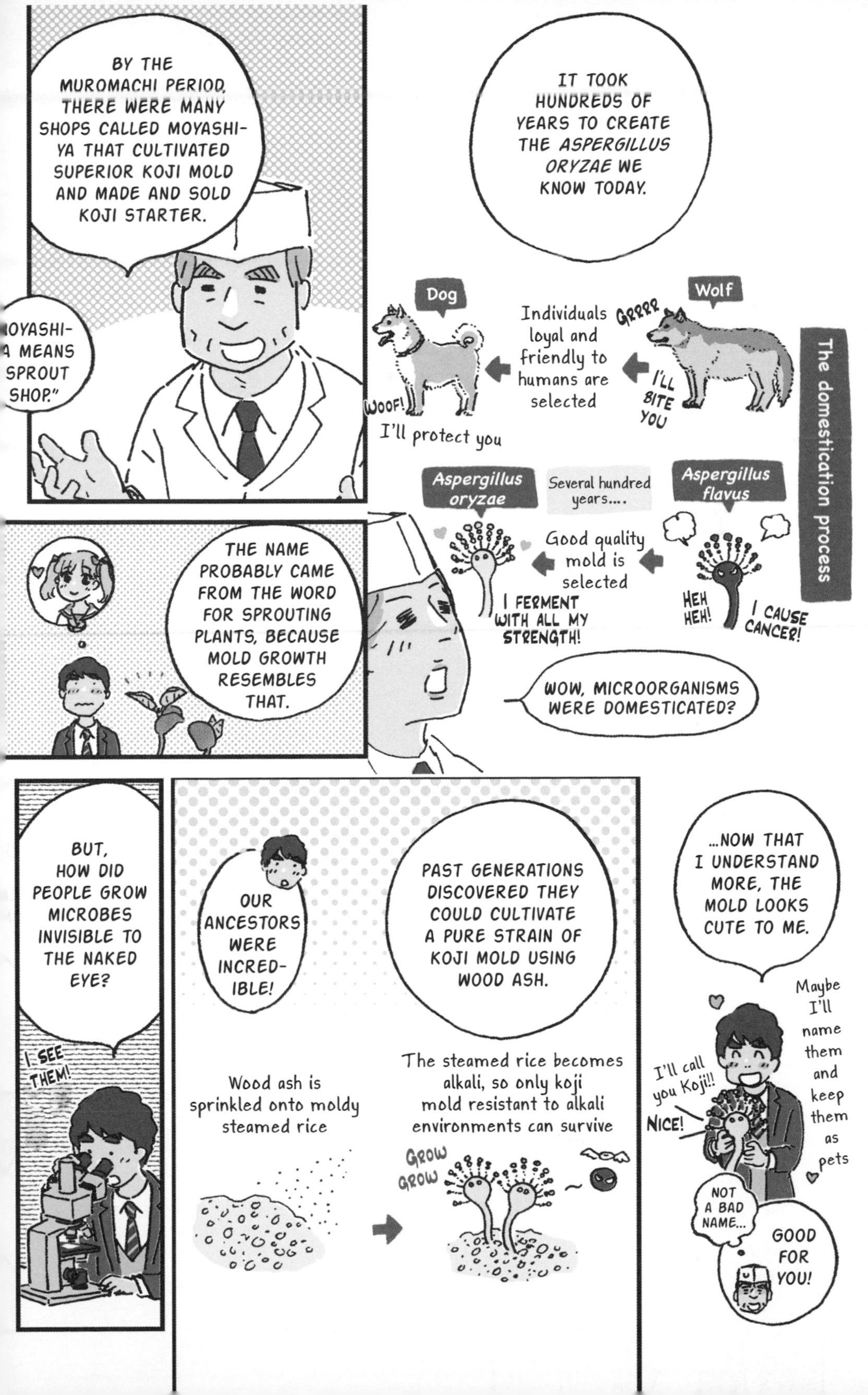

BY THE MUROMACHI PERIOD, THERE WERE MANY SHOPS CALLED MOYASHI-YA THAT CULTIVATED SUPERIOR KOJI MOLD AND MADE AND SOLD KOJI STARTER.
OYASHI-A MEANS SPROUT SHOP."
THE NAME PROBABLY CAME FROM THE WORD FOR SPROUTING PLANTS, BECAUSE MOLD GROWTH RESEMBLES THAT.
IT TOOK HUNDREDS OF YEARS TO CREATE THE ASPERGILLUS ORYZAE WE KNOW TODAY.
The domestication process
Wolf
GRRRR
I'LL BITE YOU
Individuals loyal and friendly to humans are selected
Dog
WOOF!
I'll protect you
Aspergillus flavus
HEH HEH!
I CAUSE CANCER!
Several hundred years....
Good quality mold is selected
Aspergillus oryzae
I FERMENT WITH ALL MY STRENGTH!
WOW, MICROORGANISMS WERE DOMESTICATED?
BUT, HOW DID PEOPLE GROW MICROBES INVISIBLE TO THE NAKED EYE?
I SEE THEM!
PAST GENERATIONS DISCOVERED THEY COULD CULTIVATE A PURE STRAIN OF KOJI MOLD USING WOOD ASH.
OUR ANCESTORS WERE INCRED-IBLE!
Wood ash is sprinkled onto moldy steamed rice
The steamed rice becomes alkali, so only koji mold resistant to alkali environments can survive
GROW GROW
...NOW THAT I UNDERSTAND MORE, THE MOLD LOOKS CUTE TO ME.
Maybe I'll name them and keep them as pets
I'll call you Koji!!
NICE!
NOT A BAD NAME...
GOOD FOR YOU!

Koji: The Powerhouse of Japanese Cuisine

Harnessing a mold that grows on rice

Seasonings such as soy sauce, miso, mirin and vinegar are all fermented using koji mold. Let's take a look at this behind-the-scenes powerhouse of Japanese cuisine.

Koji mold refers to the spores of a certain type of mold, while koji refers to grains inoculated with this mold. There are various types of koji mold, but here we will focus on *Aspergillus oryzae*.

It is not clear when koji mold was first used, but the earliest written reference is in the *Harima-no-kuni fudoki* (Record of the Customs and Lands of Harima Province)[1] a text from the 8th century. One of the passages in this text tells of steamed rice being offered to the gods but becoming wet and moldy, so people made sake from it and presented it to the gods for a feast. Mold grown on steamed rice is koji mold. At this time, people already knew that sake could be made from moldy rice. Koji mold evolved to meet the needs of sake brewers who wanted to produce good-tasting sake on a consistent basis.

---

1 *Harima-no-kuni fudoki* is Japan's oldest geographical record, compiled around 715. It contains a description of how rice was soaked in the Nukui River behind Niwata Shrine in Shiso, Hyogo Prefecture. Mold grew on the rice, resulting in delicious sake.

Figure 1 How Koji Mold Propagates

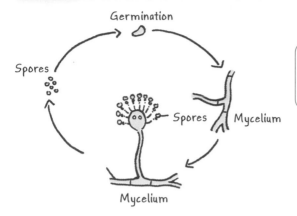

Germination

Spores

Spores

Mycelium

Mycelium

SPORES ARE LIKE SEEDS OF PLANTS.

Figure 2 How to Make Koji Starter (Traditional Method)

① Sprinkle steamed rice with wood ash and mold strain (protobacteria).

② Koji mold is cultured in a wooden tray called a *koji-buta*.

③ Spores germinate, mycelium grows, and after 5 to 6 days, many spores are produced.

④ The moldy rice is dried and passed through a sieve to separate out the spores for use.

The koji starter is ready!

What is koji starter?

Generally, the term refers to koji spores produced for brewing. They are added to steamed rice when making koji. In the brewing industry, koji starter is also called seed koji.

GREEN POWDER EVERYWHERE! IT'S LIKE GRASS IS SPROUTING.

TODAY, MANY KOJI STARTER MAKERS DO NOT USE WOOD ASH, INSTEAD USING AN ASEPTIC CHAMBER.

Today, many sake breweries use koji starter to make sake (see Figures 2 and 5). Before koji starter was invented, koji was made using the *tomodane* method, in which koji successfully made from naturally occurring mold was saved and used as starter for the next koji. However, the quality of koji made using this method was unreliable, and often failed due to contamination by various bacteria. Koji starter was developed to combat this problem. The key to making the starter was to add alkaline wood ash to the steamed rice. This caused alkali-sensitive bacteria to die, leaving only the alkali-resistant koji mold alive and resulting in the successful cultivation of pure koji mold. It was a revolutionary idea for humans to control microorganisms themselves, outside of producing fermented foods. In the Muromachi period (1336–1573), making and selling koji starter became a business.[2] Six hundred years ago, a one-of-a-kind bio-industry was established, cultivating a fungus unique to Japan.

How mold and yeast fermentation work together

The three major microorganisms responsible for fermentation are mold, yeast and bacteria. Koji mold is a widely used mold, baker's yeast and wine yeast are well-known yeasts, and lactic acid bacteria is a commonly used bacteria. Mold is the largest organism of the three, and its functions are complex. Bacteria are small and simple. Yeast is somewhere in between (Figure 3). In the next section, we'll look at the function of microorganisms during sake production.

---

2 In the Muromachi period, shops specializing in the sale of koji starter began opening in Kyoto and present-day Aichi Prefecture. The industry thrived until the Meiji Era (1868–1912). Even today, producers of miso, soy sauce and sake (with the exception of a few large soy sauce makers) use koji starter produced by these companies. However, less than 10 koji starter companies remain in Japan.

Figure 3 Mold, Yeast, and Fungi Sizes

Koji mold
(Aspergillus oryzae)

Koji spores 4—8 μm
(1 micrometer (μm) = 1/1000 mm)

Yeast spores 4—8 μm

Bacteria (cocci) About 1 μm

Incidentally....

A virus is about .1 μm

MOLDS ARE HUGE!

Diameter of mycelium 8—13 μm

A dense network of mycelium grow in the rice

Koji mold is the national fungus of Japan

In 2006, koji mold was recognized as Japan's "national fungus" by the Japanese Society of Brewing Science. The previous year, the National Institute of Advanced Industrial Science and Technology (AIST)[3] decoded the entire genome of koji mold and announced that it had approximately 12,000 genes.[4] The researchers discovered that koji mold had many genes for enzymes involved in the synthesis and degradation of protein, carbohydrates and lipids, providing scientific support for its high fermentation potential.

---

3 This institute organized a consortium for genome analysis of *Aspergillus oryzae* and conducted joint research with National Institute of Technology and Evaluation.
4 Published on the *Nature* website in 2005.

Figure 4 Winemaking Process

Grape juice

Alcoholic fermentation { ◄ Yeast

↓ Wine

Figure 5 Japanese Sake Brewing Process (Undiluted Sake)

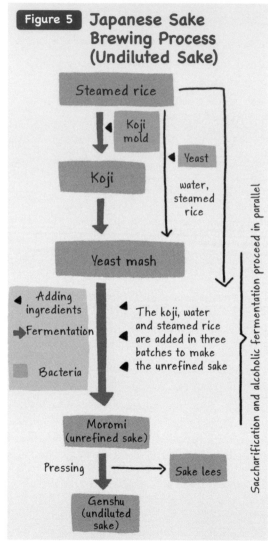

Steamed rice

◄ Koji mold

Koji

◄ Yeast

water, steamed rice

Yeast mash

Adding ingredients

Fermentation

Bacteria

The koji, water and steamed rice are added in three batches to make the unrefined sake

Moromi (unrefined sake)

Pressing ──► Sake lees

Genshu (undiluted sake)

Saccharification and alcoholic fermentation proceed in parallel

Figure 5-2 Saccharification by Koji Mold

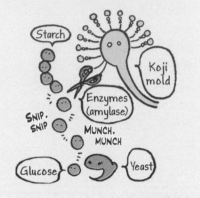

Starch

Koji mold

Enzymes (amylase)

SNIP, SNIP

MUNCH, MUNCH

Glucose

Yeast

Amylase, an enzyme produced by koji mold, breaks down the rice starch into small portions and converts it to glucose.

Japanese sake is made using a process called multiple parallel fermentation, in which saccharification and alcoholic fermentation take place at the same time.

Saccharification
Enzymes from koji mold break down starch from rice into glucose.

Alcoholic fermentation
Yeast decomposes glucose into alcohol and carbon dioxide.

AFTER THIS PROCESS, SAKE IS FILTERED, HEATED, STORED, AND DILUTED WITH WATER.

COMPARED TO WINE, MAKING JAPANESE SAKE IS COMPLICATED.

Alcoholic beverages are made by the alcoholic fermentation of sugar. The most readily available sugars in nature are found in fruits. Naturally, the world's first alcoholic beverages were fruit wines. Grapes are the most commonly used fruit, yielding a type of wine that has been enjoyed for more than 8,000 years. To make it, yeast is added to grape juice and allowed to ferment (Figure 4).

Sake is made from rice, and the brewing process is quite a bit more complicated. Two fermentations take place in parallel, one using koji mold and the other using yeast. When koji starter is sprinkled on steamed rice to produce koji, the mycelia of koji fungi grow rapidly and break down starch, the main component of rice, to produce sugar (saccharification). Yeast then breaks down these sugars into alcohol and carbon dioxide (alcoholic fermentation), producing sake. Saccharification is necessary because the starch in rice consists of thousands of glucose molecules, making it too large for yeast to break down. Yeast is only able to do its work after koji mold, with its large size and high capacity for decomposition, converts the starch into sugar (Figure 5-2).

Fermentation is primarily carried out by microorganisms such as molds and yeasts, but it is the enzymes[5] they secrete that do the actual work. To draw an analogy, microorganisms such as mold and yeast are the carpenters, and enzymes are their carpentry tools. Fermentation is the process by which microorganisms use their own enzymes to break down and transform organic matter. Koji mold in particular is a treasure trove of enzymes, which it secretes. One typical enzymes is amylase, which breaks down starch and converts it into sugar; this enzyme creates sweetness. Another is protease, which breaks down proteins and converts them into amino acids, producing umami (see page 105).

---

5 Enzymes are proteins that cause certain chemical reactions. During fermentation, microorganisms use their enzymes to break down organic matter and obtain energy.

The birth of miso and soy sauce

Koji mold changed with the development of sake production. Later, it gave rise to miso and soy sauce. Miso and soy sauce share a common root in hishio,[6] a salted fermented food introduced from China. The *Engishiki* (Regulations and Laws of the Engi Era), a book from the 10th century, makes reference to "misho" along with hishio. The word "miso" is thought to have evolved from misho, which means "something that has not yet become hishio."

Originally a byproduct of hishio, miso eventually came to be produced intentionally, and a product called Kinzanji miso[7] became popular. In the Kamakura period (1185–1333), a Zen monk named Shinchi Kakushin is said to have learned how to make it while apprenticing at Kinzanji Temple in China, and after returning to Japan passed on the technique to the people of Yuasa, in the Kishu Domain. The liquid that separated and collected at the bottom of vats of Kinzanji miso tasted so good that people started using it, which is said to be the origin of soy sauce.

In the 17th century, Dutch merchants brought soy sauce to Europe, where it became popular. The French *Encyclopédie* compiled in 1765 includes an entry on soy sauce, praising it as a sauce that enhances the flavor of meat dishes, can be stored for a long time, and imparts deep flavor in very small quantities. Today, soy sauce is such a global condiment that hardly a kitchen in the world can be found without a bottle on hand.

---

6 In China, hishio existed as early as the 11th century BCE At that time it was a type of salty fermented paste made from the meat of birds, mammals and fish. By the 2nd century BCE, it was being made from soybeans.

7 A specialty of Wakayama, Chiba, and Shizuoka prefectures, Kinzanji miso is a type of namemiso, a flavored miso eaten as a side dish or accompaniment to sake.

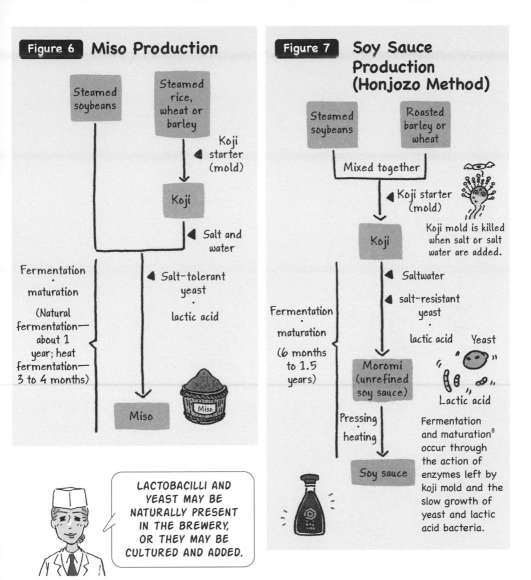

Figure 6 Miso Production

Steamed soybeans
Steamed rice, wheat or barley
Koji starter (mold)
Koji
Salt and water
Fermentation
•
maturation
(Natural fermentation—about 1 year; heat fermentation—3 to 4 months)
Salt-tolerant yeast
•
lactic acid
Miso
Miso

Figure 7 Soy Sauce Production (Honjozo Method)

Steamed soybeans
Roasted barley or wheat
Mixed together
Koji starter (mold)
Koji
Koji mold is killed when salt or salt water are added.
Saltwater
salt-resistant yeast
•
lactic acid
Yeast
Fermentation
•
maturation
(6 months to 1.5 years)
Moromi (unrefined soy sauce)
Lactic acid
Pressing
•
heating
Soy sauce
Fermentation and maturation[8] occur through the action of enzymes left by koji mold and the slow growth of yeast and lactic acid bacteria.

LACTOBACILLI AND YEAST MAY BE NATURALLY PRESENT IN THE BREWERY, OR THEY MAY BE CULTURED AND ADDED.

Koji starters for miso and soy sauce

Miso contains both amylase, an enzyme that converts starch into sugar, and protease, an enzyme that breaks down soy protein. Soy sauce does not need as much sweetness, so koji starters with more protease are typically preferred for its production.

8 Maturation is the process by which enzymes in food change the flavor over time. Unlike fermentation, it is not caused by microorganisms.

Fermentation, a global cooking trend

Fermenting food has many advantages. It improves preservation, increases nutritional value, creates new flavors and aromas, and improves digestion. Many local fermented foods have developed around the world, originally with the goal of enhancing preservation (see pages 96–97).

Once a traditional processing method, fermentation has recently gained worldwide attention as a revolutionary way of transforming how ingredients taste. The trend started at noma,[9] a restaurant in Copenhagen, Denmark that began experimenting with fermentation in 2008. Noma has focused on exploring new flavors using local ingredients. The restaurant's chefs consider fermentation a cooking method, and have created unprecedented flavors in their

Koueki kokusan-kou (Cultivation of Industrial Crops) (Digital Collections, National Diet Library)

Soy sauce production in a farming village, depicted in an agricultural science book published in 1859. In the upper right, roasted soybeans and steamed barley are being mashed with koji mold.

---

9 Noma opened in 2003 and has earned top place in The World's 50 Best Restaurants ranking in 2010, 2011, 2012, 2014 and 2021. René Redzepi is the chef.

fermentation lab (see page 107). Since 2016, more and more restaurants in Europe and the United States have adopted fermentation, and many chefs are now buying koji starter from Japan to use in their cooking.

In Japan, fermented foods are being reevaluated in the wake of the shiokoji (a paste for seasoning and marinating) boom that occurred around 2010. Japan was the first country in the world to create umami[10] through fermentation. A variety of fermented foods throughout Japan take advantage of the power of local microorganisms. Knowing about them enriches our food culture.

Figure 8 **Fermented Foods Grouped by the Microorganisms That Create Them**

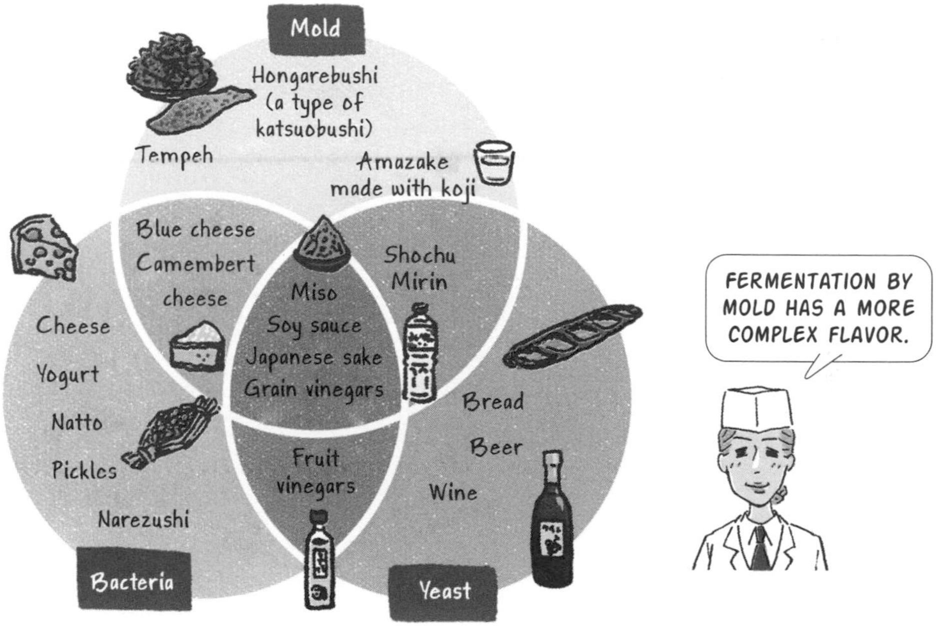
Mold
Hongarebushi (a type of katsuobushi)
Tempeh
Amazake made with koji
Blue cheese
Camembert cheese
Shochu
Mirin
Miso
Soy sauce
Japanese sake
Grain vinegars
Cheese
Yogurt
Natto
Pickles
Narezushi
Fruit vinegars
Bread
Beer
Wine
Bacteria
Yeast
FERMENTATION BY MOLD HAS A MORE COMPLEX FLAVOR.

10 See the chapter on umami, pages 98 to 107.

The Big Picture | Fermented Foods Around the World

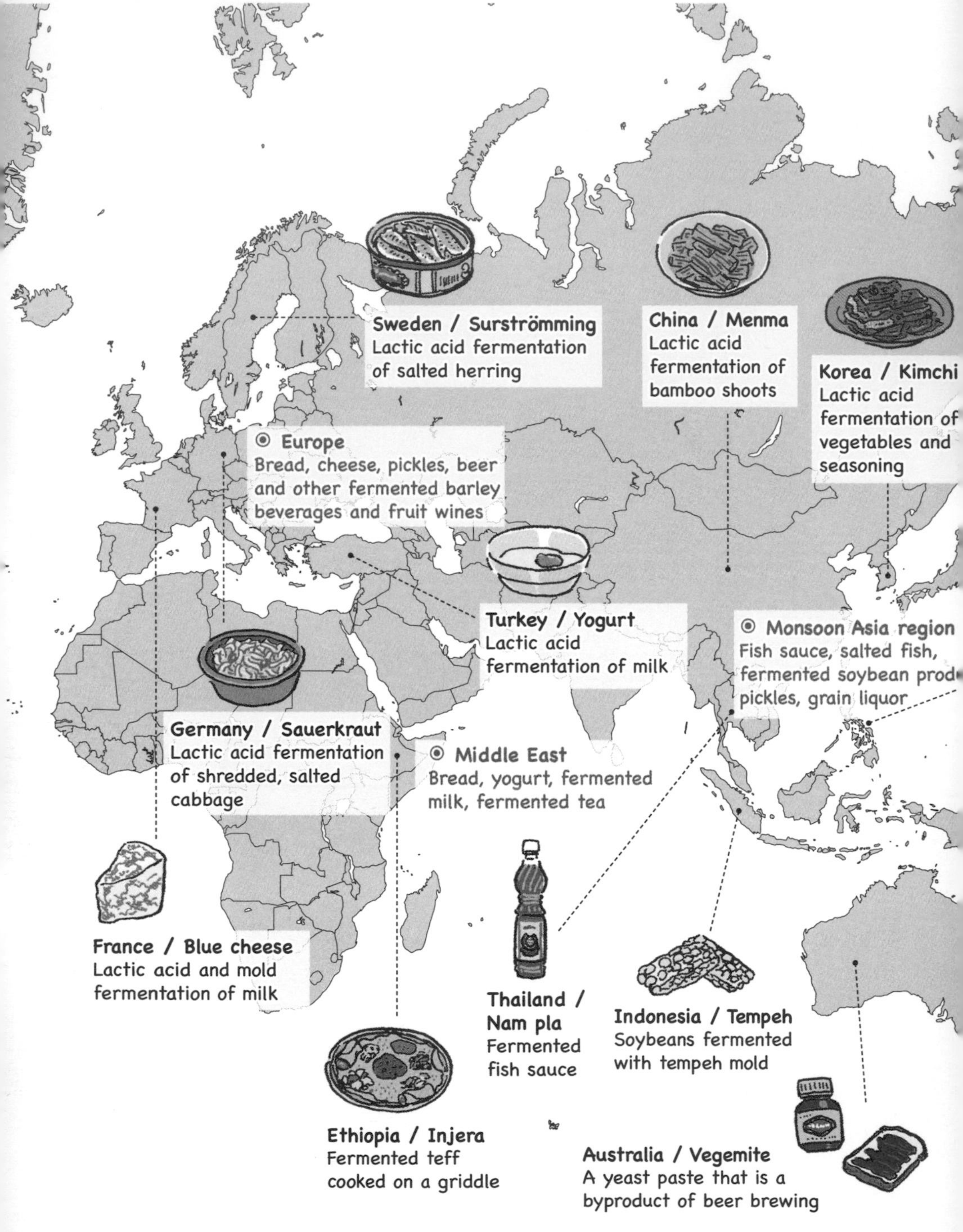

Sweden / Surströmming
Lactic acid fermentation of salted herring
China / Menma
Lactic acid fermentation of bamboo shoots
Korea / Kimchi
Lactic acid fermentation of vegetables and seasoning
◉ Europe
Bread, cheese, pickles, beer and other fermented barley beverages and fruit wines
Turkey / Yogurt
Lactic acid fermentation of milk
◉ Monsoon Asia region
Fish sauce, salted fish, fermented soybean prod
pickles, grain liquor
Germany / Sauerkraut
Lactic acid fermentation of shredded, salted cabbage
◉ Middle East
Bread, yogurt, fermented milk, fermented tea
France / Blue cheese
Lactic acid and mold fermentation of milk
Thailand / Nam pla
Fermented fish sauce
Indonesia / Tempeh
Soybeans fermented with tempeh mold
Ethiopia / Injera
Fermented teff cooked on a griddle
Australia / Vegemite
A yeast paste that is a byproduct of beer brewing

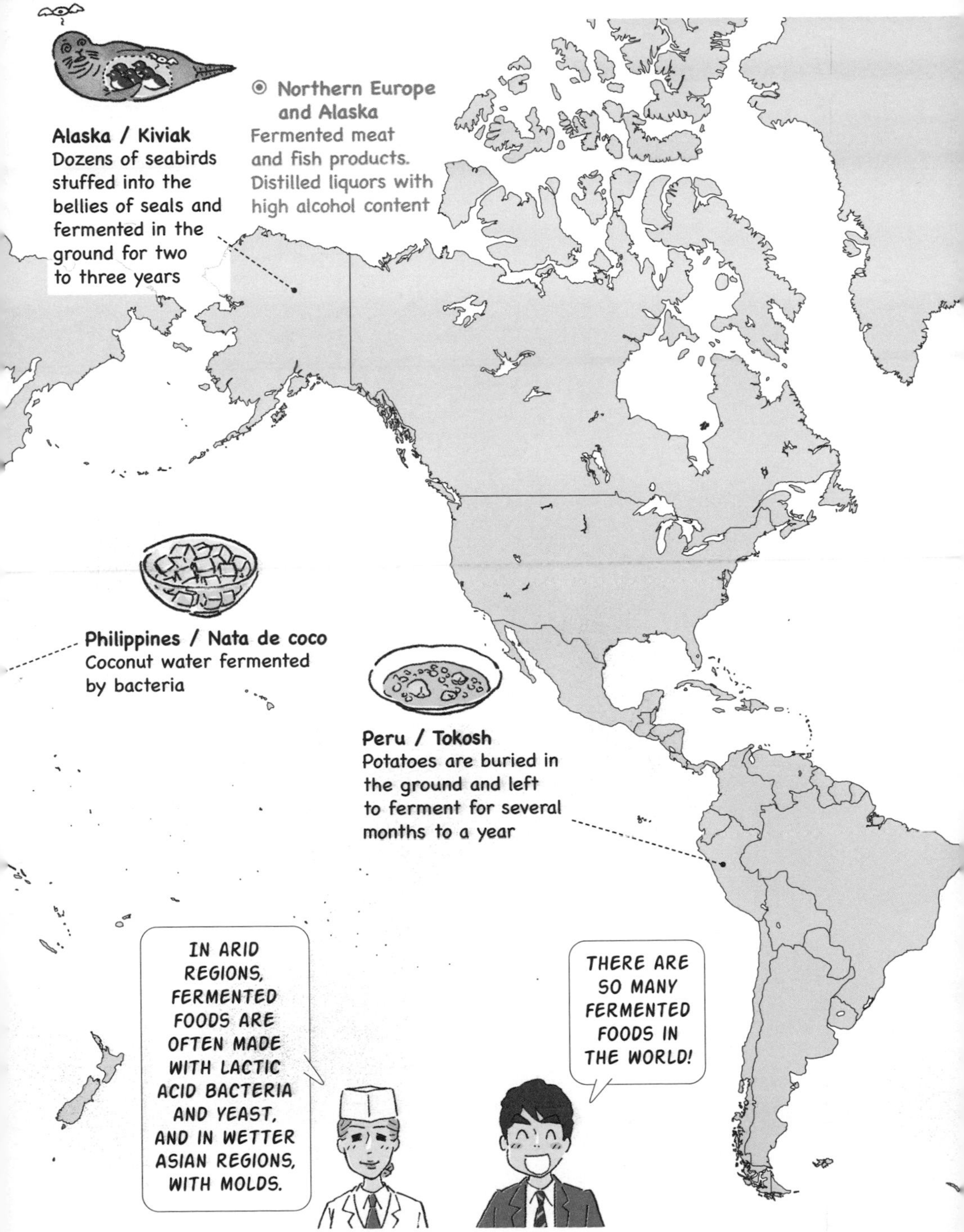
Alaska / Kiviak
Dozens of seabirds stuffed into the bellies of seals and fermented in the ground for two to three years
◉ Northern Europe and Alaska
Fermented meat and fish products. Distilled liquors with high alcohol content
Philippines / Nata de coco
Coconut water fermented by bacteria
Peru / Tokosh
Potatoes are buried in the ground and left to ferment for several months to a year
THERE ARE SO MANY FERMENTED FOODS IN THE WORLD!
IN ARID REGIONS, FERMENTED FOODS ARE OFTEN MADE WITH LACTIC ACID BACTERIA AND YEAST, AND IN WETTER ASIAN REGIONS, WITH MOLDS.

Umami, the Fifth Flavor

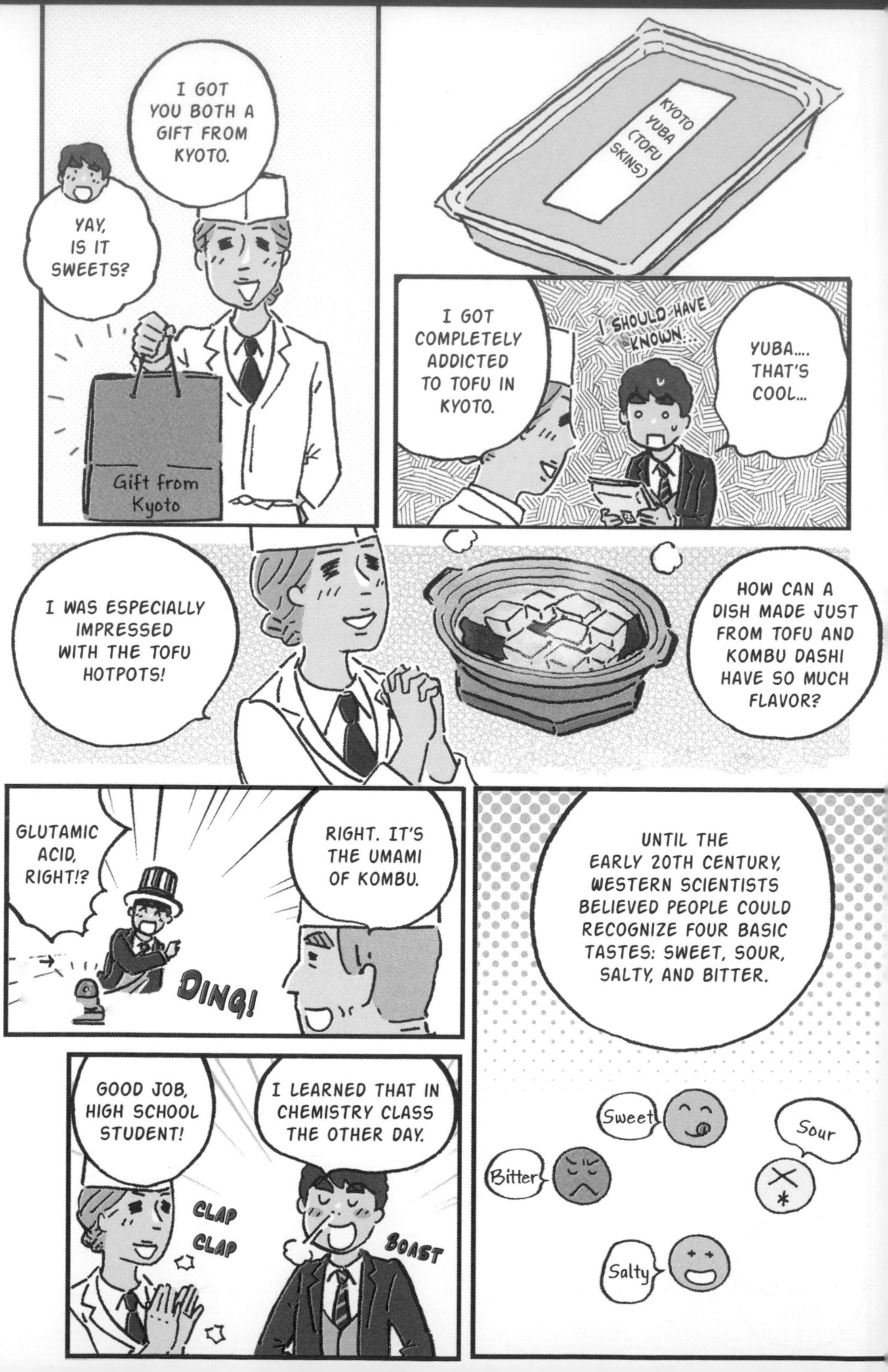

I GOT YOU BOTH A GIFT FROM KYOTO.
YAY, IS IT SWEETS?
Gift from Kyoto
KYOTO YUBA (TOFU SKINS)
I GOT COMPLETELY ADDICTED TO TOFU IN KYOTO.
I SHOULD HAVE KNOWN...
YUBA.... THAT'S COOL...
I WAS ESPECIALLY IMPRESSED WITH THE TOFU HOTPOTS!
HOW CAN A DISH MADE JUST FROM TOFU AND KOMBU DASHI HAVE SO MUCH FLAVOR?
GLUTAMIC ACID, RIGHT!?
DING!
RIGHT. IT'S THE UMAMI OF KOMBU.
GOOD JOB, HIGH SCHOOL STUDENT!
I LEARNED THAT IN CHEMISTRY CLASS THE OTHER DAY.
CLAP CLAP
BOAST
UNTIL THE EARLY 20TH CENTURY, WESTERN SCIENTISTS BELIEVED PEOPLE COULD RECOGNIZE FOUR BASIC TASTES: SWEET, SOUR, SALTY, AND BITTER.
Sweet
Sour
Bitter
Salty

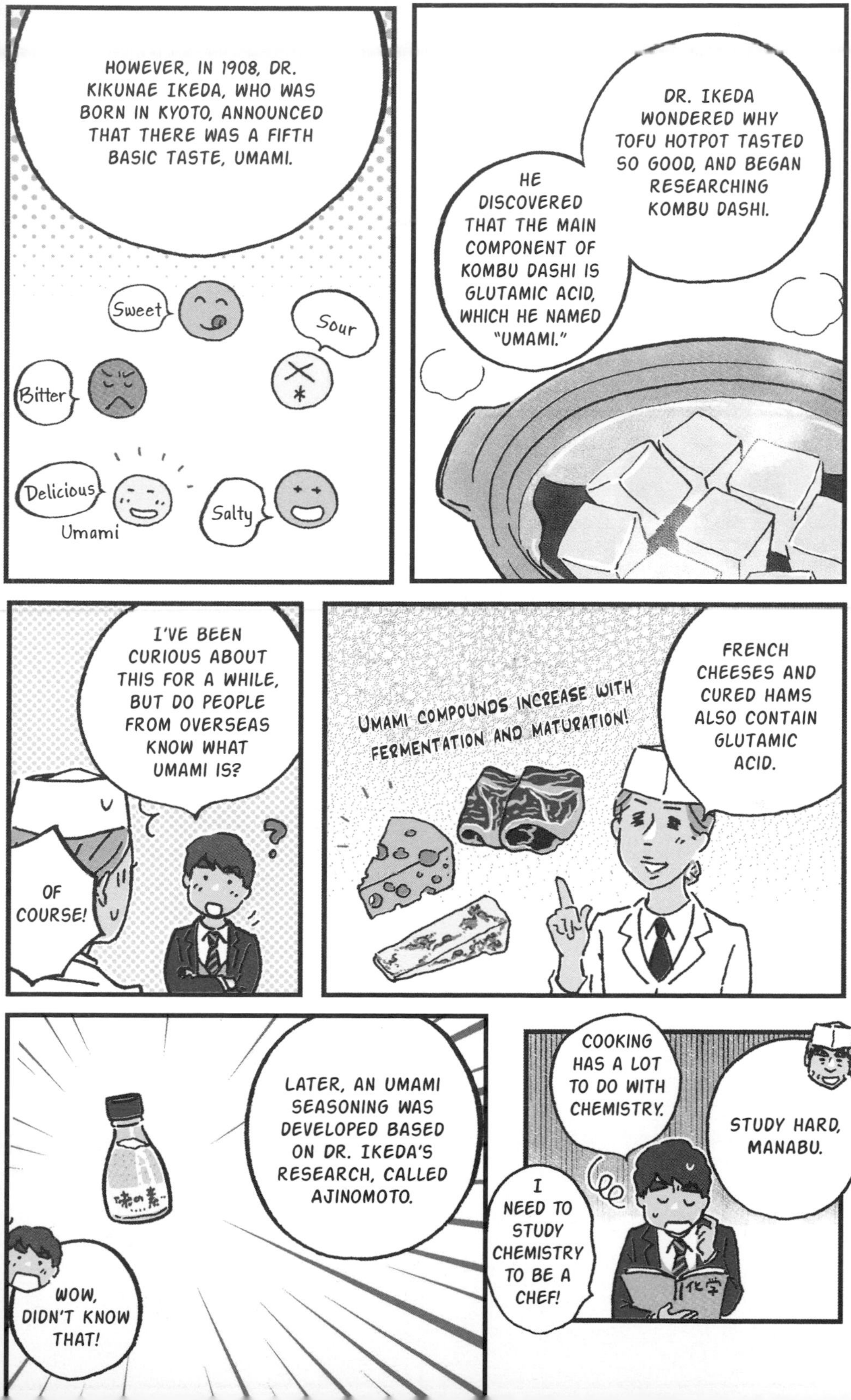
HOWEVER, IN 1908, DR. KIKUNAE IKEDA, WHO WAS BORN IN KYOTO, ANNOUNCED THAT THERE WAS A FIFTH BASIC TASTE, UMAMI.
Sweet
Sour
Bitter
Delicious
Umami
Salty
DR. IKEDA WONDERED WHY TOFU HOTPOT TASTED SO GOOD, AND BEGAN RESEARCHING KOMBU DASHI.
HE DISCOVERED THAT THE MAIN COMPONENT OF KOMBU DASHI IS GLUTAMIC ACID, WHICH HE NAMED "UMAMI."
I'VE BEEN CURIOUS ABOUT THIS FOR A WHILE, BUT DO PEOPLE FROM OVERSEAS KNOW WHAT UMAMI IS?
OF COURSE!
FRENCH CHEESES AND CURED HAMS ALSO CONTAIN GLUTAMIC ACID.
UMAMI COMPOUNDS INCREASE WITH FERMENTATION AND MATURATION!
LATER, AN UMAMI SEASONING WAS DEVELOPED BASED ON DR. IKEDA'S RESEARCH, CALLED AJINOMOTO.
WOW, DIDN'T KNOW THAT!
COOKING HAS A LOT TO DO WITH CHEMISTRY.
STUDY HARD, MANABU.
I NEED TO STUDY CHEMISTRY TO BE A CHEF!
化学

The Fifth Basic
Taste Goes Global

A Japanese scientist discovers umami

Humans perceive five basic tastes: sweet, sour, salty, bitter, and umami. Umami was discovered by the Japanese physical chemist Kikunae Ikeda. Ikeda was born in Kyoto in 1864 and studied in Germany after graduating from the chemistry department at the Imperial University (now the University of Tokyo). After returning to Japan, he became a professor at his alma mater. While in Germany, Ikeda had been impressed by the physique and diet of the German people, and in 1907, he began researching the flavor components of kombu in hopes of remedying the nutritional deficiencies of the Japanese people. Ikeda had read an article by the medical doctor Hiizu Miyake arguing that good taste promotes digestion. He believed that if he could analyze the flavor of kombu dashi, it would become possible to industrially produce a delicious seasoning that would improve the health of the Japanese people. In 1908, he succeeded in extracting about an ounce (30 grams) of glutamic acid[1] crystals from about 10 gallons (38 kilograms) of kombu dashi. Ikeda discovered that the delicious flavor of the dashi came from monosodium glutamate and named the taste substance "umami." In the same year, Ikeda invented and patented a process for manufacturing seasonings with monosodium glutamate as the main ingredient. This invention is widely considered one of Japan's ten greatest inventions.

---

1 Glutamic acid itself tastes sour and is hard to dissolve in water. Ikeda discovered that dissolving it in water and neutralizing it with sodium hydroxide to make sodium glutamate resulted in a delicious flavor.

In 1913, Shintaro Kodama, a student of Ikeda's, discovered that inosinic acid is the umami component of katsuobushi (bonito flakes). In 1957, Akira Kuninaka of the Yamasa Soy Sauce Research Institute discovered guanylic acid, the umami component of dried shiitake mushrooms. At the same time, Kuninaka also discovered a synergistic effect of umami in which guanylic acid and sodium glutamate combine to produce an astonishing amplification of umami.

Figure 1 How We Sense Umami

Flavor components
Tongue surface
epithe-lium
Taste receptor cells
Taste buds
About 50 μm diameter
Gustatory nerves
To the brain

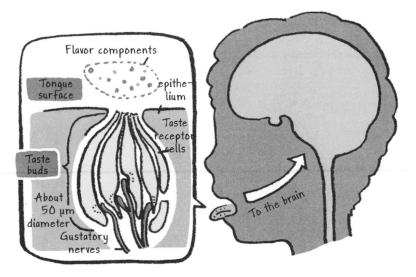

Taste receptor cells in the taste buds are classified into types I–IV, with type II cells being receptive to umami, sweet, and bitter tastes, and type III cells being receptive to sour tastes.

Scientists at Kyushu University discovered the nerves that transmit the taste of fat in 2019, and Kyoto Prefectural Medical University published research on salt taste reception in 2008.

Taste buds on the epithelium of the tongue are comprised of 50 to 150 taste cells, which contain receptors for umami. Taste receptors receive umami dissolved in saliva or water and transmit a tantalizing signal to the gustatory nerve, which sends the signal to the brain, where the taste is perceived.

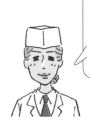

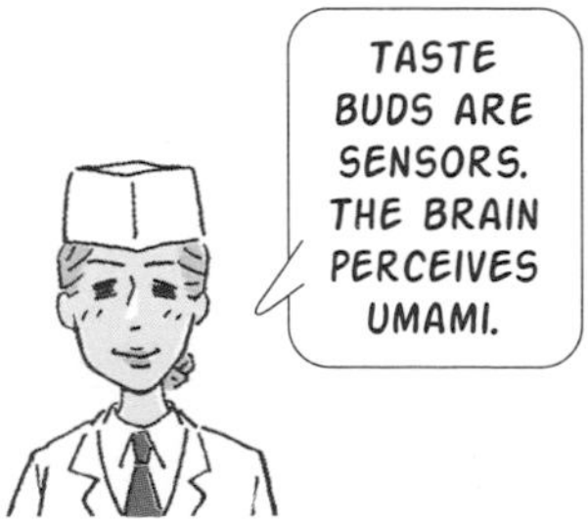

TASTE BUDS ARE SENSORS. THE BRAIN PERCEIVES UMAMI.

Table 1 Umami Content of Various Foods (mg/100g)

	Ingredient	Glutamic acid	Inosinic acid	Guanylic acid
Vegetables and mushrooms	Makombu kelp	1610–3200		
	Nori	550–1350	1–40	3–80
	Tomatoes	150–250		
	Dried shiitake mushrooms	1060		150
	Enoki mushrooms	90		50 (when cooked)
Seafood and seafood products	Niboshi (dried anchovies)	40–50	350–800	
	Katsuobushi	30–40	470–700	
	Tiger shrimp	120	90	
	Tuna	1–10	250–360	
	Oysters	40–150	20	
	Anchovies	630		
	Fermented squid	620		
Meat and dairy products	Pork	10	230	
	Chicken	20–50	150–230	
	Beef	10	80	
	Cured ham	340		
	Parmesan cheese	1200–1680		
Fermented foods	Natto	140		
	Fish sauce	950		
	Soy sauce	400–1700		
	Miso	200–700		
	Kimchi	240		

(Source: Umami Information Center website)

AMINO ACID AND NUCLEIC ACID UMAMI FLAVORS HAVE A SYNERGISTIC EFFECT WHEN COMBINED.

The two main types of umami components

Amino acid type

Amino acids are the smallest constituent units of protein. Protein is tasteless but produces a sweet and savory taste when broken down into smaller pieces and converted into amino acids. Glutamic acid is an amino-acid-type umami component.

Nucleic acid type

Essential for creating new cells, nucleic acids are divided into DNA and RNA. They are composed of phosphate, salts, and sugars called cleotides. Inosinic acid and guanylic acid are nucleic-acid-type umami components. Inosinic acid is abundant in animal products and guanylic acid in mushrooms.

Although umami was discovered in 1908, Western scientists were skeptical about its existence. They considered umami to be a combination of sweet, salty, bitter and sour tastes. In 2002, a team of researchers at the University of Miami demonstrated that cells in the tongue's taste buds (Figure 1) contain receptors that detect monosodium glutamate. This finally led to the international recognition of umami's existence. As more foods are scientifically analyzed, it has become clear that umami is not limited to certain ingredients, but rather is universally present in seafood, meat, vegetables, fermented foods, and more (Table 1).

Figure 2 **Glutamic Acid Content in Breast Milk and Kombu Dashi**

Glutamic acid
30
20
10
19mg /100g
22mg /100g
Breast milk
Kombu dashi

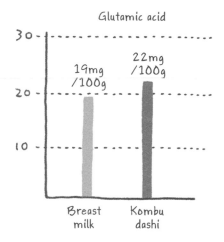

(Created from Umami Information Center website data)

Breast milk contains almost as much glutamic acid as kombu dashi. All living organisms produce glutamic acid in their bodies, and it is present in amniotic fluid in the mother's womb. For babies, umami is a taste they have been familiar with since before birth.

BREAST MILK IS RICH IN GLUTAMIC ACID. THAT'S WHY BABIES INSTINCTIVELY LIKE UMAMI!

Table 2 Elements of Deliciousness

Element		
Sweet	Basic flavors	Widely accepted flavors
Salty	Basic flavors	Widely accepted flavors
Sour	Basic flavors	Widely accepted flavors
Bitter	Basic flavors	Widely accepted flavors
Umami	Basic flavors	Widely accepted flavors
Spicy		Widely accepted flavors
Astringent		Widely accepted flavors
Fatty		Widely accepted flavors
Fragrance	Sense of smell	
Texture on the teeth and tongue	Sense of touch	
Temperature	Sense of temperature	
Color, shininess	Sense of sight	
Shape	Sense of sight	
Sound (of chewing)	Sense of hearing	
External environment (atmosphere, temperature, humidity, etc.)		
Food experience (food habits, food poisoning, food culture, etc.)		
Internal biological environment (health, psychological state, etc.)		

(Based on *Umami tte nan daro* (What is Umami?) by Kenzo Kurihara (Iwanami Junior Shinsho))

What signals do the basic tastes send?

- Sweet taste signals sugar (energy source)
- Salty taste signals minerals
- Acidity signals decomposition
- Bitterness signals toxicity
- Umami signals protein

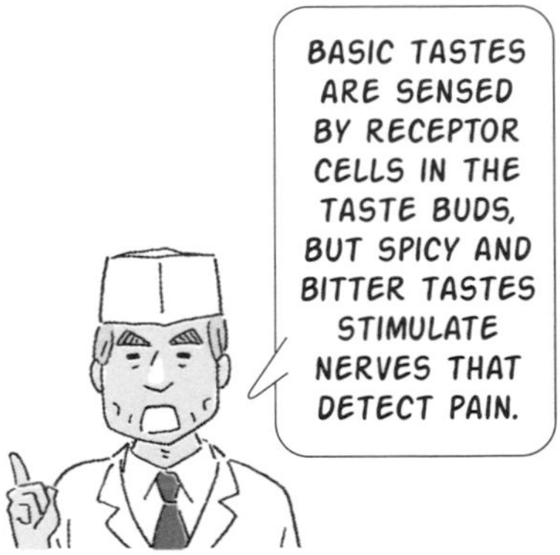
BASIC TASTES ARE SENSED BY RECEPTOR CELLS IN THE TASTE BUDS, BUT SPICY AND BITTER TASTES STIMULATE NERVES THAT DETECT PAIN.

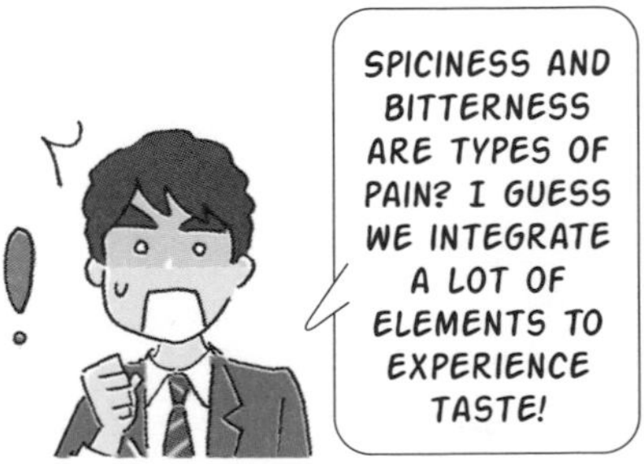
SPICINESS AND BITTERNESS ARE TYPES OF PAIN? I GUESS WE INTEGRATE A LOT OF ELEMENTS TO EXPERIENCE TASTE!

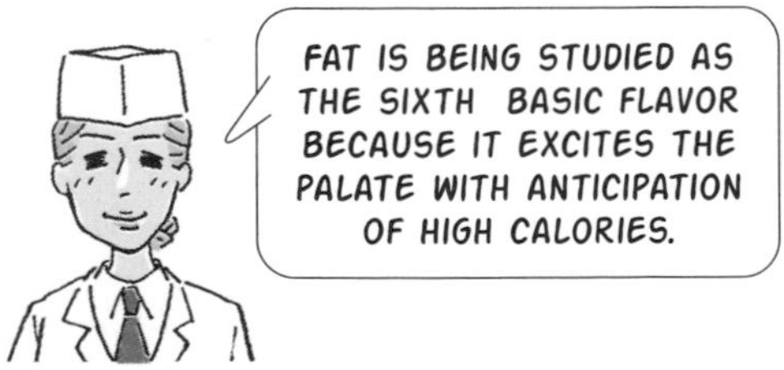
FAT IS BEING STUDIED AS THE SIXTH BASIC FLAVOR BECAUSE IT EXCITES THE PALATE WITH ANTICIPATION OF HIGH CALORIES.

Why we love umami

Let's take a look at umami from the perspective of taste sensations. Babies look satisfied when they are given umami foods. While sweet and lightly salty tastes are also favorable to them, they are averse to bitter and sour tastes.[2] These responses suggest that people are born with an innate preference for umami, sweet and salty tastes.

Each basic taste has its own physiological significance. Taste is the sense that responds to these sensations and distinguishes between edible and inedible foods. Carbohydrates are a key sweet-tasting nutrient. Since carbohydrates are a source of energy, sweetness signals the presence of energy. Salty taste signals minerals that are essential for life. In contrast, bitterness is a warning for poisons, and acidity for decomposition. So what does umami signal? Protein. Protein is an important nutrient that is the building block of the body, so it is natural that we instinctively seek out and enjoy its taste.

Proteins are giant molecules of interlinked amino acids. Protein itself has no taste, but when it is broken down into amino acids, they are small enough to be recognized by the taste sensors on the tongue, giving rise to umami taste. We can therefore view umami as a signal sent by amino acids.

2 Umami Information Center website

Tasty food without the fat

The history of how fermented foods were developed through the manipulation of koji mold (see pages 84 to 97) is, from a different perspective, a history of how we learned to create umami. Why has there been such an emphasis on umami in Japan? After years of avoiding meat, the Japanese diet lacked animal protein and fats. Umami was highly sought after as a way to make rice taste good without relying on these ingredients.

Traditional Japanese cuisine revolves around fish and vegetables, with umami as a core flavor. By contrast, in most parts of the world including Europe and the United States, dishes rich in meat, fats, oils, and spices are considered feast foods. Until the 1960s, Japanese cuisine was widely viewed as peculiar. However, the sushi boom in the U.S. in the 1970s (see page 141) and the growing health consciousness of consumers led to a worldwide appreciation of Japanese cuisine. In particular, awareness of umami has grown dramatically over the past decade or so. Umami will surely continue to attract increasing attention in terms of both taste and health.

DASHI IS MADE UP ALMOST ENTIRELY OF UMAMI COMPONENTS. IT BRINGS OUT THE UMAMI OF OTHER INGREDIENTS AND IS THE ESSENCE OF JAPANESE CUISINE.
WESTERN CHEFS ARE STARTING TO PRIORITIZE THE INHERENT UMAMI OF INGREDIENTS OVER FATS, TOO.
DASHI IS A COMFORT FOOD FOR ME.

The Big Picture

International Umami Innovations

The Japanese word "umami" has been adopted into other languages. The concept is recognized globally, and in Europe and the United States, foods using local umami ingredients are being developed.

Fermented foods from the world's top restaurant

Denmark's noma (see page 95) ferments local ingredients to bring out the best flavors, creating unique new foods. For example, they make "deer-bushi" from aged deer legs, "peaso" from peas, and beef fermented with koji mold.

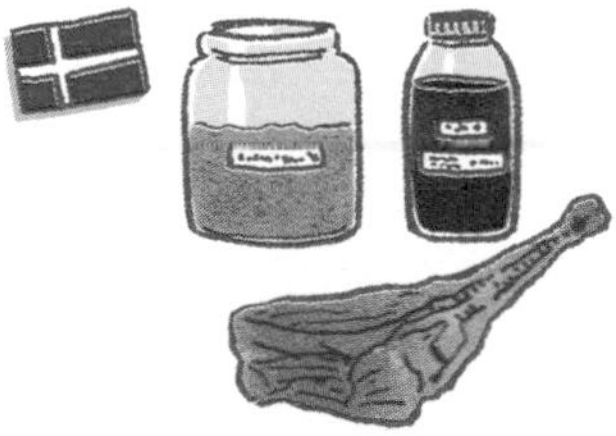

Umami seasonings in supermarkets

Major supermarkets and seasoning brands in the U.K. and U.S. are offering umami seasonings.

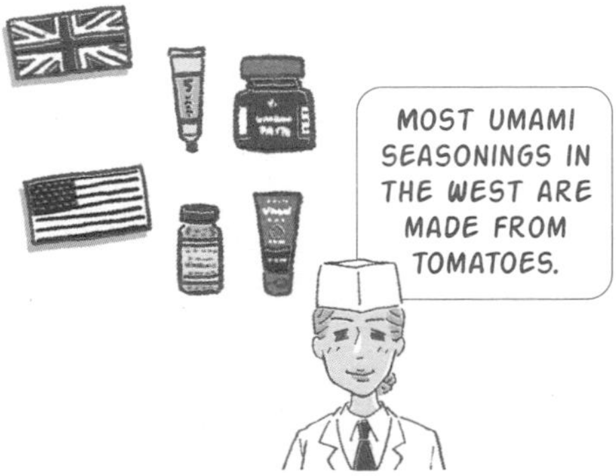
MOST UMAMI SEASONINGS IN THE WEST ARE MADE FROM TOMATOES.

Umami burgers from Los Angeles

The first Umami Burger restaurant opened in Los Angeles in 2009 and landed in Japan in 2017. The burgers are seasoned with "umami dust," a powder made from crushed kombu, dried shiitake mushrooms and katsuobushi, and served with a soy-sauce-based "umami master sauce."

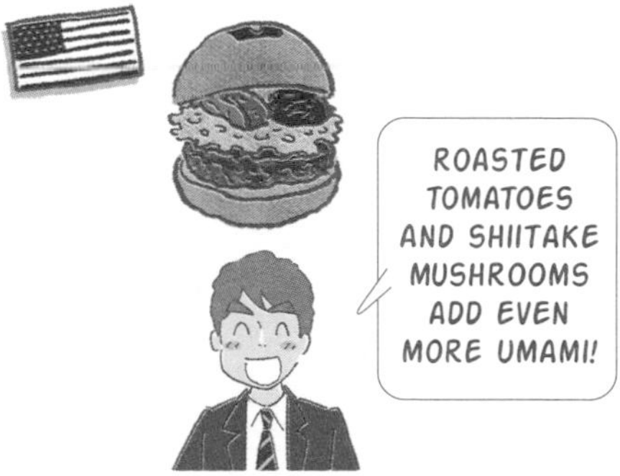
ROASTED TOMATOES AND SHIITAKE MUSHROOMS ADD EVEN MORE UMAMI!

Umami holds promise for preventive medicine

Research has shown that the addition of umami can help reduce overeating by giving the brain a sense of fullness even with low fat, sugar, and salt. This is expected to benefit health by preventing lifestyle diseases.

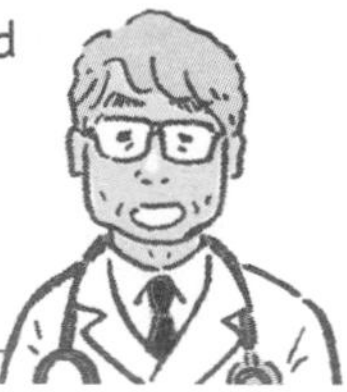

FEATURE

Japanese Food Words in the Global Vocabulary

As Japanese cuisine grows more popular around the world, the Japanese names of more dishes and ingredients are becoming familiar in other countries.

One of those words is bento. Although portable meals exist in many countries, the bento, a colorful meal packed into a small box, is unique to Japan. The bento box is said to have originated in the Azuchi-Momoyama period (1568–1603), when it became popular among the upper classes to take a hand-held stacked lunchbox with them to cherry-blossom-viewing and autumn-leaf-viewing parties. In the Edo period (1603–1867), *makunouchi* bentos appeared, to be eaten between acts of plays. When the railroads opened in the Meiji Era (1868–1912), there was a boom in *ekiben* (train station bentos).

In recent years, homemade bento boxes, especially *charaben* (character bentos) have become trendy, attracting attention overseas as well.

Japanese terms that are understood abroad

Cooked foods etc.	
sushi	すし
sashimi	刺身
sukiyaki	すきやき
tempura	天ぷら
yakitori	焼き鳥
takoyaki	たこ焼き
tonkatsu	とんかつ
teriyaki	照り焼き
ramen	ラーメン
udon	うどん
bento	弁当

Ingredients etc.	
daikon	大根
edamame	枝豆
tofu	豆腐
miso	味噌
natto	納豆
wasabi	わさび
kombu	昆布
nori	海苔
dashi	だし
mirin	みりん

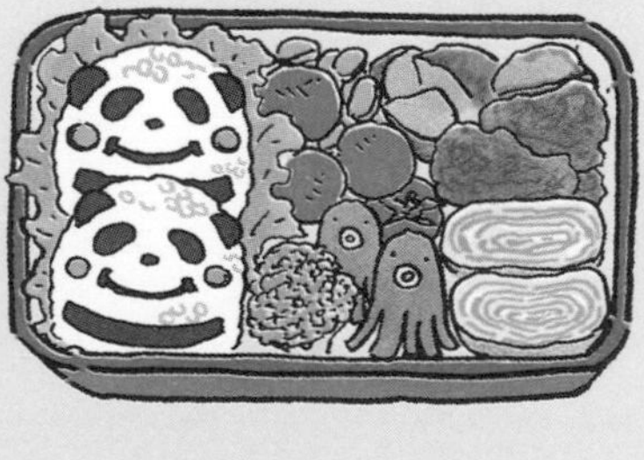

Charaben, short for "character bento," use foods to represent people, animals, anime characters and scenery. The charaben boom has spread overseas thanks to social networking sites.

PART 2

A Brief History of Feast Foods and Sushi

- The Heian Period: Aristocratic Banquets
- The Kamakura Period: Zen Monks Create a Cuisine
- The Muromachi Period: Classic Samurai Feasts
- The Azuchi-Momoyama Period: Tea Ceremony Food
- The Edo Period: Commoners Join the Party
- The History of Sushi, from the 7th Century to Today

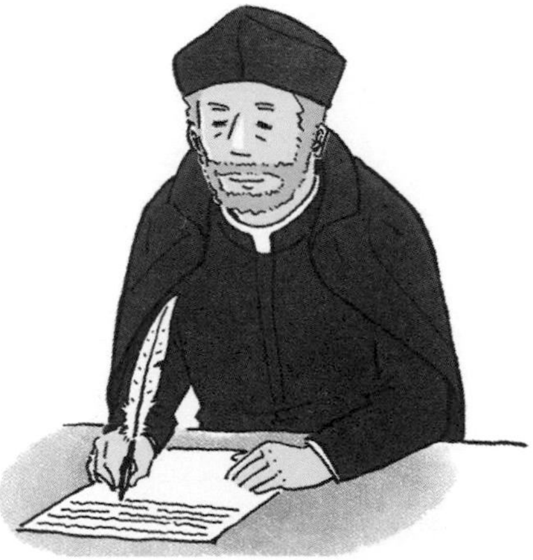

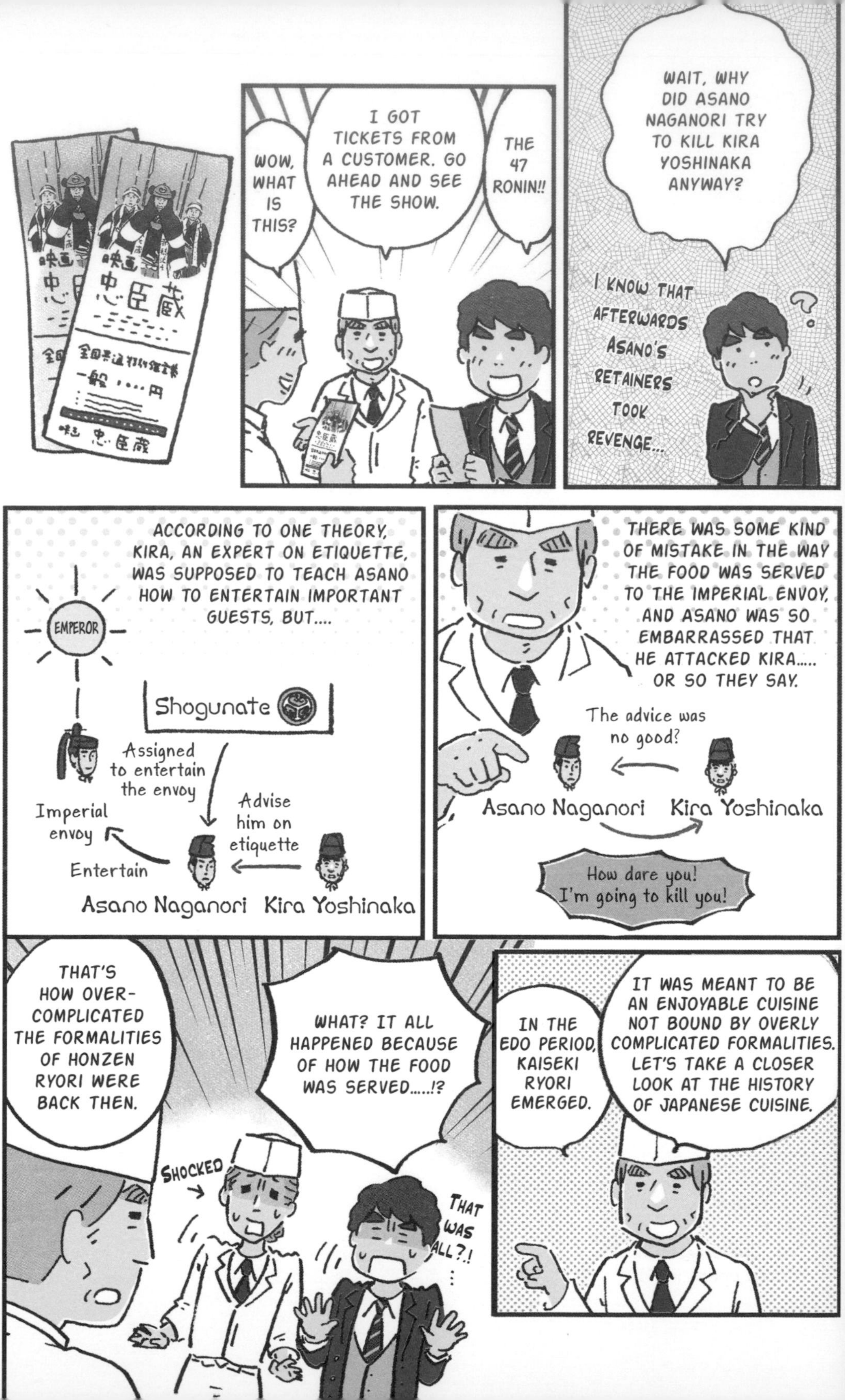
映画
忠臣蔵
一般 ....円
忠臣蔵
WOW, WHAT IS THIS?
I GOT TICKETS FROM A CUSTOMER. GO AHEAD AND SEE THE SHOW.
THE 47 RONIN!!
WAIT, WHY DID ASANO NAGANORI TRY TO KILL KIRA YOSHINAKA ANYWAY?
I KNOW THAT AFTERWARDS ASANO'S RETAINERS TOOK REVENGE...
ACCORDING TO ONE THEORY, KIRA, AN EXPERT ON ETIQUETTE, WAS SUPPOSED TO TEACH ASANO HOW TO ENTERTAIN IMPORTANT GUESTS, BUT....
EMPEROR
Shogunate
Assigned to entertain the envoy
Imperial envoy
Entertain
Advise him on etiquette
Asano Naganori
Kira Yoshinaka
THERE WAS SOME KIND OF MISTAKE IN THE WAY THE FOOD WAS SERVED TO THE IMPERIAL ENVOY, AND ASANO WAS SO EMBARRASSED THAT HE ATTACKED KIRA..... OR SO THEY SAY.
The advice was no good?
Asano Naganori
Kira Yoshinaka
How dare you! I'm going to kill you!
THAT'S HOW OVER-COMPLICATED THE FORMALITIES OF HONZEN RYORI WERE BACK THEN.
WHAT? IT ALL HAPPENED BECAUSE OF HOW THE FOOD WAS SERVED.....!?
SHOCKED
THAT WAS ALL?!
IN THE EDO PERIOD, KAISEKI RYORI EMERGED.
IT WAS MEANT TO BE AN ENJOYABLE CUISINE NOT BOUND BY OVERLY COMPLICATED FORMALITIES. LET'S TAKE A CLOSER LOOK AT THE HISTORY OF JAPANESE CUISINE.

Chronology of Japanese Feast Styles

Taikyo ryori (imperial court cuisine)

The Heian period (794–1185)
Feasts are held frequently by court nobles, and taikyo ryori is served. The *Engishiki* (completed 927) contains a description of "misho" (see page 92).

The Kamakura period (1185–1333)

Honzen ryori (formal cuisine)

The Muromachi period (1336–1573)
The honzen ryori style is established.

The Azuchi Momoyama period (1568–1603)

The Edo period (1603–1867)

Kaiseki ryori (banquet cuisine)

1717
The famed restaurant Yaozen opens in Edo.

Shojin ryori (Buddhist vegetarian cuisine)

1244
Zen master Dogen founds Eiheiji Temple and publishes *Tenzo kyokun* (Instructions for the Cook), an essay on shojin ryori.
1254
Zen master Shinchi Kakushin brings miso-making techniques back from China's Kinzanji temple

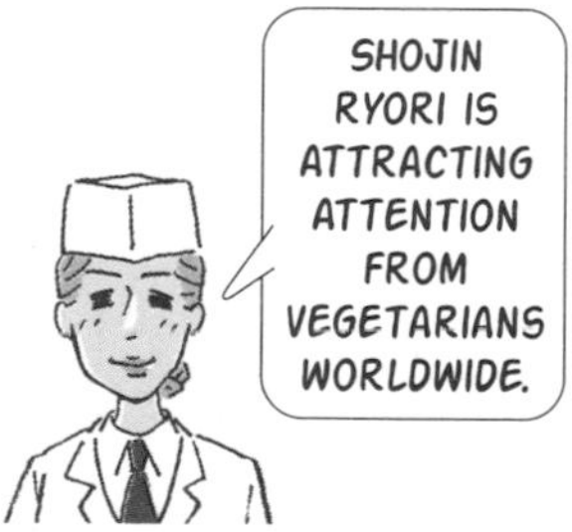
SHOJIN RYORI IS ATTRACTING ATTENTION FROM VEGETARIANS WORLDWIDE.

1654
Zen Master Ingen returns to Japan from China and introduces fucha cuisine, Chinese-style shojin ryori.

Chakaiseki ryori (tea ceremony cuisine)

815
Eichu returns to Japan from China and presents Emperor Saga with dancha (tea made by pounding steamed tea leaves in a mortar).
1191
Eisai introduces powdered green tea from Chi.

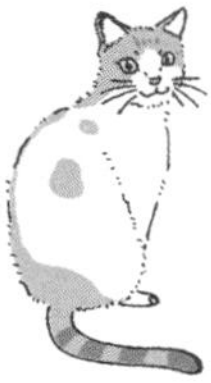

Murata Juko (1422–1502)
Establishes wabicha tea ceremony.
Takeno Jo-o (1502–1555)
Seeks the ideal of wabicha.
Sen no Rikyu (1522–1591)
Establishes the etiquette of wabicha and chakaiseki tea ceremony.
1587
Toyotomi Hideyoshi holds a great tea ceremony at Kitano Shrine in Kyoto. Toyotomi, Sen no Rikyu, and others serve as hosts.

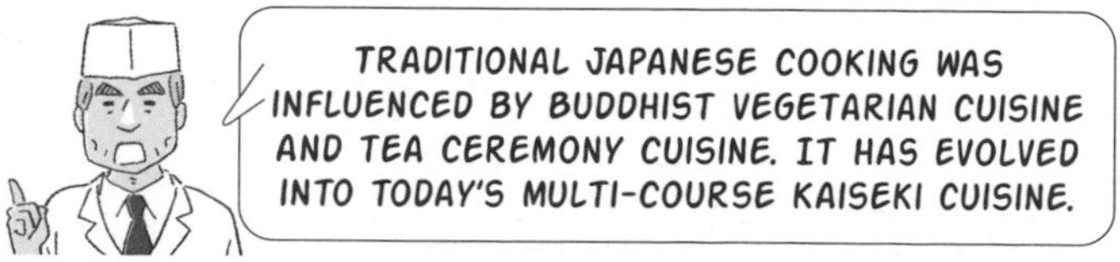
TRADITIONAL JAPANESE COOKING WAS INFLUENCED BY BUDDHIST VEGETARIAN CUISINE AND TEA CEREMONY CUISINE. IT HAS EVOLVED INTO TODAY'S MULTI-COURSE KAISEKI CUISINE.

The Heian Period

(794–1185)

Taikyo Ryori

Aristocratic Banquets

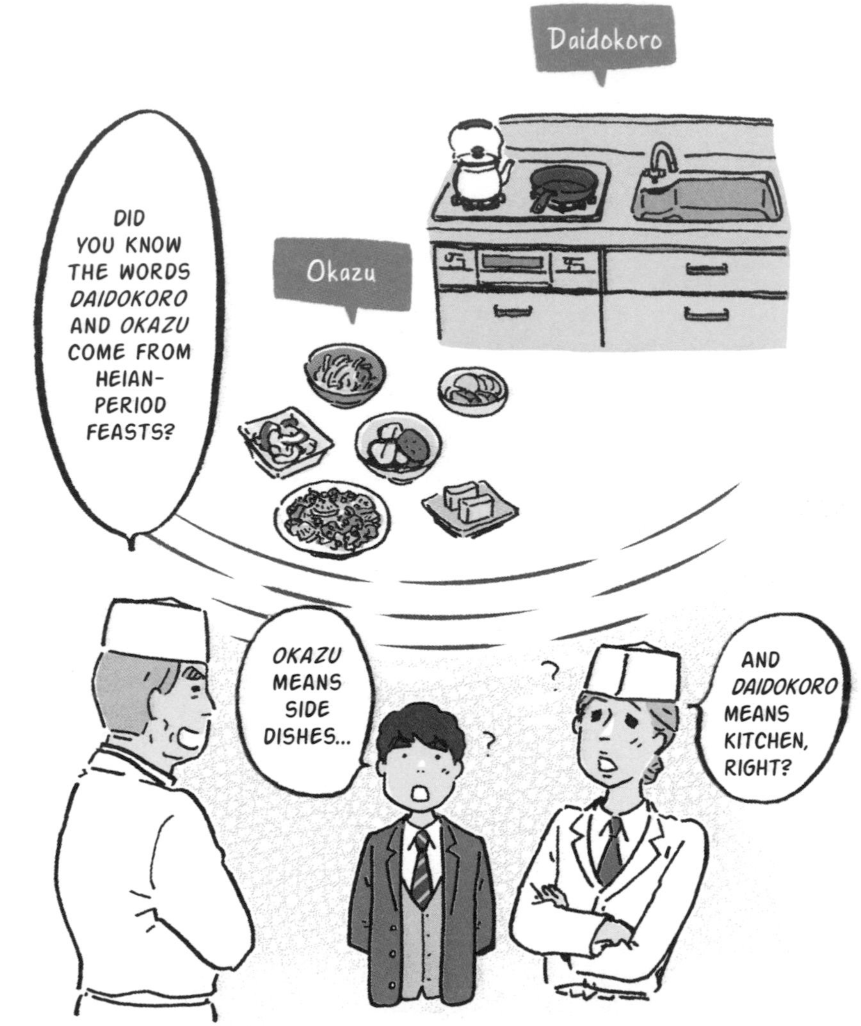
Daidokoro
Okazu
DID YOU KNOW THE WORDS DAIDOKORO AND OKAZU COME FROM HEIAN-PERIOD FEASTS?
OKAZU MEANS SIDE DISHES...
?
?
AND DAIDOKORO MEANS KITCHEN, RIGHT?

Eating with your eyes in the Chinese style

Taikyo ryori is considered the oldest culinary style in Japan, dating to the Heian period. The word *taikyo* means "grand feast," and taikyo ryori was feast cuisine served by the Fujiwara clan and other high-ranking aristocrats who held political power in the Heian period and invited the emperor and the imperial family to their banquets.

The everyday words *okazu*, meaning dishes served with rice, and *daidokoro*, meaning kitchen, originate in this style of cooking. *Okazu* is written using the character for "number" (数). In the days of taikyo ryori, a meal with many side dishes was considered a feast, and side dishes were called *kazumono*, meaning "numerous items." The honorific "o" was likely added later to make *okazu*. The word *daidokoro* comes from a rectangular table called a *daiban*[1] on which the feast was laid out. The place where the table stood was called *daibandokoro* (*–dokoro* means place), later shortened to *daidokoro*.

In this period, China's Tang Dynasty (618–907) was widely admired for having the world's most advanced technology and culture, and for this reason taikyo ryori was influenced by Chinese culture. The use of a tabletop (*daiban*), metal spoons, and an even number of plates were imitations of the Chinese style.

If you look at the large feast illustration from the *Ruiju zoyosho* (Miscellany of Related Topics) on page 114, you will see that guests sat in front of and behind the *daiban*. Directly in front of each guest was a heaping bowl of rice, chopsticks, a spoon and seasonings (salt, vinegar and hishio in this illustration)[2].

---

1 *Daiban* were vermilion or black lacquer tables. "Long tables" were approximately 94" long x 43" wide x 18" high (240 cm x 90 cm x 46 cm) and "cut tables" were half that length.

2 Salt, vinegar and hishio were placed in front of *kugyo*, courtiers in the top three ranks at the imperial court. Formal guests of the imperial family also got a fourth condiment, sake. Only salt and vinegar were placed in front of lower-ranking diners.

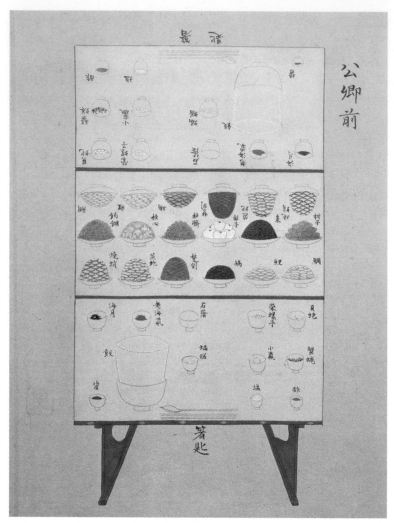

Ruiju zoyosho/Kugyo mae (Miscellany of Related Topics Vol. 1, Before the Lord) (Tokyo National Museum collection) Image: TNM Image Archives

This 12th century scroll describes the feasts, room decorations, and costumes used in court ceremonies at the time. The illustration above depicts a table for court nobles at a feast held by Fujiwara no Tadamichi to celebrate the inauguration of a minister, to which members of the imperial family were invited. Guests sat in front and behind the *daiban* (table), with heaping bowls of steamed rice, seasonings (salt, vinegar and soy sauce), chopsticks and spoon in front of them and many other dishes in the middle, such as Chinese sweets, fruits, fish and pheasant.

Although the taikyo-ryori feast was richly varied and gorgeous to look at, many of the dishes were either raw items or dried fish and poultry, which guests dipped in their own condiments. It was a feast to be enjoyed with the eyes more than the taste buds.

These feasts were ceremonial and had their roots in sacred food offerings to the gods (see page 62). Scholars believe that the strict rules for preparing the feast were also due to the ritualistic meaning contained in the act of partaking of food with the gods. For the nobility, banquets were important business, and it was more important that the rules be followed than that the guests have fun. The strict rules for cooking and eating and the emphasis on a beautiful presentation of food to the gods and others are characteristics of Japanese cuisine that continue to this day.

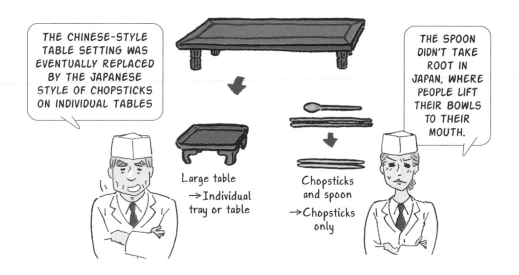

THE CHINESE-STYLE TABLE SETTING WAS EVENTUALLY REPLACED BY THE JAPANESE STYLE OF CHOPSTICKS ON INDIVIDUAL TABLES
Large table
→Individual tray or table
Chopsticks and spoon
→Chopsticks only
THE SPOON DIDN'T TAKE ROOT IN JAPAN, WHERE PEOPLE LIFT THEIR BOWLS TO THEIR MOUTH.

The Kamakura Period

(1185–1333)

Shojin Ryori

Zen Monks Create a Cuisine

DID YOU KNOW THAT SAYING "ITADAKIMASU" BEFORE WE EAT COMES FROM SHOJIN RYORI?

WOW, IT GOES ALL THE WAY BACK TO THE KAMAKURA PERIOD!

The medieval roots of modern manners

Until the early Heian period (794–1185), the imperial family and aristocracy were the leaders of food culture. However, in the late Heian and Kamakura periods (12th to early 14th centuries), Zen Buddhist monks who studied Buddhism in China during the Song Dynasty brought back culture and scientific technology as well as Buddhism, which greatly influenced Japanese food culture. The next style of food to emerge was shojin ryori, the Buddhist vegetarian cuisine popularized by Zen monks.

The custom of saying "Itadakimasu" (I humbly receive) before eating and "Gochisosama" (thank you for the feast) with hands pressed together when finished with a meal originates from the teachings of Dogen,[3] the Zen monk who introduced shojin ryori to Japan.[4] Dogen traveled to Song Dynasty China in the first half of the 13th century to study Zen Buddhism. There, temple meal attendants taught him that cooking, which was considered a menial chore in Japanese temples at the time, was an important part of Buddhist training. Upon his return to Japan, Dogen realized that the teachings of the Buddha Dharma could be found even in food, and he wrote two books, *Tenzo kyokun* (Instructions for the Cook)[5] and *Fushuku hanpo* (The Dharma of Taking Food) that provide profound insight into food and how to prepare it. The teachings in these books form the basis of shojin ryori. Dogen taught that even plants have life, that human life exists at the expense of other lives that have become food, and that we should be grateful for the gift of life. The books also instruct monks to not talk during meals, not clatter dishes, and not leave food on the table.

The lifestyles of the samurai who came to power during the Kamakura period were more frugal than those of the nobility. Zen

---

3 Dogen (1200–1253) was the founder of Japan's Soto Zen sect.
4 Dogen is said to have originated the custom of saying "Itadakimasu" before and "Gochisosama" after a meal, but the practice spread nationwide only in the Showa era (1926–1989).
5 *Tenzo kyokun* (1237) describes the mindset and methods of the monks in charge of cooking at Zen temples. *Fushuku hanpo* (1246) describes how monks should eat their food.

Buddhism[6] spread in part because it suited the temperament of the samurai, who were disciplined and sturdy. As a result, Zen Buddhist etiquette was incorporated into the manners of aristocrats and warriors who practiced it.

Dashi in Buddhist cooking

Shojin ryori is based on Buddhist precepts and is prepared using only plant-based ingredients, without meat or fish. This has fostered a tradition in Japanese cuisine of focusing on the deliciousness of vegetables.

Cooking methods also greatly advanced with shojin ryori. New cooking methods such as stewing, dressing and deep frying were added to the already common methods of boiling and grilling. One of the most significant changes was the increase in simmered dishes seasoned with dashi. Seasoning foods during the cooking process was a major difference from the taikyo ryori of the nobility. Most

Kakuran-no-onna from *Yamai no soshi* (Woman with a Stomach Illness from Diseases and Deformities) (National Diet Library Digital Collection)

This 12th century picture scroll depicts various illnesses. Here a woman uses a grinding bowl and pestle.

With the introduction of grinding bowls and stones in the Kamakura period, it became possible to easily grind wheat and soybeans into flour, which was used to make udon (wheat noodles), soba (buckwheat noodles), and tofu.

BEFORE THE GRINDING BOWL WAS INTRODUCED, FOOD WAS POUNDED IN A MORTAR CALLED AN *USU*.

---

6 Zen Buddhism is a Mahayana Buddhist sect that trains the mind and body through Zen meditation and other rigorous practices in order to attain *satori* (enlightenment).

importantly, dashi[7] was used to simmer ingredients. The custom of using dashi originated in shojin ryori.

After Zen monks brought the *suribachi* grinding bowl and pestle back from China, which made the process of grinding and mashing easier, it became common to toss various ingredients with dressings. Pulverizing miso in a *suribachi* made the miso dissolve more easily, which led to the spread of miso soup in the Kamakura period.

In the Heian period, chefs who cut up fish and birds were called *hocho-nin*, or knife men (see page 81). By contrast, the chefs who prepared shojin ryori were called *chosai-nin*, or vegetable preparers. These *chosai-nin* laid the foundation for today's simmered dishes, soups and dressed dishes. Their skills were the driving force behind the development of Japanese cooking into a full-fledged cuisine.

五十七番
庖丁

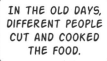

Shokunin zukushi uta-awase (Poetry Contest by Various Artisans) (National Diet Library Digital Collections)

The book depicts a competition said to date to the Muromachi period. On the right, a samurai knife man breaks down a carp, while on the left a Buddhist priest prepares dumplings.

IN THE OLD DAYS, DIFFERENT PEOPLE CUT AND COOKED THE FOOD.

7 At the time, kombu and katsuobushi were not yet widely used, so dashi was a vegetarian soup stock.

The Muromachi Period

(1336–1573)

Honzen ryori

Classic Samurai Feasts

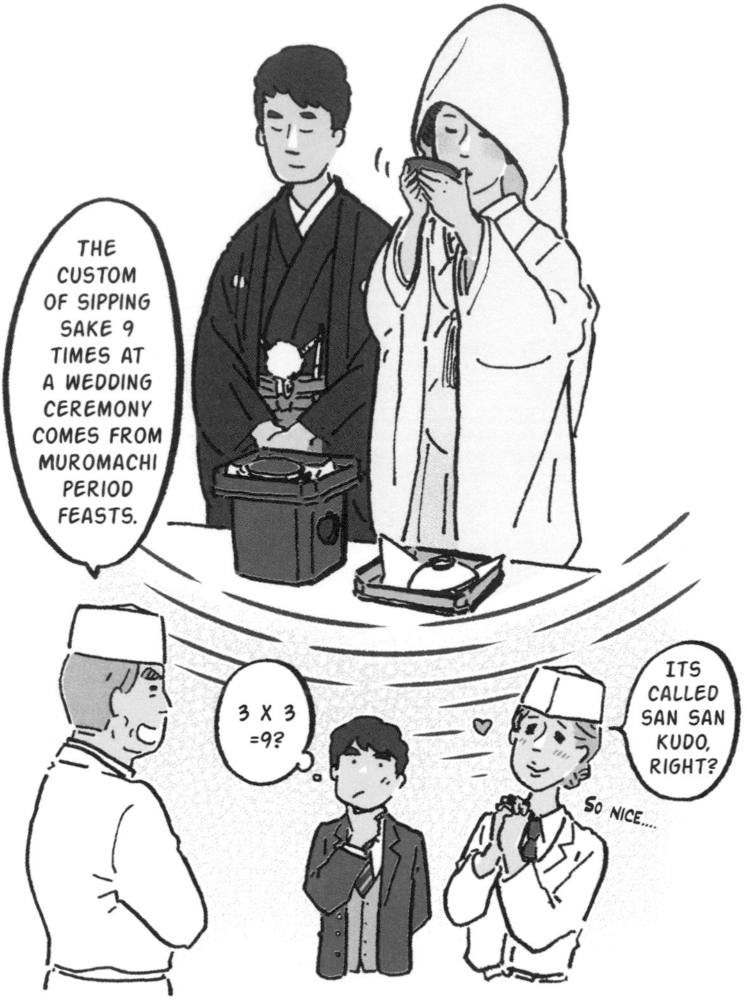
THE CUSTOM OF SIPPING SAKE 9 TIMES AT A WEDDING CEREMONY COMES FROM MUROMACHI PERIOD FEASTS.
ITS CALLED SAN SAN KUDO, RIGHT?
3 X 3 =9?
SO NICE...

The custom of serving in individual dishes

In the Muromachi period, the shogunate was established in Kyoto, and the samurai, influenced by the nobility, developed a unique culture. Honzen ryori is the feast cuisine they established in this period. It incorporated the ceremonial elements of taikyo ryori and the cooking techniques of shojin ryori, becoming the basis for later forms of Japanese cuisine.

While taikyo ryori feasts consisted of many dishes arrayed on a large tabletop, in honzen ryori feasts individual dishes were placed in front of each guest for their personal use. Previously an even number of dishes had been served because even numbers were favored in China, but in Japan odd numbers were considered auspicious, and in this period an odd number of dishes began to be served. People also stopped using spoons and ate only with chopsticks.

The honzen ryori format at a banquet begins with a ceremony called *shiki-sankon*[8] in which sake is offered to the guests. Serving a set of foods that go with sake and then offering three sake cups, one large, one medium, and one small, before removing the whole set is called *ikkon*, or one kon. The *shiki-sankon* repeats an *ikkon* three times with different foods and drinks, for a total of nine cups of sake offered to the guests. The *san-san-kudo* ceremony at Shinto weddings, in which a bride and groom take three sips each from three sake cups, comes from the *shiki-sankon* ceremony. The most important feasts in samurai society were those in which the shogun visited the residence of a feudal lord or a feudal lord visited the residence of a vassal. The *shiki-sankon* was a ritual to confirm the master-servant relationship through sake, and was an indispensable part of these formal feasts. It is said that the concept of *omotenashi* (hospitality), in which a person of lower rank entertains his or her superiors, originated in honzen ryori.

In this type of cuisine, multiple individual trays of food were arranged around the main tray. The number of trays was often either three, five, or seven, with three being most common and seven being most luxurious. They were all set out at the same time.

---

8 The *sankon* is a ritual for exchanging sake dating to the Heian period (794–1195), in which sake was served in large cups that were passed around from the top to the bottom of the table. Over time, the custom changed so that each person was given their own cup, resulting in the *shiki-sankon* form of the ceremony.

The meal was considered the main event while sake was secondary, and the original format was to eat various dishes with rice and drink sake afterwards. Each tray always included soup. The main tray had a soup to drink with rice, and later trays had clear soups to accompany sake.

The lasting influence of honzen ryori

The one soup, three side dish format (*ichiju sansai*) that continues to this day in Japanese cuisine derives from the honzen ryori style of cooking. Books written in the late 16th century describe meals with one soup and three side dishes as well as two soups and five side dishes,[9] using the terms -*ju* for soup and -*sai* for side dishes as we do today. The custom of serving rice on the left and soup on the right also comes from honzen ryori.

The use of dashi combining kombu and katsuobushi started during this period as well. In the Kamakura period, vegetarian stock was used in shojin ryori. In the Muromachi period, with the development of marine transportation, kombu from Hokkaido and katsuobushi from the south were brought to Kyoto, resulting in the combination of these two ingredients. Whereas miso was used extensively in shojin ryori, soy sauce started to be used more in honzen ryori.

The "knife men" of old Japan

Knife men (see page 81) made their presence felt during the development of honzen ryori from the Muromachi period to the early Edo period (17th century). There were various styles or schools of knife men. In addition to the Shijo-ryu, a traditional court noble school of practice, there was also the Ikuma-ryu, which handled the ceremonies of the Kamakura shogunate, and the Okusa-ryu and Shindo-ryu, both of which were patronized by the Muromachi shogunate. Each school developed its own rules and regulations for honzen ryori, passing them down as secret or esoteric knowledge.

---

9 The *Yukishi shinhatto*, a set of laws issued in 1556, includes a description of *ichiju sansai*.

Menu for a feast for Shogun Ashikaga Yoshiteru on the last day of March, 1561 held by Miyoshi Nagayoshi

Shiki-sankon		**Double tray of appetizers ▪ Sake ▪ Decorative fowl ▪ Decorative sea bream**
Konbu (offerings)	First tray	Bird ▪ Turtle shell ▪ Soup with mochi
	Second tray	Dried squid ▪ Shellfish ▪ Sea bream
	Third tray	Dried squid ▪ Octopus ▪ Hishioiri*
Zenbu (main meal)	Main tray	Salted fowl ▪ Grilled food ▪ Salted entrails of sea cucumber ▪ Dressed dish ▪ Rice gruel** ▪ Pickles ▪ Fish cakes ▪ Sea bream
	Second tray	Crucian carp ▪ Jellyfish ▪ Sea bream soup ▪ Sea snails ▪ Salted dried mullet roe ▪ Shrimp ▪ Soup
	Third tray	Crab ▪ Two kinds of soup
	Fourth tray	Sake-steamed dish ▪ Abalone ▪ Whale soup
	Fifth tray	Mackerel sushi ▪ Quail eggs ▪ Dried squid ▪ Flathead soup
	Sixth tray	Pike conger ▪ Red clams ▪ Shrimp soup
	Seventh tray	Dolphinfish ▪ Snipes ▪ Crucian carp soup
	Savories	Devil's tongue jelly ▪ Wheat gluten ▪ Walnuts ▪ Chestnuts ▪ Root vegetables ▪ Nori ▪ Kombu ▪ Skewered dried persimmons
Konbu (offerings)	Fourth tray	Noodles ▪ Pressed confection ▪ Rice crackers
	Fifth tray	Dried shark ▪ Dried squid ▪ A basket of root vegetables
	Sixth tray	Dumplings ▪ Pressed confection ▪ Sashimi
	Seventh tray	Pike conger ▪ Green vegetable ▪ Shrimp
	Eighth tray	Three-part tray ▪ Pressed confection ▪ Skipjack tuna
	Ninth tray	Shrimp ▪ Sushi ▪ Dolphin
	Tenth tray	Red bean jelly ▪ Pressed confection ▪ Red clams
	Eleventh tray	Pike conger ▪ Sea snails ▪ Octopus
	Twelfth tray	Fish soup ▪ Pressed confection ▪ Fuka Shark
	Thirteenth tray	Dried fish ▪ Sake-steamed dish ▪ Soup with dried fish
	Fourteenth tray	Wrapped dried squid ▪ Sea snails ▪ Whale
	Fifteenth tray	Dolphinfish ▪ Jellyfish ▪ Flathead
	Sixteenth tray	Thrushes ▪ Small sea bream ▪ Duck
	Seventeenth tray	Salted dried mullet roe ▪ Hamaguri clam ▪ Sea bass

Adapted from *The History of Japanese Food* by Nobuo Harada (Shibunkaku Publishing)

This was the menu when Miyoshi Nagayoshi, who controlled the Kinki region during the Muromachi period, received the shogun. First, Miyoshi, the shogun, and his entourage performed the shiki-sankon ceremony in a separate room, then moved to a larger room where the sankon were served again. After the meal ended, sake was again served. This was followed by the konbu, or offering. Noh, kyogen, and dance performances were held between offerings, and the feast lasted until late at night or into the next morning.

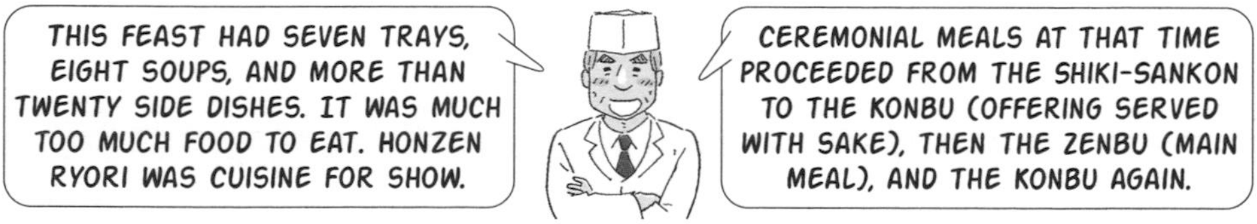
THIS FEAST HAD SEVEN TRAYS, EIGHT SOUPS, AND MORE THAN TWENTY SIDE DISHES. IT WAS MUCH TOO MUCH FOOD TO EAT. HONZEN RYORI WAS CUISINE FOR SHOW.
CEREMONIAL MEALS AT THAT TIME PROCEEDED FROM THE SHIKI-SANKON TO THE KONBU (OFFERING SERVED WITH SAKE), THEN THE ZENBU (MAIN MEAL), AND THE KONBU AGAIN.

*Ground, salted fish or poultry paste simmered with miso and minced mountain yams, topped with yuzu peel.
**If the main tray had gruel or mochi soup, no other soup was served.

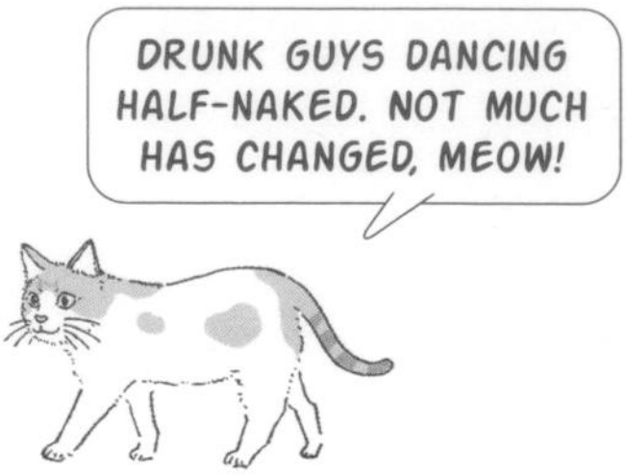
DRUNK GUYS DANCING HALF-NAKED. NOT MUCH HAS CHANGED, MEOW!

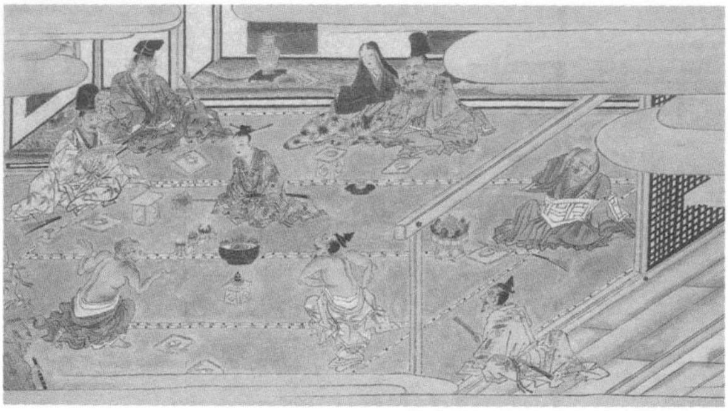

Here, Nagamochi, a court nobleman who loved to drink, is holding a lavish drinking party in spring. He preaches the virtues of sake and criticizes teetotalers.

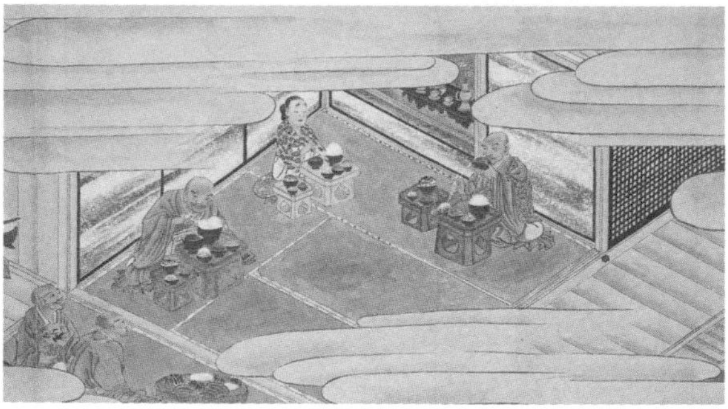

In this autumn scene, two monks who like to eat are invited to a samurai household, joined by the son and heir of the family. The food for the guests is served in heaping portions.

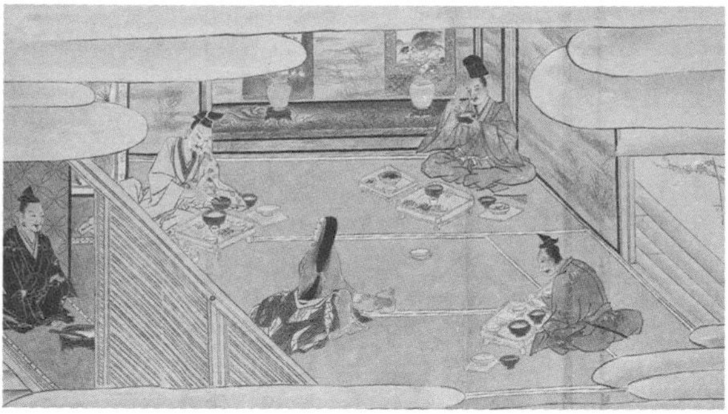

A banquet scene with the samurai Nakanari family. They are enjoying sake and rice. This is a three-part honzen ryori meal: the first tray is in the center, the second tray is on the right and the third tray is on the left as seen from the guest's perspective.

Shuhanron emaki (Illustrated Debate Over Wine and Rice) (National Diet Library Digital Collections)

This picture scroll was made by Kano Motonobu and his studio in the early 16th century. It tells the story of a debate between a court nobleman who likes to drink, a monk who likes to eat, and a samurai who likes both drinking and eating but emphasizes moderation.

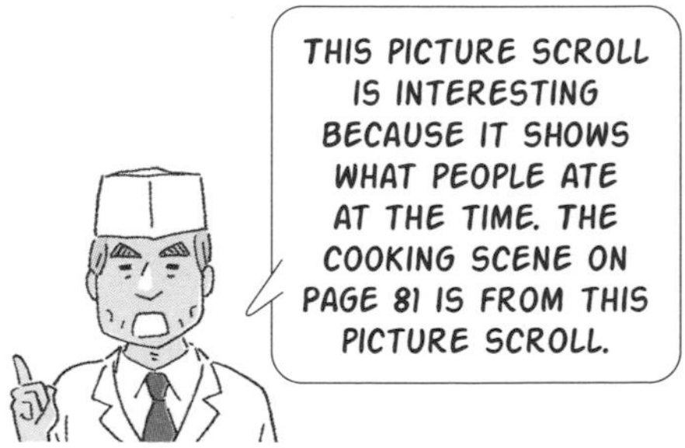
THIS PICTURE SCROLL IS INTERESTING BECAUSE IT SHOWS WHAT PEOPLE ATE AT THE TIME. THE COOKING SCENE ON PAGE 81 IS FROM THIS PICTURE SCROLL.

As a ceremonial cuisine, honzen ryori emphasized elegance, and the large quantities of food displayed on the table were for viewing, not eating. From the number of dishes to the seating arrangements that indicated status, to the way food was cut and the culinary etiquette, the rules of the knife men were so complex that they could only be understood by upper-class intellectuals. By the 19th century, honzen ryori had become a mere formality. It was simplified and passed on as ceremonial cuisine for weddings, funerals, and other such occasions. It was still sometimes served at wedding ceremonies until around the 1920s.

A honzen ryori meal

Fifth tray
Take-home food
Fourth tray
Grilled food
Main tray
Simmered dish
Vinegared dish
Pickles
Rice
Soup
Third tray
Vinegared dish
Sashimi
Soup
Second tray
Dressed dish
Simmered dish
Soup

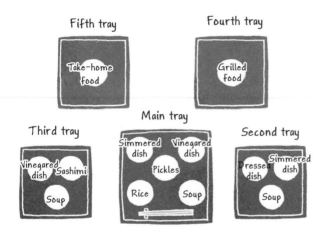

HONZEN RYORI DECLINED AFTER THE MEIJI ERA AND IS RARELY SEEN TODAY, BUT IT'S STILL IMPORTANT TO KNOW ABOUT THIS AUTHENTIC FORM OF JAPANESE CUISINE.

Main tray: Rice, miso soup, simmered or steamed dish, vinegary vegetable dish, pickles

2nd tray: Clear soup, simmered dish, dressed dish

3rd tray: Fish soup, sashimi, vinegared or dressed dish

4th tray: Grilled whole fish or similar item, usually taken home by the guest

5th tray: Food meant to be taken home by the guest

The Azuchi-Momoyama Period
(1568–1603)

Chakaiseki ryori
Tea Ceremony Food

THE PRACTICE OF SERVING HOT DISHES IN SUCCESSION AS SOON AS THEY ARE MADE DATES TO THE TEA CEREMONY CUISINE OF THE AZUCHI-MOMOYAMA PERIOD

WHAT ABOUT FRENCH MULTI-COURSE MEALS, EMMA?

IT WASN'T UNTIL THE LATE 19TH CENTURY, UNDER RUSSIAN INFLUENCE, THAT MULTI-COURSE MEALS STARTED BEING SERVED IN FRANCE.

THAT'S EVEN MORE RECENT THAN IN JAPAN!

The advent of the multicourse meal

The foundations of modern Japanese feast cuisine were established by the honzen ryori of the Muromachi period (1336–1573). With the development of the tea ceremony (chanoyu[10]) in the Azuchi-Momoyama period, chakaiseki ryori[11]—the food served at tea ceremonies—took the best of honzen ryori and shojin ryori and refined them with an emphasis on spirituality. In honzen ryori, the priority was on arranging food in a highly formal way, and the food was prepared days in advance in quantities too great to actually eat. In chakaiseki ryori, on the other hand, there were fewer dishes served more simply, but warm, well-prepared food was presented as soon as it was ready. The style was more in line with the essence of cooking, with the focus on flavor. In honzen ryori food is arranged spatially, with everything presented at once. In chakaiseki ryori, it is arranged chronologically, with each dish brought out only after the previous one is finished. This was a revolutionary change in the way food was served.

Let us briefly trace the history of chanoyu. Tea was introduced to Japan in the Kamakura period (1185–1333) along with vegetarian cuisine, and the tea ceremony took root in Zen Buddhist monasteries. In the Muromachi period, the tea ceremony became a highly entertaining event that was accompanied by drinking and feasting. In those days, tea was considered a kind of intoxicating drink, similar to alcohol, and a drinking banquet with sake was usually held after the tea ceremony. Reacting to this, the tea master Murata Shuko created a style of tea ceremony called wabicha that was held in a simple tea room without ostentatious elements. Wabicha was passed down to Shuko's disciple Takeno Jo-o and perfected by Sen no Rikyu.[12]

---

10 The host invites guests and prepares tea for them.
11 Chakaiseki cuisine is also called kaiseki ryori, using different characters from the formal kaiseki ryori meals described in the next chapter. To avoid confusion between these two distinct styles of food, we use the term chakaiseki here.
12 Sen no Rikyu (1522–1591) was a great tea master of the Azuchi-Momoyama period. Founder of the Senke school of tea ceremony.

Sen no Rikyu invents tea ceremony cuisine

Sen no Rikyu's greatest innovation in the tea ceremony was to cut out the drinking and feasting element. Rikyu also invented chakaiseki ryori as a light meal eaten before the tea ceremony. Prior to that, the food served at tea ceremonies was not much different from ordinary banquet food, often consisting of two soups and five side dishes. Rikyu reduced extraneous elements and defined the ideal meal as one soup and three sides. A meal consisting of rice, soup, and the three sides—a simmered dish, a grilled dish, and a dish called mukozuke (usually sashimi or a vinegared dish)—became the basic form of chakaiseki ryori and, by extension, of Japanese cuisine for many years to come.

Incidentally, in Rikyu's time, the characters 会席 were generally used

Example of chakaiseki menu

Rice · soup · mukozuke
↓
Simmered dish
↓
Grilled dish
↓
Shii-zakana
↓
Hashi-arai
↓
Hassun
↓
Pickles and yuoke
↓
Sweets, tea

The first 3 courses make up the *ichi-ju sansai* (one soup and three sides). Since it is a tea ceremony meal, sake is not consumed after the third course. The shii-zakana is either a dressed dish or a vinegared dish. The hashi-arai is a lightly seasoned soup. The hassan includes something from the sea and something from the mountains, after which the host and guest share a drink. The yuoke or "hot tub" is filled with scalding water, which is poured over the leftover rice to make a kind of rice porridge.

Arrangement of dishes for chakaiseki

Mukouzuke
Rice
Soup

Rice, soup, and mukouzuke are served on an oshiki tray. The portion of rice is enough for one or two bites, and the soup is made with miso. The mukouzuke is a vinegared dish or sashimi. After the guests have eaten the rice and soup, the host offers the first round of sake. Only after drinking this do they eat the mukozuke.

TO MAKE IT CLEAR YOU'RE TALKING ABOUT TEA CEREMONY CUISINE, YOU CAN SAY CHAKAISEKI.
KAISEKI RYORI (懐石料理) AND KAISEKI RYORI (会席料理) ARE OFTEN CONFUSED, BUT THEY ARE TWO VERY DIFFERENT THINGS.

for this type of kaiseki meal. When a new and very different style of kaiseki ryori emerged in the late 19th century, the characters 懐石 began being used to distinguish the older style of kaiseki ryori from the newer one. According to legend, a Zen monk in training warmed himself by putting hot stones (石) in his bosom (懐) to quench his hunger, leading to this style of writing "kaiseki" for tea ceremony cuisine.

Treasuring the moment

Another reason chakaiseki holds an important place in the history of Japanese cuisine is that it added a message of seasonality and celebration to the meal. This is largely due to the spirit of *ichigo-ichie*, which in tea ceremony refers to cherishing each unique encounter as a once-in-a-lifetime experience.

In addition to emphasizing seasonal ingredients and the timing with which dishes were served, people also paid careful attention to tableware and presentation, and took great care in decorating the tea room and garden.

Hospitality is reflected in the way guests are treated, and this philosophy has been passed down through the generations as an essential part of the Japanese culinary aesthetic.

A *hassun* tray. The name refers to the size of the tray, which has a square rim measuring about 9.5 inches (24 cm). The seam in the rim is placed on the far side, and bamboo chopsticks complete the setting.

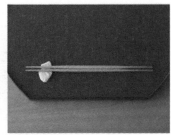

Rikyu chopsticks used in chakaiseki. These cedar chopsticks are pointed at both ends, thick and flat in the middle, and usable from both ends. In chakaiseki, chopsticks are placed on the right edge of the tray before the meal and on the left edge after the meal.

SEN NO RIKYU IS SAID TO HAVE PERSONALLY SHARPENED PIECES OF CEDAR TO MAKE CHOPSTICKS FOR GUESTS ON THE DAY THEY WERE INVITED TO DINE.

FEATURE

Japan's Food Culture Through the Eyes of Missionaries

At the end of the 16th century, Jesuit missionaries who came to Japan from Europe to preach Christianity enthusiastically collected information on the lifestyles of the Japanese people and sent reports back to their home countries. *Treaty on the contrasts and differences between Europe and Japan* by Portuguese Jesuit missionary Luís Fróis[13] and *History of the Japanese Church* by João Rodrigues Tçuzu[14] both include commentary on food. Their observations feel fresh even today.

From *Treaty:*

- We eat everything with our hands. Japanese men and women eat with two sticks (chopsticks) from childhood.
  (Europeans started using forks in the 17th century.)
- We eat wheat bread. Japanese eat rice boiled without salt.
  (White rice without salt apparently seemed odd to him.)
- We can eat well without soup. Japanese cannot eat without soup.
- We start drinking as soon as the meal begins. Japanese people usually start drinking after the meal is over.
  (In those days, the meal was followed by sake drinking.)

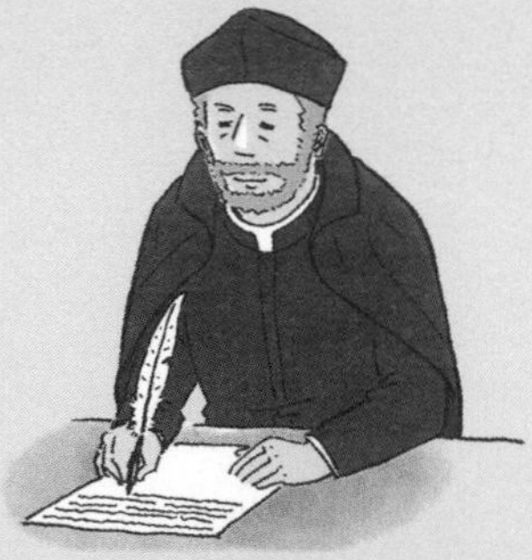

13 Luís Fróis (1532–97) came to Japan in 1563 at the age of 31 and lived there for the rest of his life.

14 João Rodrigues Tçuzu (1561–1633) came to Japan in 1577 and was expelled by Tokugawa Ieyasu in 1610.

- We eat while chatting, but we do not sing or dance. Japanese eat in silence, but dance and sing when they finish eating.
- In Europe, women usually prepare meals. In Japan, it is the men who prepare the food. And the upper class think it is a noble thing to go to the kitchen to cook.
  (In those days, formal feasts were prepared by a male "knife man" [see page 81].)

The missionaries turned their focus on the tea ceremony, which was flourishing at the time, as an appropriate site for missionary activity.

History of the Japanese Church evaluates the cuisine of the tea ceremony and describes honzen ryori and chakaiseki as follows:

- About honzen ryori: The food is chopped into bite-sized pieces and served on the dining table, so it is cold and tasteless, and among the various dishes only the soup was served hot. The more solemn the banquet, the greater the number of soups and the more varied they were. Precious fish, cranes, swans, wild ducks, and so on are the preferred meats. Only the meat of hunted game is used, never that of domesticated animals or birds. They consider animals raised at home unclean and think it cruel to kill animals they have reared themselves.
- About chakaiseki: Cold foods whose only purpose is decorative have been abandoned in favor of warm, well-cooked dishes served at the appropriate time. The dishes are of quality and substance.

Many of Sen no Rikyu's disciples were Christian feudal lords, and some observers have pointed out the similarities between the rituals of the tea ceremony and those of the Catholic Mass.

The Edo Period

(1603–1867)

Kaiseki ryori

Commoners Join the Party

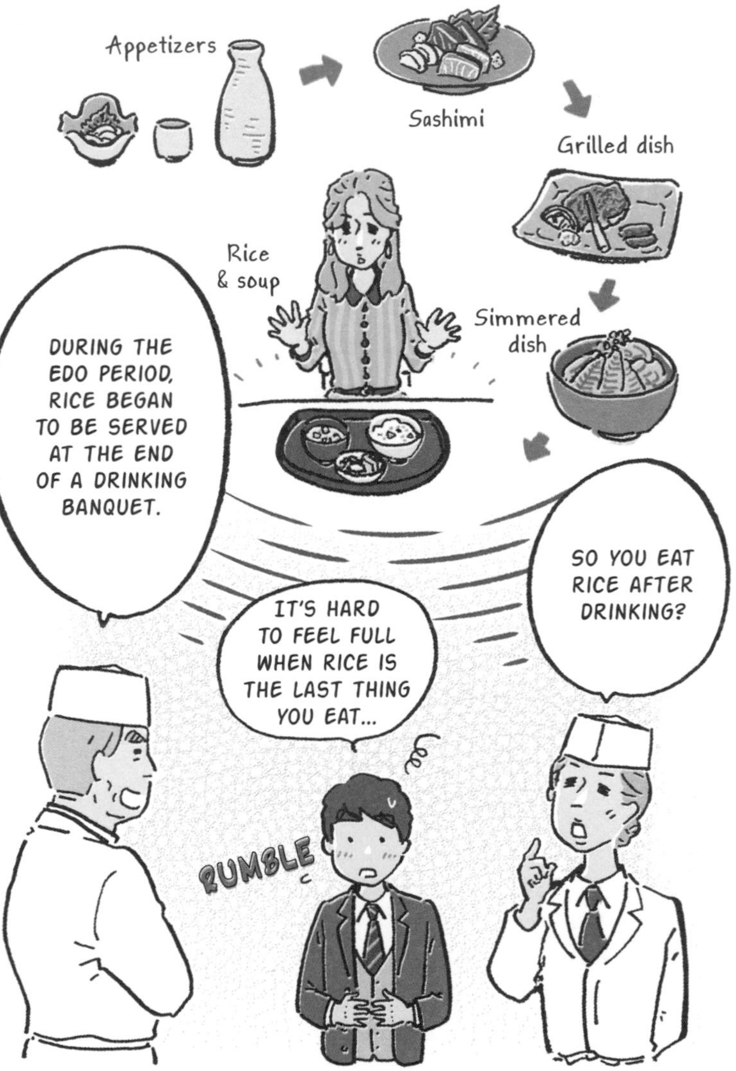

Appetizers
Sashimi
Grilled dish
Simmered dish
Rice & soup
DURING THE EDO PERIOD, RICE BEGAN TO BE SERVED AT THE END OF A DRINKING BANQUET.
SO YOU EAT RICE AFTER DRINKING?
IT'S HARD TO FEEL FULL WHEN RICE IS THE LAST THING YOU EAT...
RUMBLE

Drink first, then eat

The type of kaiseki ryori that first emerged in the Edo period is a feast cuisine based on honzen ryori but incorporating the chakaiseki ryori custom of serving freshly prepared coursed of soup, sashimi, grilled or boiled foods, and other dishes. A major change during the 265 years of the Edo period was that townspeople gained economic power and became the main actors in food culture. Prior to the Edo period, feast food was for special people of high status. Taikyo ryori was for royalty and aristocrats, shojin ryori was for Buddhist monks, honzen ryori was for samurai, and chakaiseki ryori was for the cultural elite. It was not until the Edo period that commoners were able to enjoy feast dishes, which had once been out of reach.

Significant changes also occurred in the places where food was served. Prior to the Edo period, feast food was only available in special locations that a limited number of people had access to. Taikyo ryori and honzen ryori were served at the residences of aristocrats and samurai, shojin ryori at temples, and chakaiseki ryori at tea ceremonies. However, as the urban economy developed in the 18th and 19th centuries, high-class restaurants appeared where anyone could enjoy good food and drink as long as they paid for it. The food served at such restaurants was called kaiseki ryori.

Although kaiseki ryori incorporated elements of both chakaiseki and honzen ryori, there was another significant differences from the feast cuisine of earlier times: the order of the meal and the drinking party was reversed. In the past, feasting was followed by drinking, whereas in kaiseki ryori, the meal is served after drinking. There is no strict etiquette for this type of feast. It was served at restaurants over drinks and conversation, and it continues to be enjoyed in a similar form today.

At a tea ceremony, guests wait outside until the meal is ready.

After purifying their mouths and hands, they enter the tea ceremony room through the *nijiriguchi* (crawl-through entrance).

Dining in the tea ceremony room. Instead of rimmed trays, they eat from individual honzen tables with legs.

The sake banquet begins after they leave the tea ceremony room.

Kaisekiryori saikubocho (The Craft of Kaiseki Ryori) (Collection of the National Institute of Japanese Literature)

A scene from a late-Edo period cookbook showing that in the early 1800s, food was still followed by drinking at banquets.

IT'S AN INTERESTING MIX OF THE HONZEN, CHAKAISEKI AND KAISEKI STYLES OF CUISINE.

Food stalls enjoy a boom

Edo, a metropolis of one million people, was home to a large number of men living alone, including rural samurai who came on mandatory visits to the capital called *sankin kodai* and servants from the countryside who worked in stores. The food service industry supported these men's dietary needs. In the late 1700s, mobile food stalls selling quick and easy meals began to gain popularity. Sushi, broiled eel, tempura, and soba noodles were among the most popular items. The increasing availability of seasonings such as vinegar, mirin, and soy sauce contributed to the popularity of these foods.

Edo komei kaitei zukushi: Sanya Yaozen (The Yaozen Restaurant in Sanya from the Famous Restaurants in Edo series) by Utagawa Hiroshige (National Diet Library Digital Collection)

This is one of a set of 30 ukiyo-e prints depicting famous restaurants in Edo. The word "kaitei" in the title refers to a kaiseki-ryori restaurant. Kaiseki was the name for poetry gatherings, and kaiseki ryori was served with sake at such occasions. The restaurant Yaozen was established in 1717 in Asakusa Sanya, and was said to be the best high-end restaurant in Edo.

RESTAURANTS STARTED OPENING, AND IT SEEMS PEOPLE ENJOYED EATING OUT AS MUCH AS THEY DO NOW.

Nigirizushi was made by mixing rice with vinegar, and broiled eel was created in the Kanto region after the mirin industry became firmly established. Buckwheat, which had previously been eaten as a paste called soba gaki, became more popular when a new way of using it was invented: in a dough that was rolled out and cut thin as noodles. Improvements in the quality of soy sauce also contributed to the popularity of soba. In the early Edo period, barley was used to make soy sauce, but from the mid Edo period onwards wheat was used, which improved the taste. In the early Edo period, light soy sauce from Kyoto and Osaka was most common, but by the end of the Edo period, dark soy sauce from around Edo became the standard.

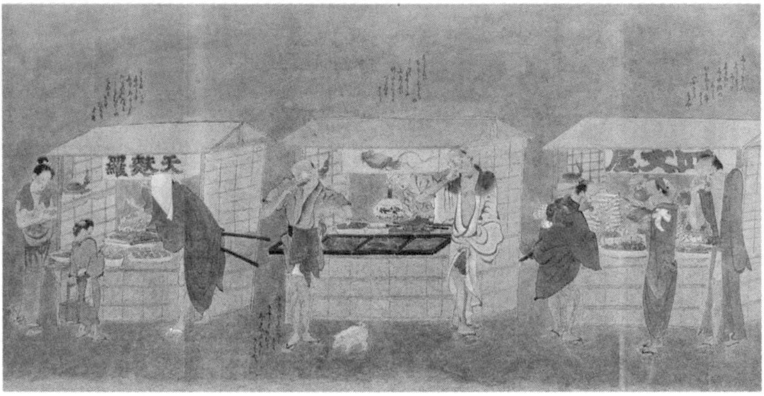
天麩羅

Kinsei shokunin zukushi ekotoba (Modern Artisans) (Digital Collections, National Diet Library)

This three-volume work by ukiyo-e artist Kuwagata Keisai depicts over a hundred craftsmen and women in Edo. From left to right: a tempura shop, a dried squid shop, and a shimonya stand. Shimonya were the Edo equivalent of dollar stores, selling all items for one four-mon coin, such as skewered oden (simmered fish cakes and vegetables).

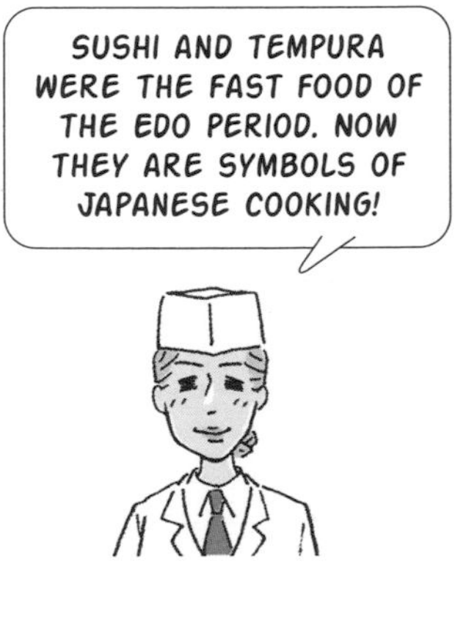
SUSHI AND TEMPURA WERE THE FAST FOOD OF THE EDO PERIOD. NOW THEY ARE SYMBOLS OF JAPANESE COOKING!

Eating becomes entertainment

The Edo period saw revolutionary changes in eating habits. People went from eating two meals a day (breakfast and supper) to three meals a day (breakfast, lunch, and dinner), establishing the basis of the modern diet. Another major development was the publication of cookbooks, which opened up the art of cooking. Previously, there had only been secret texts for each school of knife men.

Gourmands delivered their opinions on good and bad food, competitive eating contests were held, and eating became a pastime. Edo townspeople had a particular passion for seeking out the first of each seasonal food to appear on the market, which they called *hatsumono*. People believed that eating the first food of the season would extend their life by 75 days. The first bonito of the season was the most popular *hatsumono*, but people also looked forward to the first sake, soba noodles, sweetfish and mochi of the season.

Edo first-of-the-season calendar

December
January
November
Whitefish
Trout
February
Shiitake mushrooms
Monkfish
Raw cod
Sea snails
Horsetail shoots
October
Goose
March
Young ginger
Smartweed
Fiddleheads
WE STILL EAT SOME OF THESE FOODS, BUT CRANES ARE A SURPRISE!
Duck
Thrush
Pheasant
Udo shoots
Matsutake mushrooms
Young taro roots
Bamboo shoots
Fresh shiitake mushrooms
Bonito
September
Crane
Sea cucumber
April
Sweetfish
Pickling melon
Salmon
Fresh black-eyed peas
Eggplant
Snipe
August
May
July
June

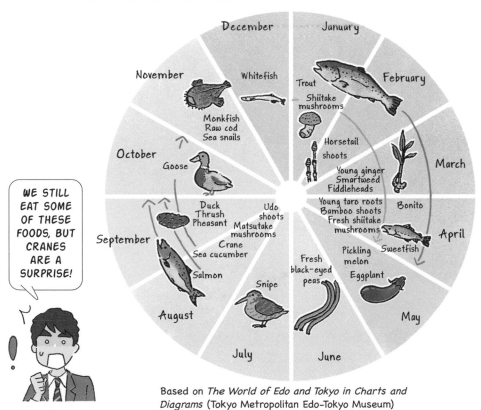

Based on *The World of Edo and Tokyo in Charts and Diagrams* (Tokyo Metropolitan Edo-Tokyo Museum)

The History of Sushi, from the 7th Century to Today

From Southeast Asian Fermented Fish to Global Favorite

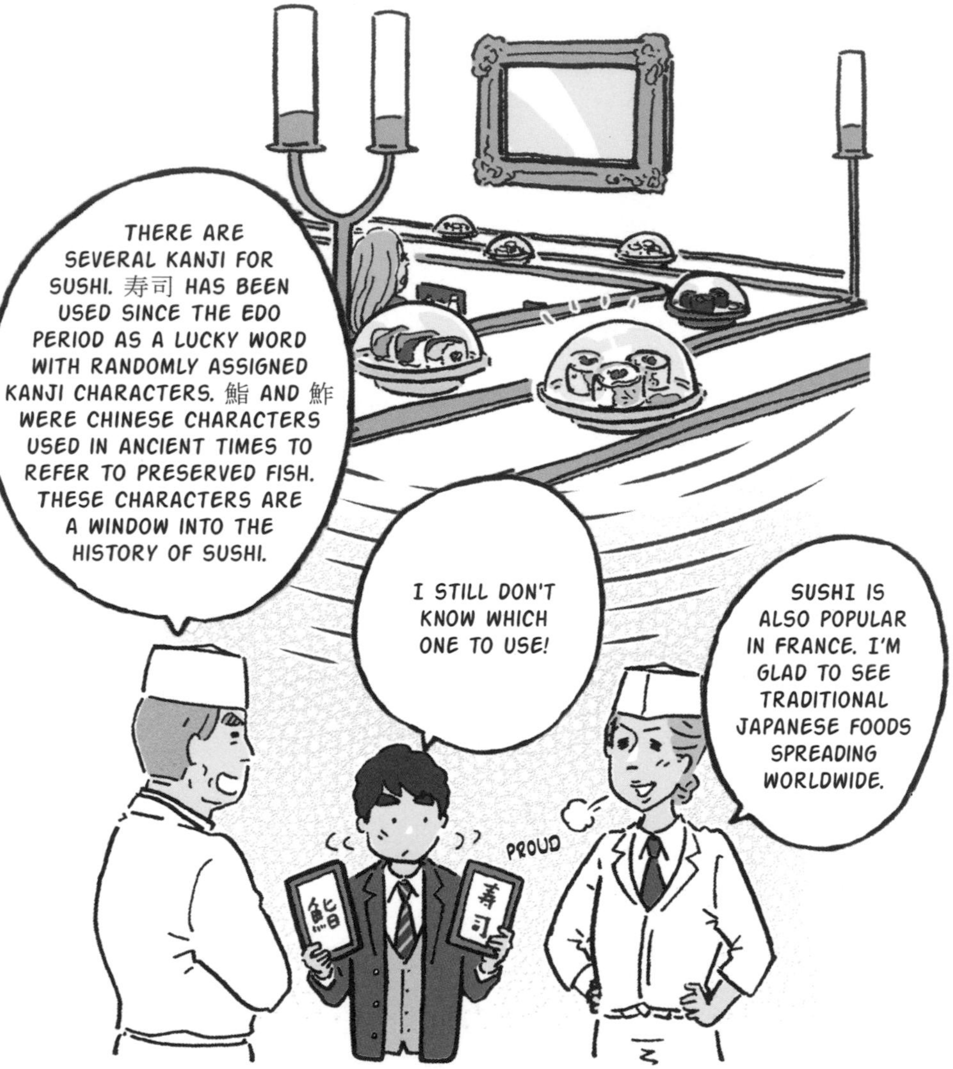
THERE ARE SEVERAL KANJI FOR SUSHI. 寿司 HAS BEEN USED SINCE THE EDO PERIOD AS A LUCKY WORD WITH RANDOMLY ASSIGNED KANJI CHARACTERS. 鮨 AND 鮓 WERE CHINESE CHARACTERS USED IN ANCIENT TIMES TO REFER TO PRESERVED FISH. THESE CHARACTERS ARE A WINDOW INTO THE HISTORY OF SUSHI.
I STILL DON'T KNOW WHICH ONE TO USE!
SUSHI IS ALSO POPULAR IN FRANCE. I'M GLAD TO SEE TRADITIONAL JAPANESE FOODS SPREADING WORLDWIDE.
PROUD
鮨
寿司

The three sushi revolutions

Sushi is now popular all over the world as a typical Japanese dish, but it did not actually originate in Japan. Sushi is thought to have first been made in Southeast Asia, from northeastern Thailand to Laos. In Thailand and Laos, rice paddies fill up with water during the rainy season, providing an abundance of fish. To preserve fish caught during the rainy season until the dry season, raw fish were mixed with salt and starchy foods such as rice. The acidity from the lactic fermentation of the starch kept the fish from spoiling. This is believed to be the original sushi.

This method of preservation was brought to China before the 5th century BCE Later, it was introduced to Japan. It was likely in use by the Nara period (710–794), since the kanji character for sushi (鮓) is written on a wooden board on the Heijo Palace grounds. The sushi of this era was a preserved food made by marinating salted fish in rice and allowing it to ferment naturally. The rice touching the fish during its long preservation period fermented and became sludgy, so it was discarded and only the fish was eaten. Sushi made in this way is called honnare. The funazushi eaten in Shiga Prefecture, said to be the oldest type of fermented sushi still being made in Japan, is honnare sushi.

In the Muromachi period (1336–1573), a type of sushi called namanare appeared. The mixture of fish and rice was fermented for a few days to a month, stopping when the rice was slightly sour but the grains had not yet disintegrated, and the rice was eaten with the fish. This was the first sushi revolution. Famous types of namanare sushi are mackerel narezushi from Wakayama Prefecture and sweetfish narezushi from Gifu Prefecture. Another type of sushi called izushi, which uses koji to speed up the fermentation of the rice and adds vegetables to the mix, was also developed. Izushi includes Ishikawa Prefecture's kaburazushi and Akita Prefecture's hatahatazushi.

In the Edo period, hayazushi, meaning quick sushi, was created by using vinegar to shorten the fermentation time. This was the second sushi revolution. At first vinegar was used to speed up the fermentation process, but eventually it was simply mixed with rice and the fermentation step was eliminated. In the 19th century, nigirizushi, a type of sushi with raw fish on top of vinegared rice, made its appearance before customers in Edo. What was once a preserved food had become an instant food.

The genealogy of sushi

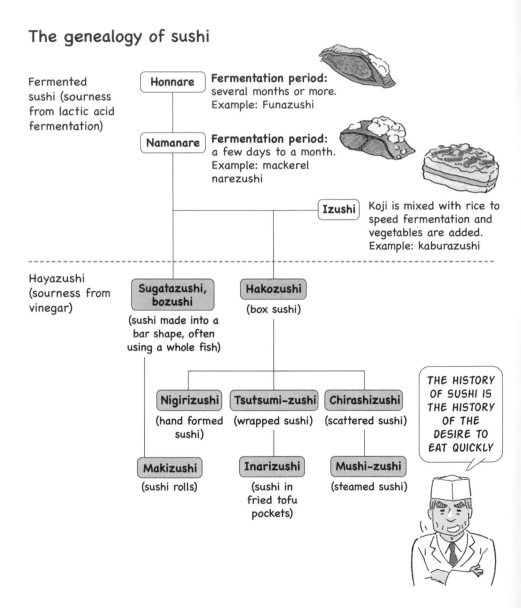

Fermented sushi (sourness from lactic acid fermentation)

Honnare — **Fermentation period:** several months or more. Example: Funazushi

Namanare — **Fermentation period:** a few days to a month. Example: mackerel narezushi

Izushi — Koji is mixed with rice to speed fermentation and vegetables are added. Example: kaburazushi

Hayazushi (sourness from vinegar)

Sugatazushi, bozushi (sushi made into a bar shape, often using a whole fish)

Hakozushi (box sushi)

Nigirizushi (hand formed sushi)

Tsutsumi-zushi (wrapped sushi)

Chirashizushi (scattered sushi)

Makizushi (sushi rolls)

Inarizushi (sushi in fried tofu pockets)

Mushi-zushi (steamed sushi)

THE HISTORY OF SUSHI IS THE HISTORY OF THE DESIRE TO EAT QUICKLY

The third sushi revolution occurred after World War II. In the midst of postwar food shortages, the Japanese government banned the restaurant business in order to seek food aid from other countries. However, sushi restaurants insisted that they were not restaurants, but rather "processors" who turned rice brought in by customers into sushi. These businesses were permitted to process one cup of rice into 10 pieces of nigirizushi. This is how nigirizushi, once a local dish in Edo, spread throughout the country.

In the 1970s, a sushi boom started in Los Angeles and expanded to other parts of the United States. In those days, *itamae* chefs would respond to customer requests and create a variety of sushi rolls on the spot. The California roll[15] in particular was a groundbreaking invention that brought Americans unaccustomed to eating raw fish closer to the world of sushi. In the late 1990s, conveyor-belt sushi restaurants opened across Europe and the United States, gaining popularity. Sushi will surely continue to change and develop just as it has in past centuries.

SUSHI CONVEYOR BELTS AND SUSHI ROBOTS HAVE A LOT TO DO WITH SUSHI'S POPULARITY OVERSEAS.

SUSHI IS APPEALING BECAUSE IT'S HEALTHY. I ALSO LIKE ITS COLOR AND SMALL, CUTE SHAPES.

A page from a 34-volume text from the late Edo period. From top: tamagoyaki (omelet), tamago-maki (dried gourd wrapped in omelet), nori maki (sushi roll with dried gourd inside), a section of a cut sushi roll, and sea eel, white fish, tuna and gizzard shad sushi.

A page from *Morisada manko* (Digital Collections, National Diet Library)

---

15 California rolls are said to have been invented by Ichiro Mashita, a sushi chef at the Tokyo Kaikan restaurant in Little Tokyo, Los Angeles, around 1967. The thick rolls are filled with avocado, imitation crab meat and other ingredients.

FEATURE

Eating in Kansai vs Kanto

In the 19th century, Edo developed its own food culture in contrast to that of Kyoto and Osaka. While seasoning in Kyoto and Osaka tended to be elegant and light, the Edo style favored a richer flavor using mirin and soy sauce. The difference between Kansai in the west (the Kyoto-Osaka region) and Kanto in the east (the greater Edo/Tokyo region) can be attributed to the difference in water quality (see page 33) and the fact that more root vegetables were grown near Edo, requiring a richer seasoning, whereas leafy greens were more common in Kansai.

	Kanto	Kansai
Dashi	Katsuo dashi + dark soy sauce	Kombu dashi + light soy sauce
Soy sauce	Dark soy sauce (darker color but less salty than light soy sauce)	Light soy sauce (lighter color but saltier than dark soy sauce)
Noodle sauce	Roughly shaved katsuobushi is simmered and flavored with dark soy sauce. The sauce is strong and dark.	Dashi made from thinly shaved katsuobushi and kombu seaweed is flavored with light soy sauce. The pale, umami-rich sauce is poured over noodles.
Zoni (mochi soup eaten at New Year's)	Grilled mochi is added to a clear soup	Round mochi is simmered in a white miso soup
Grilled eel	The eel is opened up from the back and steamed before grilling	The eel is opened up from the belly and boiled before grilling
Sushi	Nigirizushi (hand-formed sushi)	Oshizushi (pressed sushi)
Inarizushi (sushi in fried tofu pouches)	Cylindrical	Triangular
The amount of food served	More	Less
Tamagoyaki (sweet rolled omelet)	Sweet, rich flavor, browned on the outside	Less sweet, with dashi added. Tidied up afterwards with a sushi rolling mat.

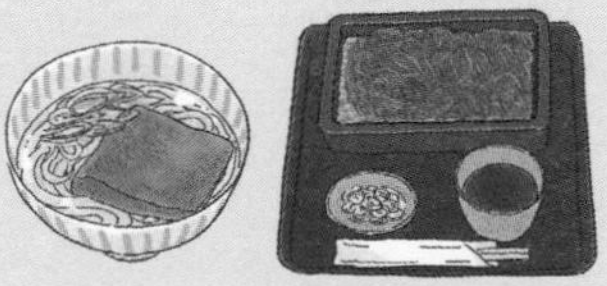

Cold soba noodles with dipping sauce were popular in Edo. The intense sauce was a quick, elegant way to add flavor. In Kansai, people favored dashi, so udon in broth was preferred.

PART 3

Putting It All Into Practice

- The Elements of Kaiseki Cuisine
- Tableware and Food Presentation
- Dining at a Traditional Japanese Restaurant

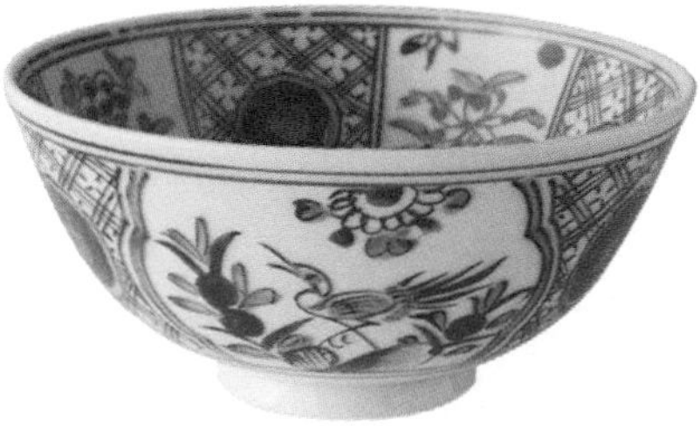

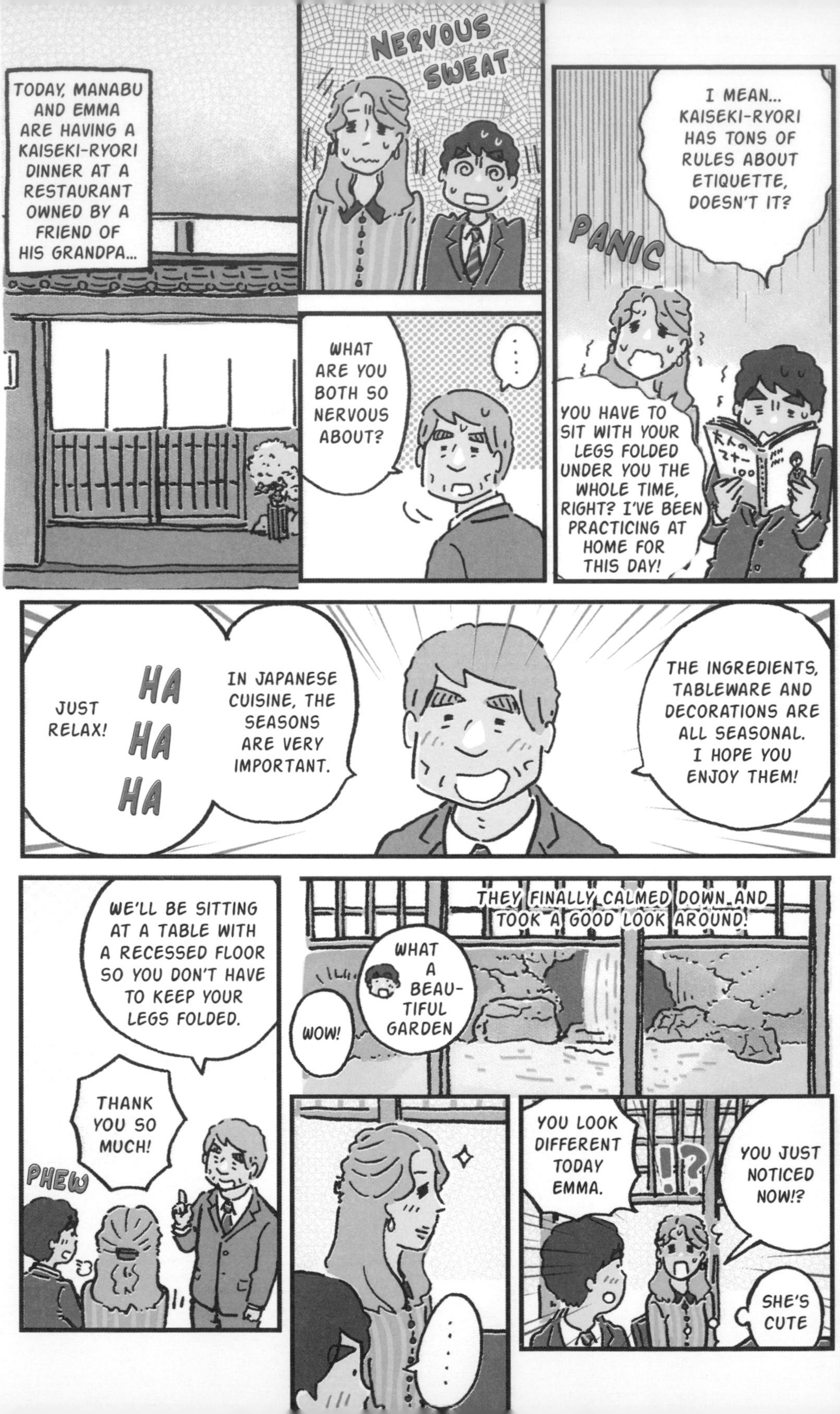
TODAY, MANABU AND EMMA ARE HAVING A KAISEKI-RYORI DINNER AT A RESTAURANT OWNED BY A FRIEND OF HIS GRANDPA...
NERVOUS SWEAT
WHAT ARE YOU BOTH SO NERVOUS ABOUT?
......
PANIC
I MEAN... KAISEKI-RYORI HAS TONS OF RULES ABOUT ETIQUETTE, DOESN'T IT?
YOU HAVE TO SIT WITH YOUR LEGS FOLDED UNDER YOU THE WHOLE TIME, RIGHT? I'VE BEEN PRACTICING AT HOME FOR THIS DAY!
JUST RELAX!
HA HA HA
IN JAPANESE CUISINE, THE SEASONS ARE VERY IMPORTANT.
THE INGREDIENTS, TABLEWARE AND DECORATIONS ARE ALL SEASONAL. I HOPE YOU ENJOY THEM!
WE'LL BE SITTING AT A TABLE WITH A RECESSED FLOOR SO YOU DON'T HAVE TO KEEP YOUR LEGS FOLDED.
THANK YOU SO MUCH!
PHEW
THEY FINALLY CALMED DOWN AND TOOK A GOOD LOOK AROUND.
WOW!
WHAT A BEAU-TIFUL GARDEN
......
YOU LOOK DIFFERENT TODAY EMMA.
!?
YOU JUST NOTICED NOW!?
SHE'S CUTE

ONCE YOU'RE SEATED, LOOK OVER THE MENU SO YOU KNOW WHAT YOU'RE EATING AND THE ORDER IN WHICH IT WILL BE SERVED.
THE MENU CELEBRATES EARLY SPRING.
HOW ELEGANT— A MENU WRITTEN IN CALLIGRAPHY!
ICHIYO RAIFUKU MEANS "WINTER IS GONE AND SPRING IS COMING."

Ichiyo Raifuku

Appetizer	Persimmon salad, smoked scallops, pickled turnip sushi with salmon roe
Soup	Lily bulb soup with crab cake, bamboo shoots, greens and yuzu
Sashimi	Tuna, tiger shrimp, sea bream
Grilled Dish	Spanish mackerel with yuzu-miso glaze, daikon steak, candied kumquat, lotus root with pickled plum
Simmered Dish	Taro root, beef, carrot, butterbur, garland chrysanthemum, sansho pepper
Steamed Dish	Tilefish with grated turnip and ginkgo nuts
Vinegared Dish	Yamaimo yam, mitsuba, carrot, lotus root
Rice, Soup, Pickles	Karasumi rice, red miso soup, pickled napa cabbage, daikon and mizuna.
Dessert	Citrus jelly

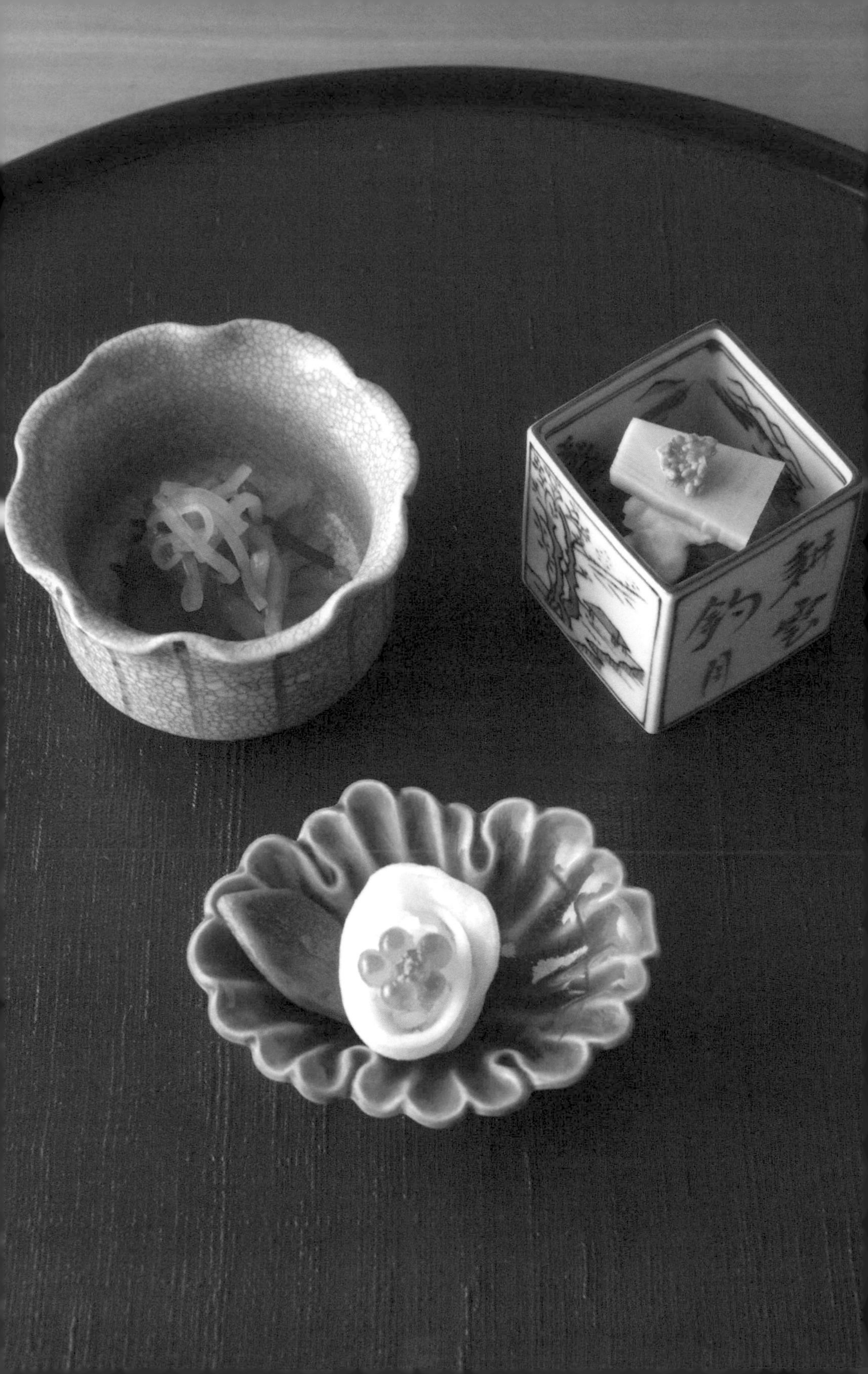

Sakizuke Appetizer

Persimmon salad ■ Smoked scallops ■ Pickled turnip sushi

The *sakizuke* is an appetizer consisting mainly of seasonal vegetables. Several small dishes are served as accompaniments to alcoholic beverages. Seasonality is especially important in this course. Here, sushi in the shape of a camellia that blooms in the cold and early bamboo shoots capture the feeling of Risshun, the first day of spring in the traditional lunar calendar.

The persimmon salad (kaki-namasu[1]) is made by tossing salted daikon radish and carrot strips with naturally sweet dried persimmon (anpo kaki), then balancing the flavor with vinegar. The smoked scallops (hotategai kunsei) are seasoned with soy sauce and topped with bamboo shoots. The sushi features thinly sliced turnip pickles (senmaizuke) wrapped around vinegared rice and garnished with salted salmon roe.

When pairing items for a *sakizuke* tray, chefs typically season each item differently and avoid repetition of cooking methods. Because odd numbers are preferred in Japanese cuisine, they avoid combinations of two or four dishes.

Kyo ware (midori kochi[2])

Sometsuke ware

Raku ware

---

1 See page 158 for more on namasu.
2 Kochi is an abbreviation for Kochi Ware, a lead-glazed pottery fired at low heat and characterized by bright colors such as yellow and green. The name "Kochi" refers to Vietnam, which was the source of similarly bright Sancai ware produced in southern China in the mid Edo period.

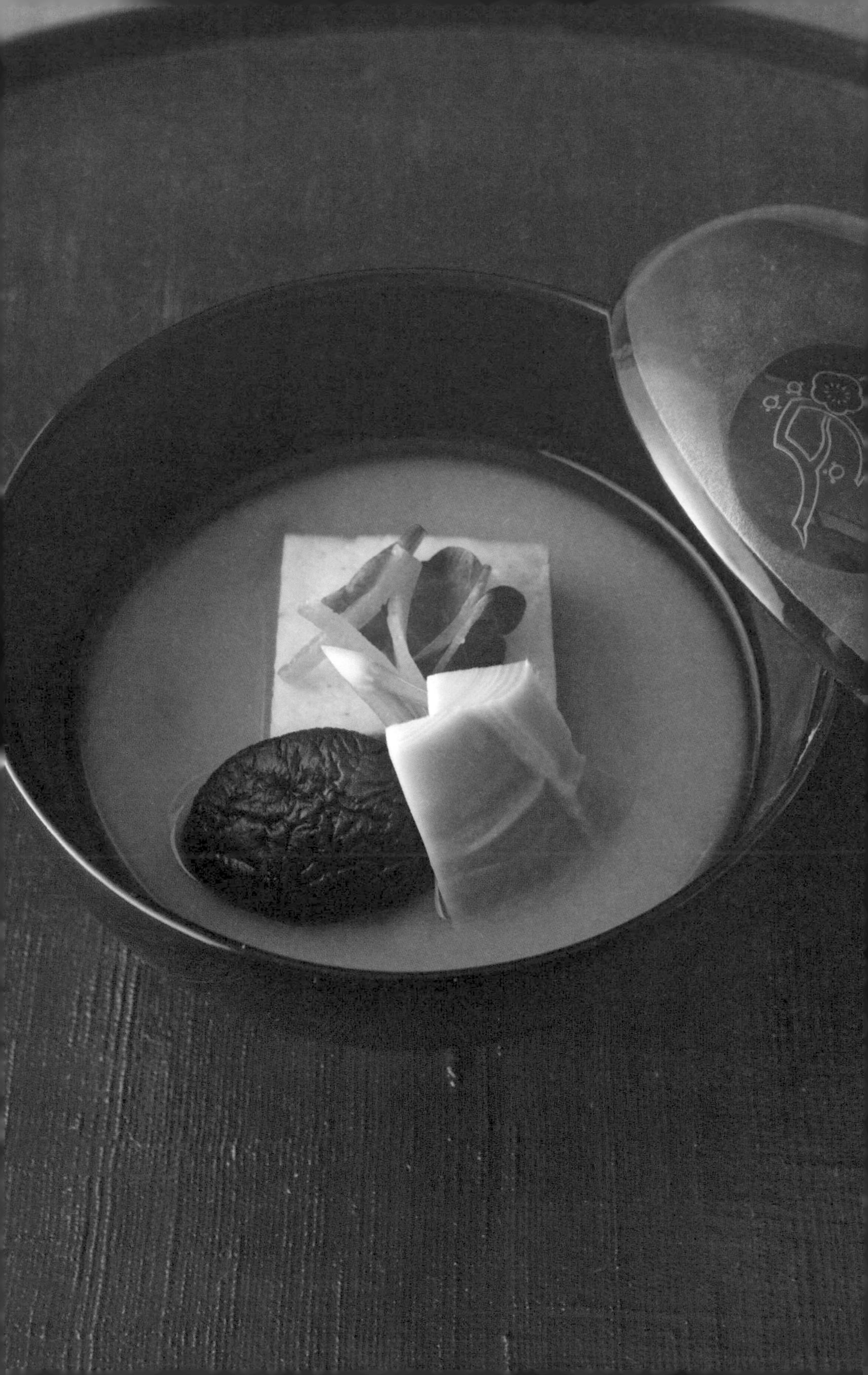

 Owan Soup

Lily bulb soup ■ Crab cake ■
Bamboo shoots, greens, yuzu

Soups (*owan*; literally "soup bowl") that allow the diner to fully enjoy the flavor of dashi are a point of pride in Japanese cuisine. They consist of four elements: the flavorful dashi broth, the featured ingredient, the supporting ingredients, and the aroma accent. *Owan* are presented with their lids on.

The base of this soup is a puree of lily bulbs thinned with dashi, and the featured ingredient is a light crab cake called kani shinjo. The lily bulb puree represents melting snow while the crab cake stands in for a lump of snow. The supporting ingredients—grilled shiitake mushrooms, bamboo shoots, and carrots cut in the shape of plum blossoms—represent bamboo shoots and soil (the dark mushrooms) peeking out from the melting snow as plum trees bloom. The aroma accent is yuzu peel cut to look like a pine needle. The soup is served with a bamboo-shaped piece of a green called uguisu-na to give the dish five colors (see page 167) and to represent the traditionally festive combination of pine, bamboo and plum. A decorative cutting technique called *mukimono*[1] is used for the carrots and yuzu.

Wajima lacquerware with maki-e in the *shikunshi*[2] pattern.

SKILLFULLY CUT GARNISHES ADD A SENSE OF THE SEASON EVEN WITHOUT REAL PLUM BLOSSOMS OR PINE NEEDLES.

---

1 A method of cutting vegetables to depict natural objects such as plants and animals. It originated in the Edo period as a way to add festiveness to the dining table and entertain guests.

2 A traditional Chinese auspicious pattern of orchids, bamboo, chrysanthemums and plum blossoms. Japan's lucky pine-bamboo-plum motif is thought to have originated in the *shikunshi* pattern. The bowl is placed with the item in season (in this case, the plum blossom) facing the diner.

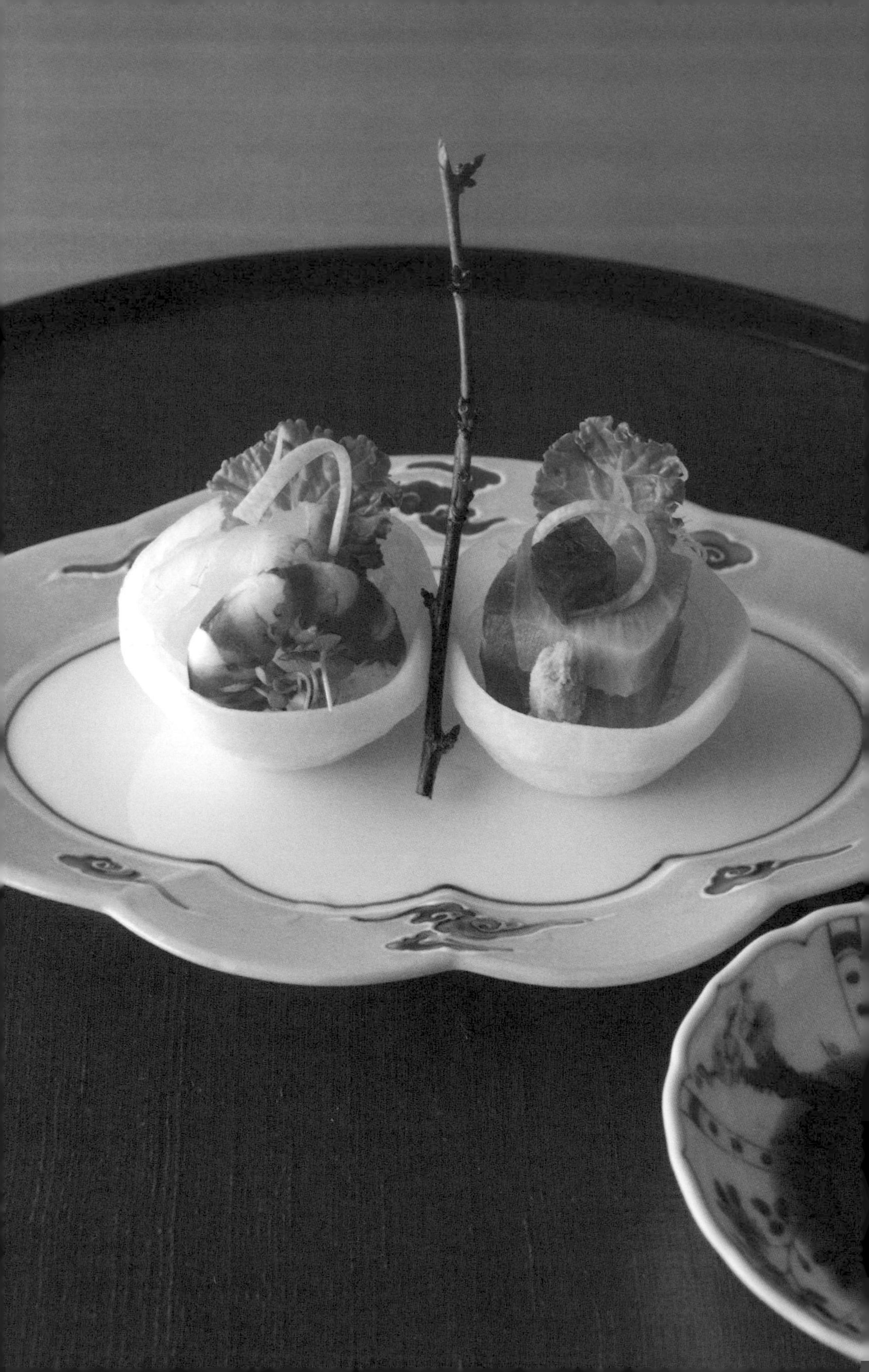

Tsukuri Sashimi

Tuna ▪ Tiger shrimp ▪ Sea Bream ▪ Wasabi, Tosa shoyu

Tsukuri is another name for sashimi, the ultimate Japanese dish that can only be made with the freshest fish and a very sharp knife. Traditionally, sashimi has been viewed as the best way to prepare fish, followed in order by steaming, grilling, frying and simmering.

Tuna, shrimp and sea bream are a perfect combination. The tuna is cut into cubes while the sea bream is cut into thin, flat slices, providing contrasting appearances and textures. Here the shrimp are quickly submerged in hot oil, a preparation method called *aburajimo*. As soon as they change color, they are plunged into cold water to accentuate their bright red tint.

The garnish adds color and three-dimensionality to the sashimi plate. Here the fish is served in tiny bowls made from paper-thin slices of daikon radish, just one technique in which the garnish becomes amusement. In another, daikon slices are fashioned into miniature spinning tops.

Yellow Kochi ware (see footnote page 146) in a *yokobai* shape representing a side view of a plum blossom.

EVEN SASHIMI OFTEN GETS A TWIST IN KAISEKI RYORI, SUCH AS INFUSING IT WITH KOMBU.

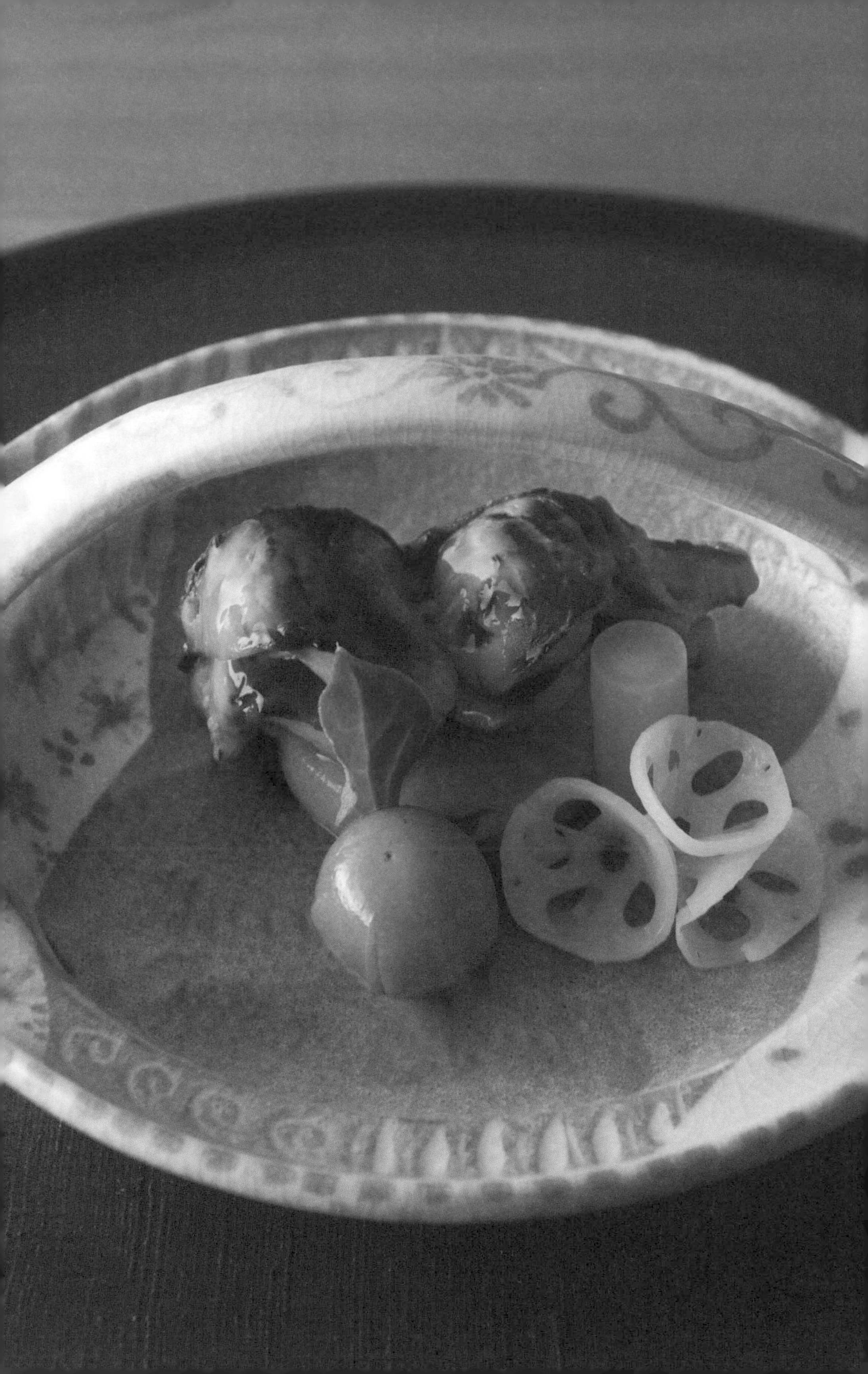

Spanish mackerel with yuzu-miso glaze ▪ Daikon steak ▪ Candied kumquat, lotus root with pickled plum, stem lettuce

Yakimono, or grilled food, is one of the main dishes on the menu. Typically it is grilled fish. An abundance of variations exist, such as marinating the fish before grilling or cooking it on a cedar plank.

Spanish mackerel with yuzu-miso glaze is a quintessential winter grilled dish. The fish is skewered before cooking to have a pattern like surging waves in the ocean, creating a festive atmosphere. A daikon radish "steak" is placed under the mackerel to give it height. A fundamental principle of plating Japanese food is to place taller elements in the back and lower ones in the front.

Palate-cleansing garnishes called *ashirai* accompany grilled foods Here, candied kumquat, lotus root seasoned with pickled plum, and stem lettuce are served.

Karatsu ware with handle

GRILLED DISHES LOOK BEST ON HEAVY POTTERY.

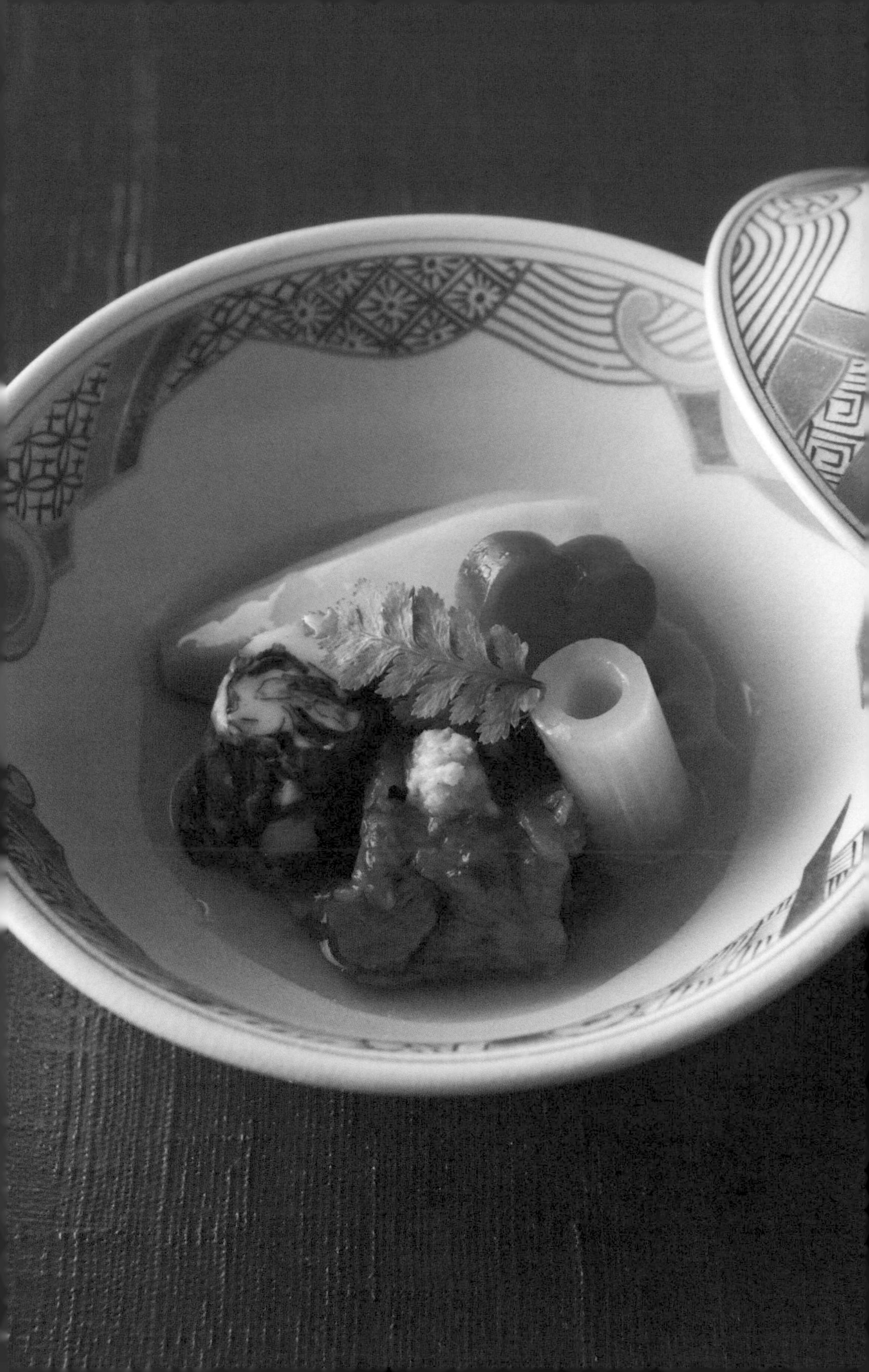

 Nimono Simmered Dish

Taro root ■ Beef ■
Carrot, butterbur, garland chrysanthemum, sansho pepper leaf

Simmered dishes featuring vegetables and other ingredients cooked in dashi with soy sauce and mirin are called nimono or takiawase. They are an essential element of Japanese cuisine, and a test of the chef's skill.

The beef is prepared in the jibu-ni style from Kanazawa, where pieces of chicken are coated with flour and simmered. Here, beef replaces chicken and buckwheat flour replaces wheat flour to create a more sophisticated dish. The combination of creamy simmered taro root, rich beef jibu-ni, and crispy simmered butterbur (fuki) stems offers an interesting contrast in textures.

For the garnish, fish paste is rolled in garland chrysanthemum leaves to represent sprouts emerging from under the snow. Carrots cut in the shape of plum blossoms and sansho pepper leaf are the other garnishes.

Colorful Kyo ware
evokes early spring

SIMMERED DISHES TEND TO BE DRAB, SO IT'S IMPORTANT TO REMEMBER THE FIVE COLORS WHEN SELECTING GARNISHES.

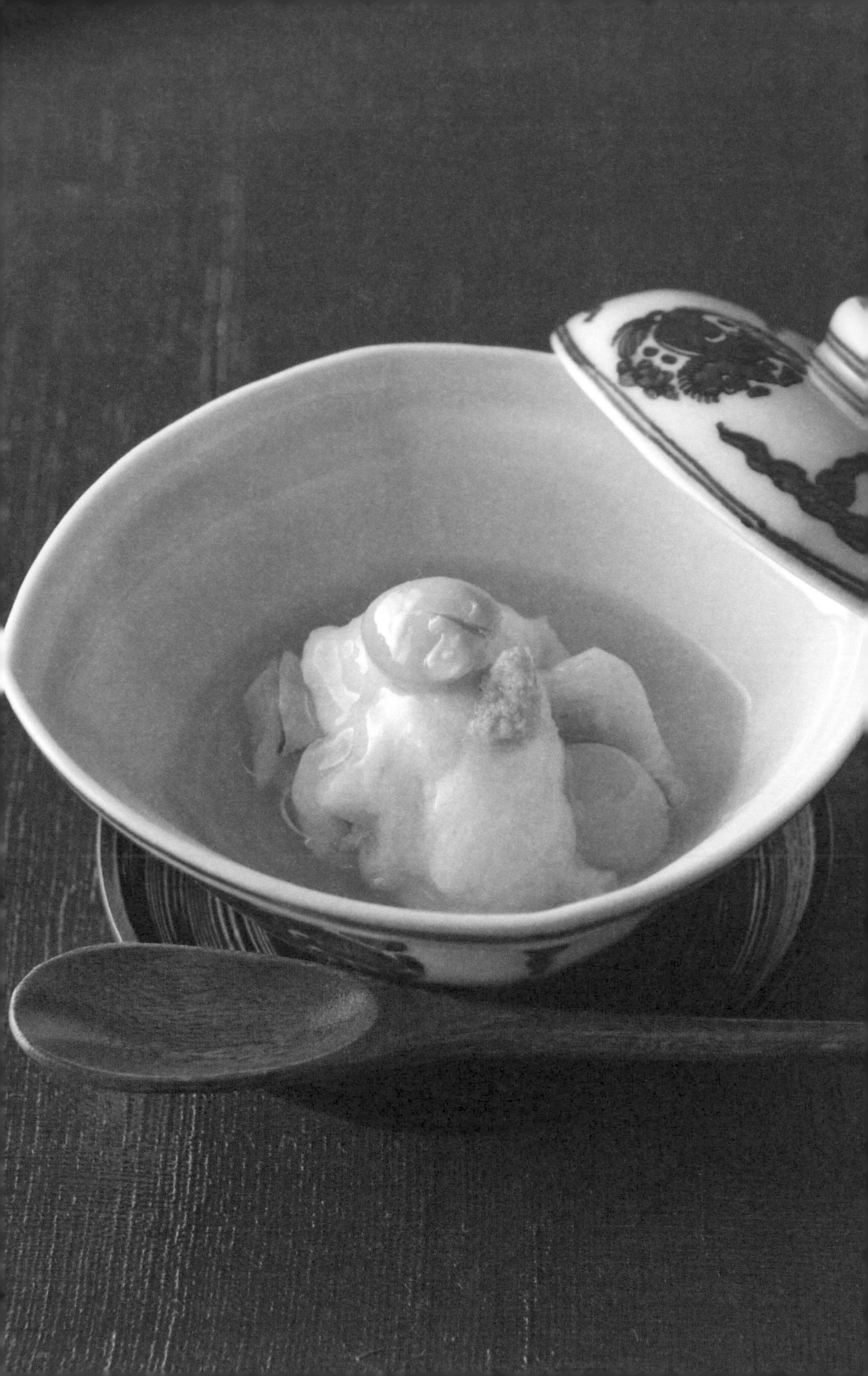

Mushimono Steamed Dish

Tilefish with grated turnip ■ Ginkgo nut, wasabi, ginan sauce

Steamed dishes, or mushimono, use indirect heat to cook the ingredients, an effective technique for delicately flavored foods such as poultry and seafood. Since seasonings cannot be added during cooking, foods are either preseasoned, or a thick sauce called "an" is poured over them after cooking.

In this dish, called kabura-mushi, white fish is topped with finely grated turnip before steaming, then served with a pale sauce called ginan. Kabura-mushi made with tilefish and large Shogoin turnips is a winter delicacy in Kyoto, with the grated turnip standing in for snow. To preserve the whiteness of the turnip, the sauce is made without ingredients that would darken it. Gin-an is so named because it appears to glow silver when light reflects off of it.

A bowl decorated with an auspicious *kara-shishi* (Chinese lion) pattern

WHEN YOU WANT TO SERVE FOOD HOT, IT'S BEST TO USE A BOWL WITH A LID.

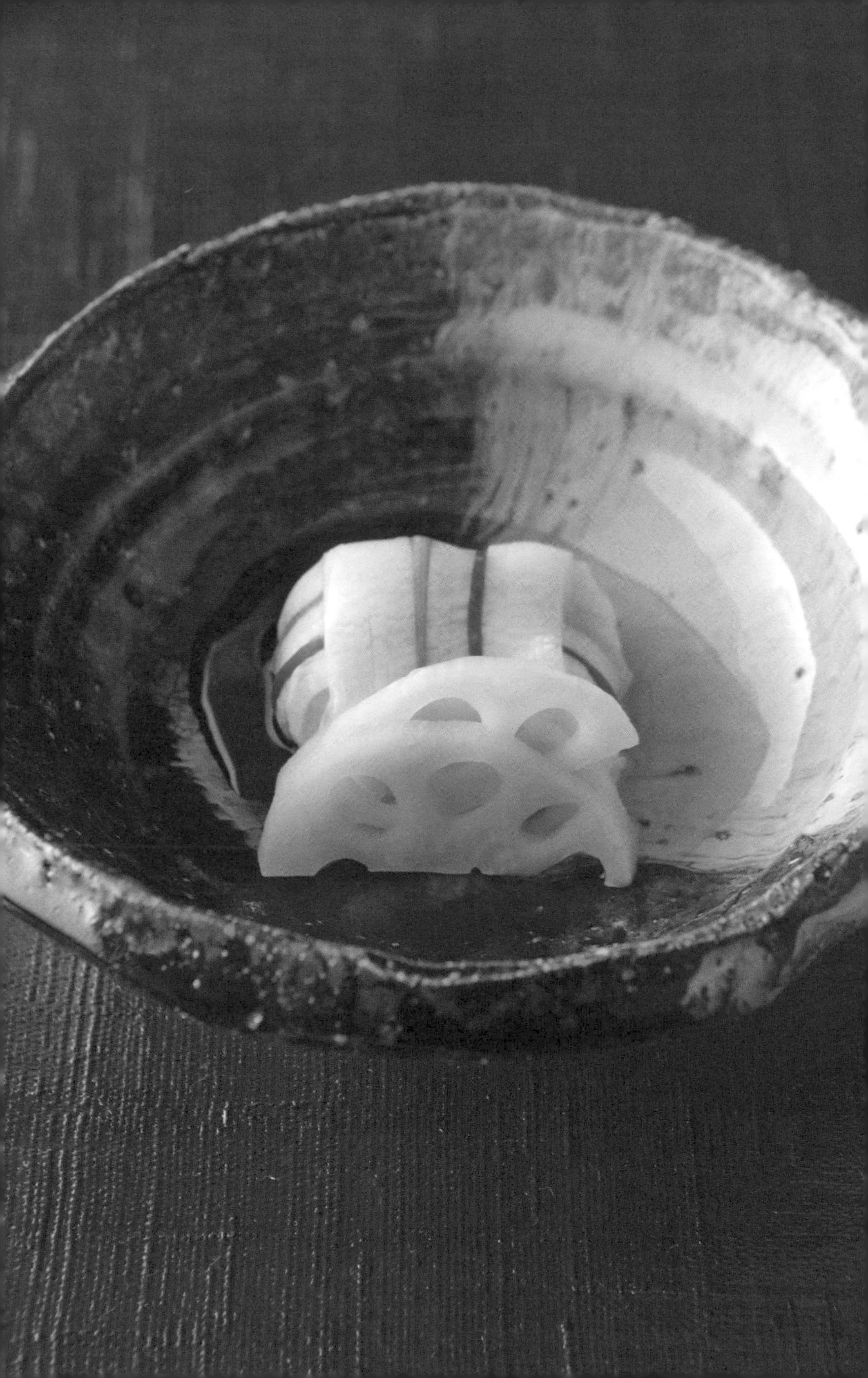

Sunomono Vinegared Dish

Yamaimo yam, mitsuba, carrot ■ Lotus root, vinegar sauce

Sunomono, or vinegar flavored dishes, are served toward the end of the meal to refresh the palate. This dish of paper-thin slices of yamaimo yam wrapped with green mitsuba and red Kyoto carrots is called shirako itomaki, and represents happiness or congratulations. It is accompanied by lotus root and a vinegar sauce.

Among Japanese chefs, dishes seasoned with vinegar are widely referred to as namasu-mono. Namasu was originally an ancient Chinese dish of thinly sliced raw meat or fish (see footnote on page 28). After arriving in Japan, it evolved in new directions, and by the Muromachi period (1336–1573), vinegar was being added. Sashimi was originally a type of namasu in which thinly sliced fish was served with gingered vinegar or a type of flavored sake called irizake.[1] After soy sauce became more common in the 16th century, people began to eat raw fish with soy sauce instead of vinegar, and sashimi became a dish of its own.

A type of Korean Karatsu ware with black and white poured glazes, representing snow melting on soil.

VINEGARED DISHES AND SASHIMI BOTH HAVE THEIR ROOTS IN NAMASU.

---

1 Irizake is made by reducing sake with pickled plums and other ingredients.

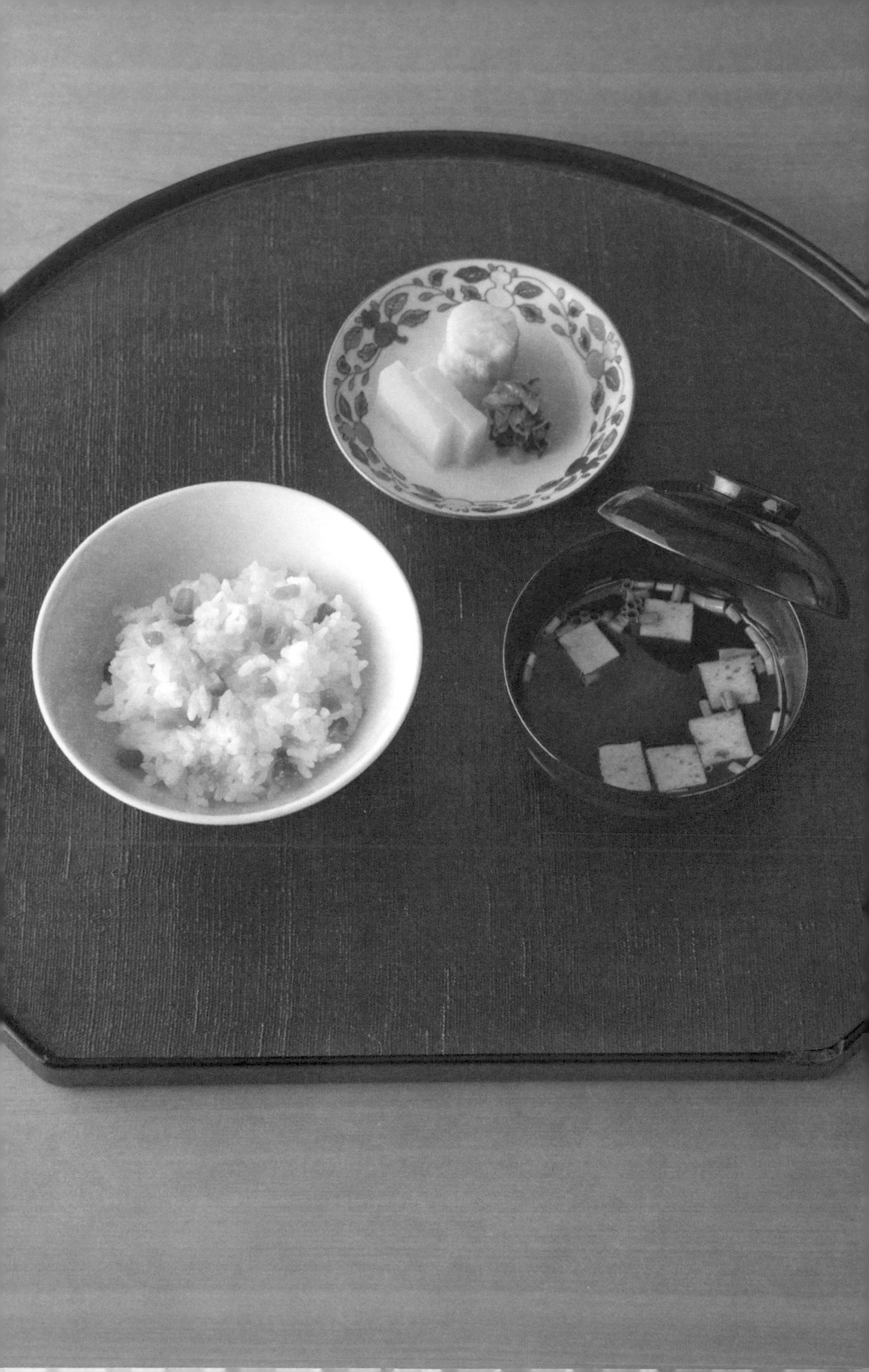

Shokuji Rice, Soup, Pickles

Karasumi rice ■ Red miso soup, tofu, mitsuba ■
Pickled napa cabbage, daikon radish, and mizuna

The final course of a kaiseki meal, save the dessert, is called the shokuji, or "meal." It typically consists of three items: a rice dish, often including other ingredients or seasonings; a soup such as clear or miso soup, called "the last bowl"; and pickles.

Karasumi rice is made with the salted, sun-dried roe sacs of mullet or other fish, a preserved food made in November. Karasumi is considered an auspicious ingredient that turns simple white rice into a delicacy.

Pickled vegetables served with the shokuji are called konomono, a word that originated in an aristocratic game of the Heian period called *monko*, or "listening to incense." Nobles warmed fragrant wood in incense burners held in their palms to appreciate the scents. To keep their sense of smell sharp, they would eat pickled daikon radish as they played. Originally, pickles were a fermented food, but today quick pickles made without fermentation are common.

Banreki akae plate

Wajima lacquerware

Arita ware

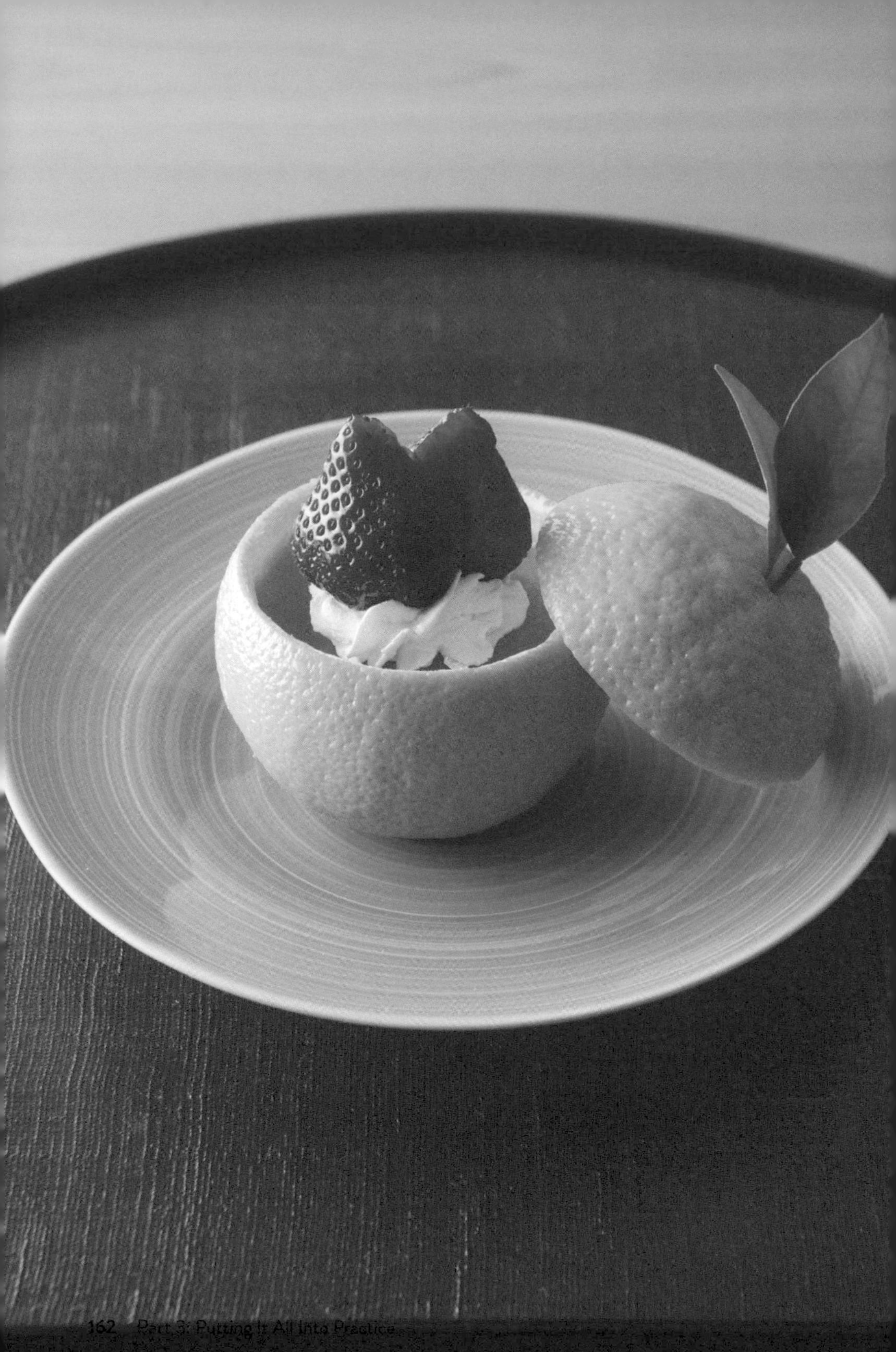

 Mizugashi Dessert

Citrus Jelly

Originally the word "mizugashi" meant fruit, but in kaiseki ryori, all desserts are called mizugashi. In addition to fresh fruits, Japanese sweets such as anmitsu and yokan and Western sweets such as sorbet and ice cream are served.

This jelly is made with sanboukan, a type of citrus fruit in season in late winter. The jelly has a smooth, refreshing mouthfeel similar to drinking cold water.

Japanese cuisine is generally free of dairy products, but the use of cream is becoming more common in desserts.

Green Kochi ware
(see footnote page 146)

IN FRENCH CUISINE YOU WANT SWEET DESSERTS, BUT JAPANESE CUISINE IS SWEET OVERALL, SO REFRESHING DESSERTS ARE PREFERRED.

Tableware and Food Presentation

Tableware as delightful as the food it holds

Tableware is one of the unique pleasures of Japanese cuisine. As you may have noticed in the kaiseki ryori meal on the preceding pages, part of what makes a Japanese meal so appealing is that the seasons are expressed not only in the food but also in the dishes that hold the food, making the meal as pleasurable to look at as it is to eat.

The distinctive Japanese way of eating, in which bowls are picked up and brought to the mouth, led to the development of ceramic and lacquerware bowls and the creation of a wide variety of vessels, both large and small. While fancy Western meals often use uniform sets of white porcelain or glassware, high-end Japanese meals feature a variety of colors, shapes and materials, such as lacquerware, earthenware and porcelain, inviting diners to enjoy the textures of the tableware as yet another element of the meal.

Earthenware versus porcelain

	Earthenware	Porcelain
Raw materials	Potter's clay etc.	Crushed pottery stone etc.
Firing temperature	1470–2280°F (800–1250°C)	2200–2550°F (1200–1400°C)
Water absorbency	Up to 10%	Close to 0%
Heat conductivity	Low	High
Texture	Soft and porous	Glassy, dense and hard
Representative regions/wares	Mino ware, Seto ware, Mashiko ware, Shigaraki ware, Karatsu ware etc.	Arita ware (also called Imari ware), Kutani ware, Tobe ware etc.

Korean Karatsu ware

Arita ware

FRENCH FOOD IS NOT SERVED ON EARTHENWARE BECAUSE IT ABSORBS OIL. FORKS AND KNIVES MAY SCRATCH IT, TOO.

The yin and yang of tableware

The fundamental concepts of yin and yang are as follows:

Yang is movement, strength, heat, brightness and lightness.

Yin is stillness, softness, coldness, darkness and heaviness.

Round vessels and those that have a calm, soft feeling are yang, while square, deep, assertive vessels are yin. For the food and the vessel to complement each other, warm-looking dishes should be served with vigorous-looking food, while more assertive dishes should be served with calmer-looking foods.

Yang

Banreki akae ware

Footed bowl

Bizen ware

Yin

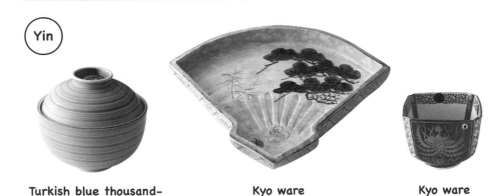

Turkish blue thousand-layer lidded bowl

Kyo ware fan-shaped bowl with pine, plum blossom and bamboo motif

Kyo ware

A BOWL WITH A LID IS A YIN VESSEL. SERVING WARM SOUP OR OTHER YANG FOODS IN A LIDDED VESSEL BRINGS HARMONY TO THE DISH.
IT'S BEST TO BALANCE EARTHENWARE AND PORCELAIN, YIN AND YANG VESSELS THROUGHOUT THE MEAL.

The rules of food presentation

Let's take a brief look at five important guidelines for presenting food.

① **Be aware of the front and back of the vessel**

As a rule, when serving food, the front of the vessel should face the guest. If you have difficulty distinguishing the front from the back, look for an inscription or mark on the back.[1]

② **Consider the food's compatibility with the vessel**

The shape and color of the food should go well with the shape and color of the vessel. The concept of yin and yang can be applied here as well. Serve square foods in round dishes and round foods in square dishes. For example if you are serving sashimi, a round vessel works well with flat or square slices. For soups, the ingredients should have angular elements to contrast with the round bowl.

Japanese names for vessel parts

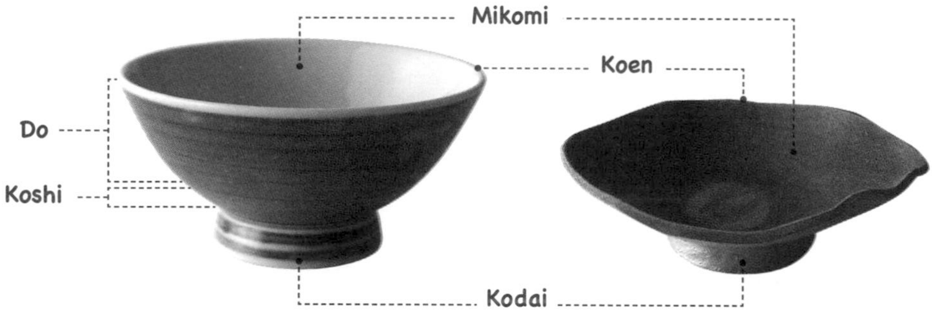
Mikomi
Koen
Do
Koshi
Kodai

Mikomi ... Inner part of the vessel.
Koen ... Rim of the vessel. Also called kuchizukuri.
Kodai ... Circular foot at the bottom of the vessel
Do ... The area between the koen and koshi (not present on shallow dishes).
Koshi ... The area between the do and the kodai (only on vessels with a protruding lower part). It is sometimes difficult to determine the boundary between the do and the koshi.

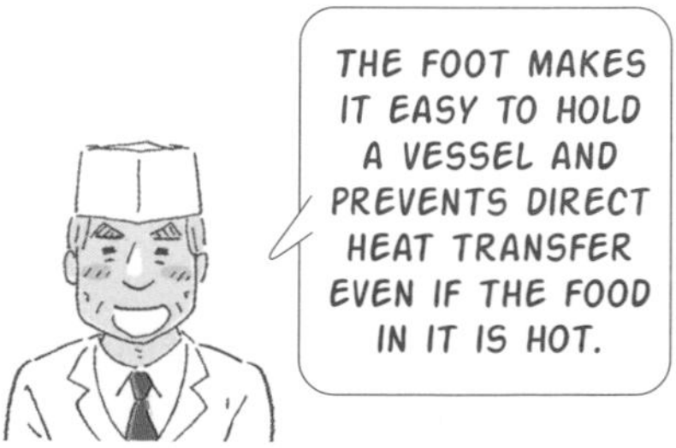
THE FOOT MAKES IT EASY TO HOLD A VESSEL AND PREVENTS DIRECT HEAT TRANSFER EVEN IF THE FOOD IN IT IS HOT.

1 The side below the inscription or mark of the artist or kiln is the front (the bottom edge if you are holding it up vertically as you look at the inscription).

③ Make the most of empty spaces

It has long been viewed as important to leave ample space around the food, rather than filling the entire the dish. Refer to the figure below for margin guidelines.

④ Create a three-dimensional effect

Food presentation customs are said have originated in offerings to the gods (see page 62). In offerings, it was customary to stack the food in tall, beautiful arrangements. Because of this tradition, Japanese cuisine is strongly focused on height in presentation.

⑤ Include the five colors

The color scheme of the food arrangements should be based on the following five colors: blue or green, red, yellow, white, and black.

⑥ Give a sense of the season

This is the most important element of Japanese cuisine. Pay attention not only to the four seasons, but also to the finer monthly changes in seasonality.

Margin guidelines for plating food

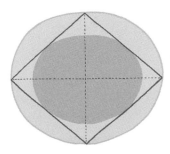

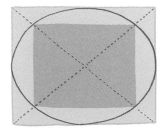

For an oval or circular vessel
Imagine a diamond positioned as on the plate above. The blue ellipse inside the diamond is the approximate area where food should be arranged.

For a rectangular or square vessel
Imagine an ellipse positioned as on the plate above. The blue rectangle is the approximate area where the food should be arranged.

IT'S BEST TO PLACE THE FOOD SLIGHTLY TOWARD THE BACK OF THE BLUE AREAS IN THE DIAGRAMS ABOVE.

Dining at a Traditional Japanese Restaurant

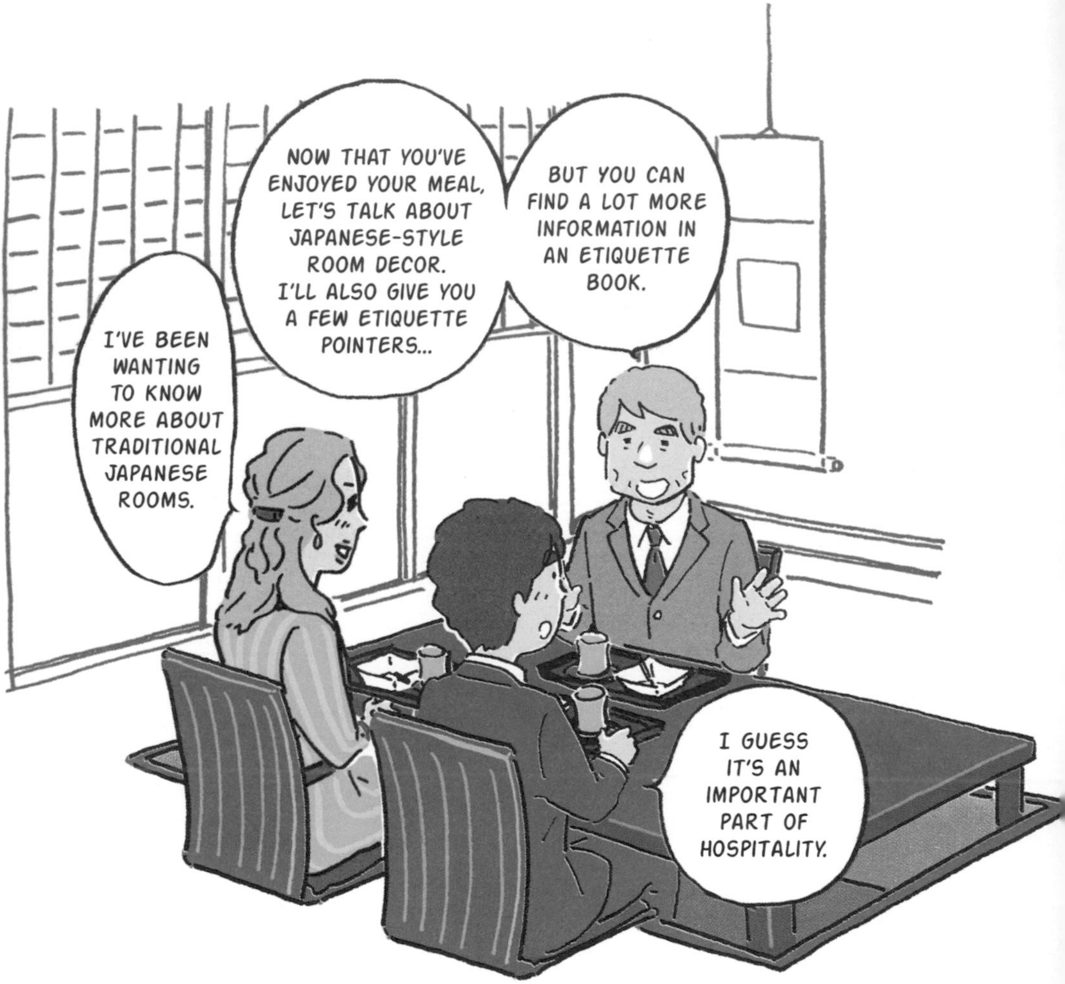
NOW THAT YOU'VE ENJOYED YOUR MEAL, LET'S TALK ABOUT JAPANESE-STYLE ROOM DECOR. I'LL ALSO GIVE YOU A FEW ETIQUETTE POINTERS...
BUT YOU CAN FIND A LOT MORE INFORMATION IN AN ETIQUETTE BOOK.
I'VE BEEN WANTING TO KNOW MORE ABOUT TRADITIONAL JAPANESE ROOMS.
I GUESS IT'S AN IMPORTANT PART OF HOSPITALITY.

The Entrance

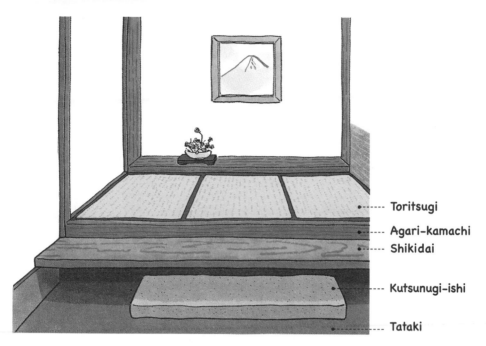

Toritsugi
Agari-kamachi
Shikidai
Kutsunugi-ishi
Tataki

Tataki ... Entryway floor
Kutsunugi-ishi ... A stone for taking off and putting on shoes and stepping inside.
Shikidai ... A board installed if the step up from the entryway is high. People sit here when putting on their shoes.
Agari-kamachi... The board on the front of the step up from the entryway.
Toritsugi... Where guests are welcomed.

How to remove shoes at the entrance

- Facing the same direction as when you came in, remove your shoes on the kutsunugi-ishi.
- Kneel on the shikidai so that your back does not face the entrance and arrange your shoes neatly.

WHEN LINING UP YOUR SHOES, BEND AT A SLIGHT ANGLE FOR A GRACEFUL LOOK.
IN NEWER BUILDINGS, THE DIFFERENCE IN LEVEL BETWEEN THE TATAKI AND THE SHIKIDAI HAS BECOME SMALLER, AND KUTSUNUGI-ISHI ARE NOT SO COMMON ANYMORE.

The kamiza (upper seat) and shimoza (lower seat) in a tatami room

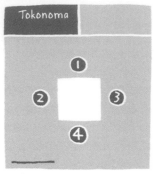

Tokonoma
1
2
3
4
Door
Tokonoma
1
3
2
4
Door
Tokonoma
1
2
4
3
Door
Tokonoma
2
1
4
3
Door

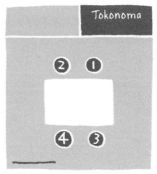

IT'S HARD TO RELAX WHEN YOU'RE SO CLOSE TO THE DOOR.
IF THE TOKONOMA ALCOVE IS NEXT TO THE DOOR, THE SEAT FARTHEST FROM THE DOOR IS THE KAMIZA.

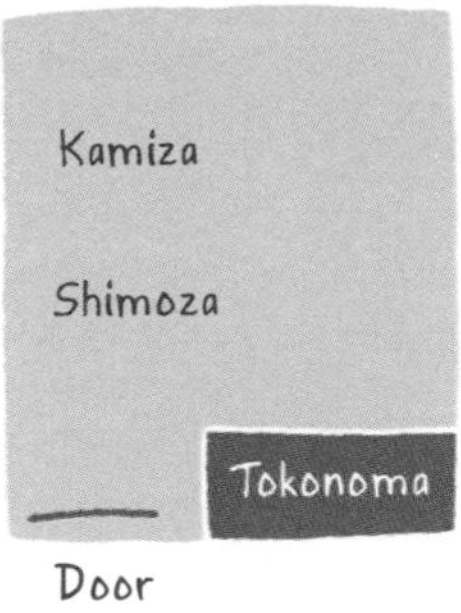

Kamiza
Shimoza
Tokonoma
Door

Who sits where?

When dining, it is important to pay attention to where each person sits. This is not a concern among friends, but it is when entertaining guests.

The term kamiza means upper seat, and shimoza means lower seat. The kamiza is for superiors and guests, while the shimoza is for subordinates and the host.

If there is a tokonoma alcove in the room, the seat closest to the alcove is the kamiza, and the seat on the opposite side is the shimoza. If there is no alcove, the seat furthest from the door is the kamiza. Take a look at the seating arrangements in the diagrams shown here. However, while these rules exist, the most important point is to make sure that the safest and most comfortable seat is the kamiza.

Seating in a tatami room with a garden

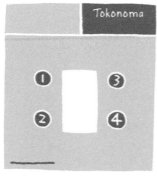

Tokonoma
1
3
2
4
Garden
Door

EVERYONE WANTS TO ENJOY A BEAUTIFUL GARDEN!
NORMALLY THE SEAT FACING AWAY FROM THE ALCOVE AND FARTHEST FROM THE DOOR IS THE KAMIZA, BUT IF THERE IS A GARDEN, THE SEATS FACING IT ARE THE KAMIZA.

Tokonoma (Hondoko style)

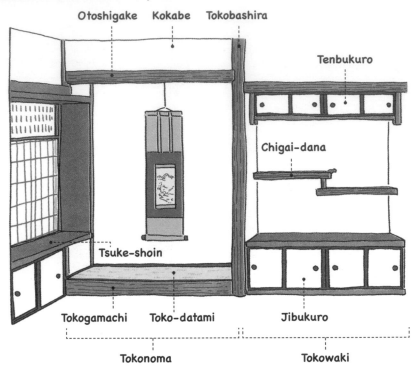

Otoshigake   Kokabe   Tokobashira

Tenbukuro

Chigai-dana

Tsuke-shoin

Tokogamachi   Toko-datami   Jibukuro

Tokonoma   Tokowaki

How changing architectural styles affected the tokonoma

- In the Muromachi period (1336–1573), the shoin-zukuri style of samurai residences was perfected. The tokonoma, or alcove, is a simplified version of the elevated rooms in these houses where dignitaries were welcomed. The hondoko style dates to this period.
- In the Azuchi-Momoyama period (1568–1603), Sen no Rikyu invented the hermitage-style tea house. He created many variations on the alcoves by altering the hondoko style. The simplest was the kabedoko, or wall alcove, in which a nail was simply driven into the wall to hang a scroll.
- The Azuchi-Momoyama period saw the emergence of sukiya-zukuri, a building style that incorporated the characteristics of the tea room. It is a simple and free but refined style that eschews the formality of the shoin-zukuri style, and is used today in traditional Japanese-style restaurants.

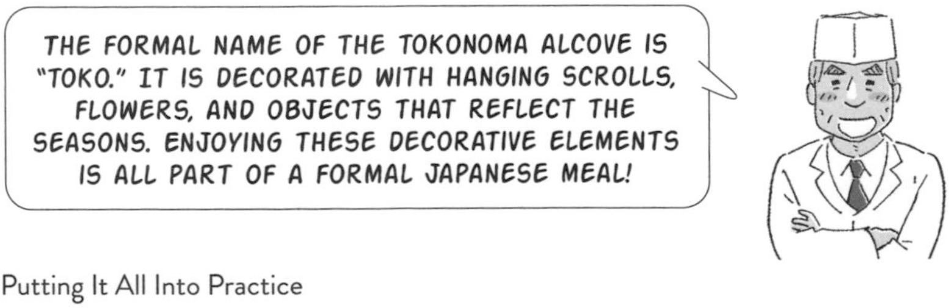

THE FORMAL NAME OF THE TOKONOMA ALCOVE IS "TOKO." IT IS DECORATED WITH HANGING SCROLLS, FLOWERS, AND OBJECTS THAT REFLECT THE SEASONS. ENJOYING THESE DECORATIVE ELEMENTS IS ALL PART OF A FORMAL JAPANESE MEAL!

Upper part of a tatami room

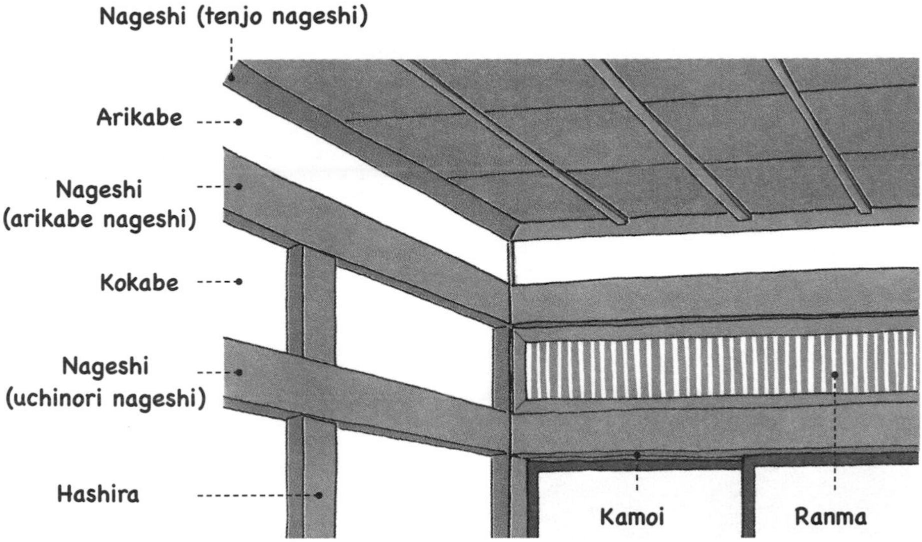

Nageshi (tenjo nageshi)
Arikabe
Nageshi
(arikabe nageshi)
Kokabe
Nageshi
(uchinori nageshi)
Hashira
Kamoi
Ranma

Kakejiku (hanging scroll)

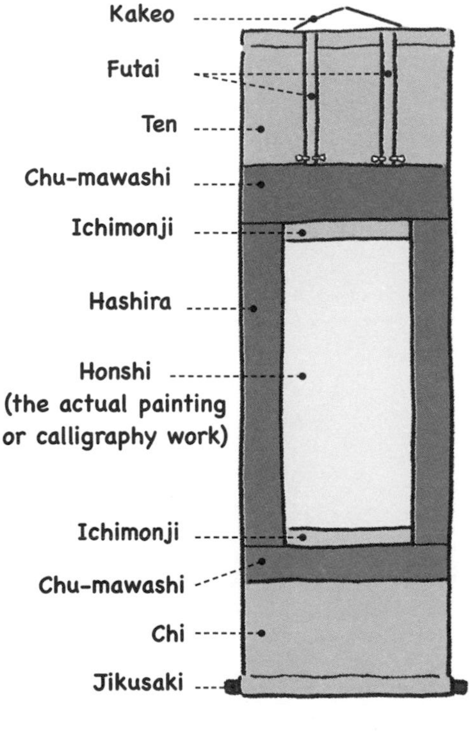

Kakeo
Futai
Ten
Chu-mawashi
Ichimonji
Hashira
Honshi
(the actual painting
or calligraphy work)
Ichimonji
Chu-mawashi
Chi
Jikusaki

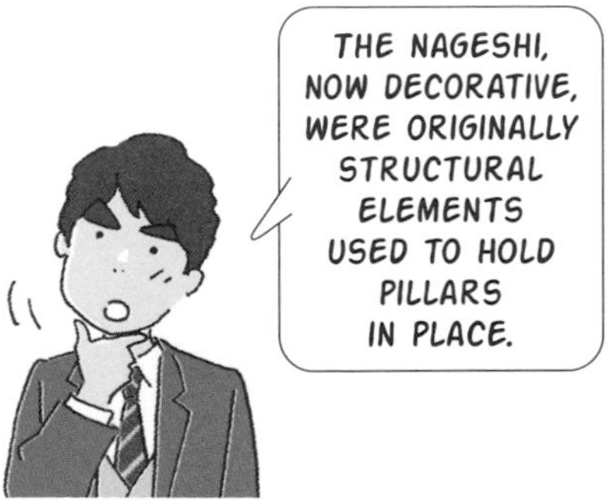

THE NAGESHI, NOW DECORATIVE, WERE ORIGINALLY STRUCTURAL ELEMENTS USED TO HOLD PILLARS IN PLACE.

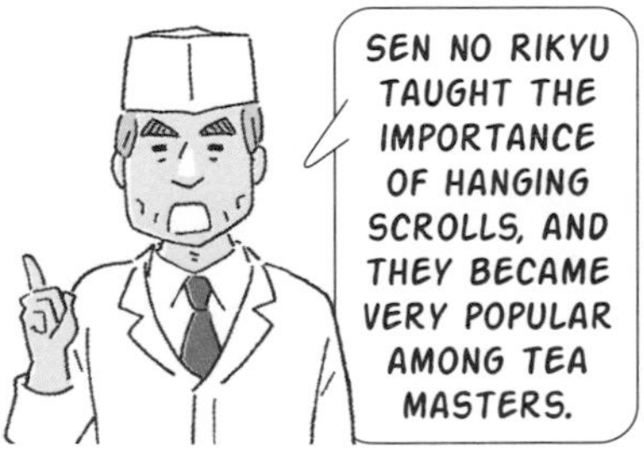

SEN NO RIKYU TAUGHT THE IMPORTANCE OF HANGING SCROLLS, AND THEY BECAME VERY POPULAR AMONG TEA MASTERS.

Can you serve a traditional Japanese meal?

LET'S SEE IF YOU KNOW THE CORRECT WAY TO PRESENT FOOD.

CHOOSE EITHER A OR B. ANSWERS AND EXPLANATIONS ARE ON PAGES 178-179.

Q1 Which way should a round tray be placed?

a

b

With the seam in front

With the seam in back

Q2 Which way should a square tray be placed?

a

b

With the seam in front

With the seam in back

Q3 Which way should a tray with a cut corner be placed?

a

b

With the cut corner on the far left

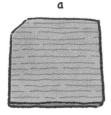

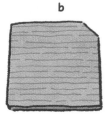

With the cut corner on the far right

Q4 Which way should a square wood tray with no seam be placed?

a

b

With the wood grain running vertically

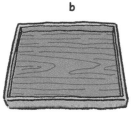

With the wood grain running horizontally

Q5 Which way should a round wood tray with no seam be placed?

a

b

With the inner tree rings on the left

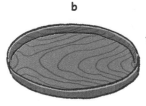

With the inner tree rings on the right

Q6 Which way should a leaf-shaped plate be placed?

a

b

With the tip on the left

With the tip on the right

Q7 How should a grilled fish be served?

a   b

With the head   With the head
to the left   to the right

Q8 How should a flatfish be served?

a   b

With the head   With the head
to the left   to the right

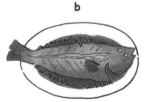

Q9 How should a piece of fish be served?

a   b

With the skin   With the skin
side up   side down

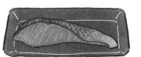

Q10 How should naruto (spiral fish paste) be served?

a   b

With the   With the spiral
spiral going   going counter-
clockwise   clockwise

Q11 Which is the top side of a zabuton cushion?

a

b

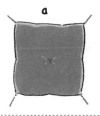

The side without the tassel

The side with the tassel

Q12 Which is the correct way to fold *kaishi* paper for celebratory occasions?

a

b

With the top layer slanting down to the right

With the top layer slanting down to the left

Use it as a plate

Use it to wipe your chopsticks

KAISHI PAPER IS SO CONVENIENT! IT'S GOOD TO KEEP A FEW SHEETS IN YOUR BAG.

Use *kaishi* paper to...

- wipe your mouth, chopsticks, and glass.
- hold down your fish when removing the bones.
- cover up the fish bones after you have finished eating the fish.
- catch drips when eating something moist.
- hold Japanese sweets, like a plate.

Answers and Explanations

Q1   a
For round wooden trays, the seam is placed in the front.

Q2   b
For square wooden trays, the seam is placed in back.

Q3   b
For cut-corner trays, the cut corner goes on the far right.

Q4   b
Square trays are placed with the wood grain running horizontally.

Q5   b
Round wooden trays are placed with the inner tree rings on the right.

Q6   a
Leaf-shaped plates are placed with the tip facing left.

Q7   a
Grilled fish is served with the head to the left. In addition, saltwater fish are served with the belly toward the front, while freshwater fish are served with the back toward the front.

JAPANESE CUISINE TENDS TO GIVE PRECEDENCE TO THE LEFT SIDE. SEE PAGE 180 FOR MORE INFO!

Q8　b

Grilled fish is generally served with the head on the left, but flatfish is an exception. If you serve flatfish with the head on the left, the back of the fish will be in front, so the head goes to the right and the belly in front.

Q9　a

Serve fish fillets so that the skin is visible, facing up.

Q10　a

Serve spiral fishcakes with the spiral going clockwise when seen by the diner.

Q11　b

The side of the zabuton cushion with the tassel in the center is the top. For a zabuton with tassels on both the top and bottom, the side with the fabric overhanging the side seams is the top.
Place the unstitched edge (the edge with no seam) so it faces the diner's knees. If the zabuton has a cover, place it so that the zipper is at the back.

Q12　a

A *kaishi* is a small sheet of Japanese paper often used in tea ceremonies and in serving Japanese cuisine. Take care when you fold the paper. For celebrations and ordinary occasions, the fold should be at the bottom, and the top edge should be slanted slightly to the right, as in Example a. For mourning, the top edge should slant to the left, as in Example b.

A ZABUTON IS SLIGHTLY LONGER THAN IT IS WIDE.

FEATURE

Should the Left Side or the Right Take Precedence?

In Japan, the left side was historically regarded as higher in rank. This is thought to be because the left, which is to the east when facing south, represented the direction of the sunrise and was considered sacred. By contrast, in ancient China the right side was considered superior.

However, each new dynasty in China tended to establish new customs, and in the later Tang Dynasty (618–907) the left became superior. Japan had frequent contact with the Tang Dynasty during this time (the Heian period in Japan), and as a result the superiority of the left side took root, especially within the government.

When determining which side is superior, point of view is crucial. For instance, on a theatrical stage, from the audience's perspective the right side is superior and the left side is inferior, but from the performers' perspective, the left side is superior and the right is inferior.

Western influence from the Meiji period (1868–1912) onward led to the current tendency in Japan to see the right side as superior. In the West, "right" means "correct," and the right side is typically the superior position. Following this custom, the portrait of Emperor Meiji was painted with the emperor on the right and the empress on the left, which later became common practice. However, traditional Japanese values are still emphasized in the world of Japanese cuisine, and left-is-superior positioning has been preserved. One indication of this is the position of the bowl of rice in place settings. Rice holds the highest status and is therefore placed on the left side of the setting as viewed by the diner.

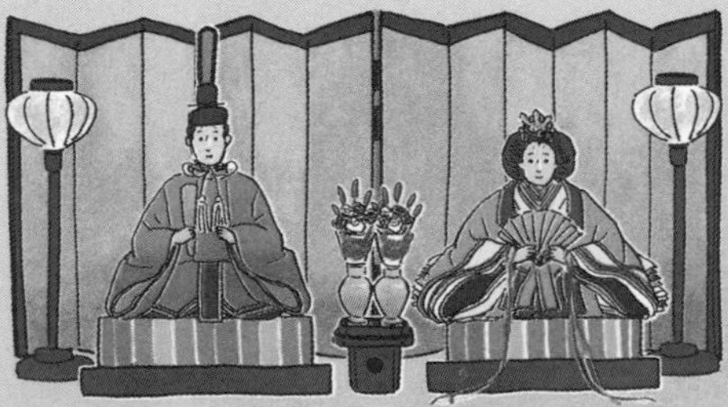

Today, hina dolls displayed for the Doll Festival are generally positioned with the doll representing the emperor on the left, in a right-is-superior position from the dolls' perspective. However, in Kyoto, where tradition is highly valued, the emperor doll is positioned on the right, representing a traditional left-is-superior position from the dolls' perspective.

Afterword

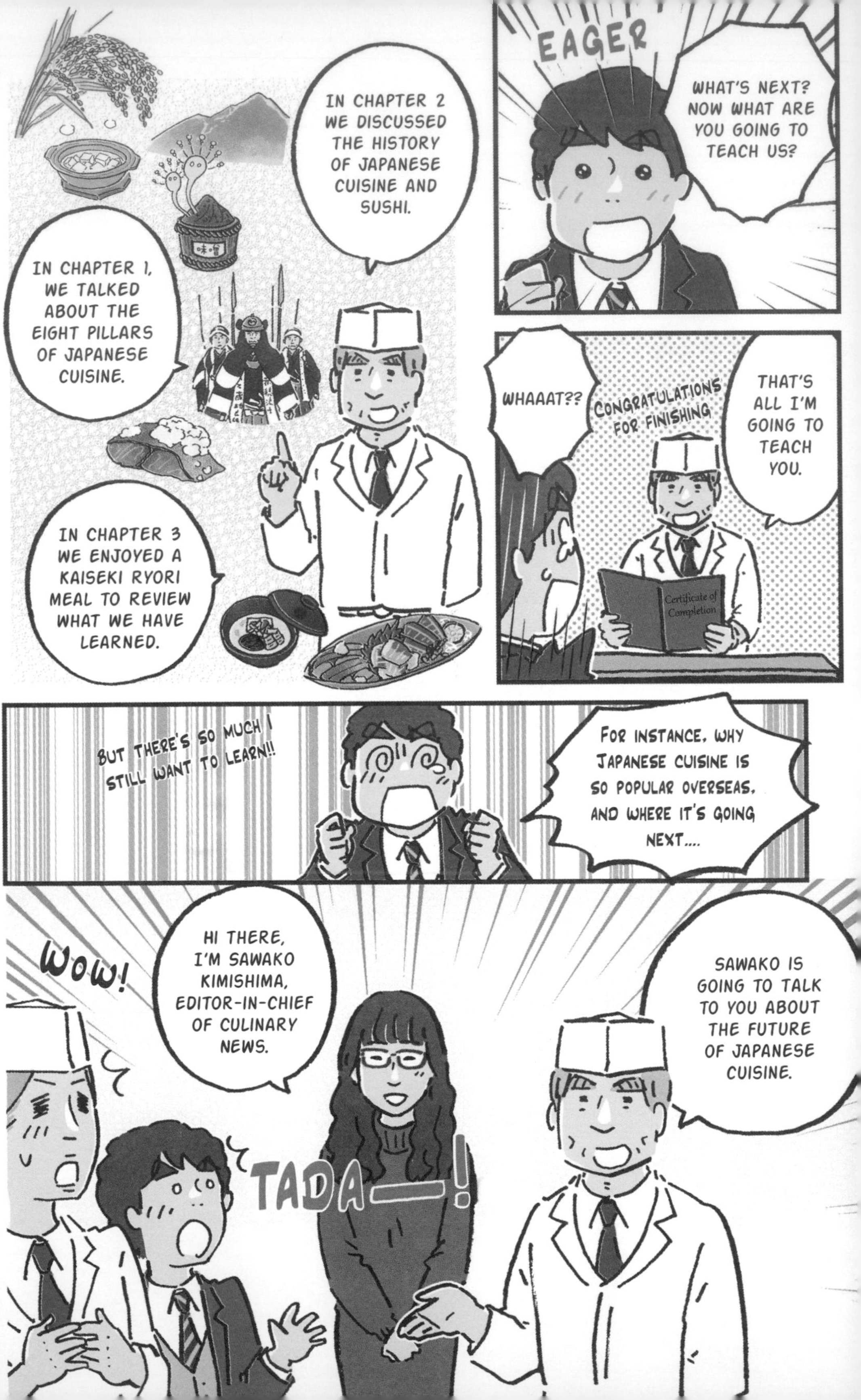
IN CHAPTER 1, WE TALKED ABOUT THE EIGHT PILLARS OF JAPANESE CUISINE.
IN CHAPTER 2 WE DISCUSSED THE HISTORY OF JAPANESE CUISINE AND SUSHI.
IN CHAPTER 3 WE ENJOYED A KAISEKI RYORI MEAL TO REVIEW WHAT WE HAVE LEARNED.
EAGER
WHAT'S NEXT? NOW WHAT ARE YOU GOING TO TEACH US?
CONGRATULATIONS FOR FINISHING
Certificate of Completion
THAT'S ALL I'M GOING TO TEACH YOU.
WHAAAT??
BUT THERE'S SO MUCH I STILL WANT TO LEARN!!
FOR INSTANCE, WHY JAPANESE CUISINE IS SO POPULAR OVERSEAS, AND WHERE IT'S GOING NEXT....
WOW!
HI THERE, I'M SAWAKO KIMISHIMA, EDITOR-IN-CHIEF OF CULINARY NEWS.
TADA—!
SAWAKO IS GOING TO TALK TO YOU ABOUT THE FUTURE OF JAPANESE CUISINE.

Why Japanese Cuisine Fascinates Chefs Around the World

The number of sushi restaurants around the world began to increase rapidly toward the end of the 20th century. To report on this trend, essayist Toyo Tamamura visited sushi restaurants in Paris, London, Amsterdam, New York and Los Angeles, and published *Around the World with Conveyor Belt Sushi* (Sekai Bunka Publishing). It came out in 2000, the millennium year.

Wherever you go, the basic structure of sushi is the same: there's vinegared rice and a filling or topping, served either as nigiri or maki rolls. The world of sushi, where the toppings and fillings provide the arena for innovation, must have been easy to grasp for people from different cultures. Sushi's colorfulness and the fact that it is both fast food and finger food have also hastened its spread.

Starting around 2010, Japanese ingredients such as soy sauce, wasabi, yuzu, sake, miso, tofu, and kombu began to enter the kitchens of overseas restaurants.

When I asked a food journalist living in Paris about the popularity of soy sauce overseas, he told me, "I don't think there is a starred restaurant in Paris that doesn't keep soy sauce in the kitchen." That's not a hard fact, of course, but if that's his sense from covering restaurants day in and day out, I imagine it is not far off the mark.

"A simple art"

Looking back, Japanese cuisine has been inspiring star chefs around the world for the past half century.

The influence of Japanese cuisine on contemporary French nouvelle cuisine has been frequently noted. Paul Bocuse, a key figure in nouvelle cuisine, first came to Japan in 1972 at the invitation of Shizuo Tsuji. The following year, 1973, the French culinary world was revolutionized by the nouvelle cuisine creed of eliminating unnecessary complexity, reducing cooking time, respecting market-influenced dishes (emphasizing ingredients), and rejecting excessively rich sauces.

French cuisine had been rich in high-protein, high-fat animal products such as fond de veau, which is made by boiling down roasted beef bones, butter, and cream, and perhaps this richness was a sign of luxury. However, it is too heavy for modern people who exercise less due to lifestyle changes. Moreover, chefs today have access to fresh ingredients thanks to advances in logistics and refrigeration technology, but rich sauces and lots of butter can mask their full flavor. Nouvelle cuisine took the heavy coat off French cuisine, which had gotten out of step with the times.

What about Japanese cuisine inspired Bocuse? The answer can be found in the title of a book by Tsuji, who invited Bocuse to Japan. *Japanese Cooking: A Simple Art*, published in the United States in 1980, is a bible of Japanese cooking, but it was the qualities captured by the phrase "a simple art" that changed the mindset of chefs like Bocuse. In other words, they realized that perhaps they had been overdoing it. Fish should be seasoned only with salt and grilled just until tender, never overcooked. Vegetables should retain their texture when boiled, and leafy greens in particular should be blanched quickly to accentuate their bright green color. French chefs experienced the intense flavors of ingredients brought out by simple cooking methods and found inspiration in Japanese cuisine, where the true value of ingredients is revealed not by adding elements but by subtracting everything superfluous.

An aesthetic rooted in terroir

The reason Japanese cuisine has become a simple art derives from Japan's climate and geography.

Due to the archipelago's long north–south axis, its climate is diverse. The complex coastline, the sixth longest in the world, provides excellent fishing grounds. About 70% of Japan is covered by forests, and rivers are steep due to the proximity of the mountains to the sea. Abundant precipitation waters the vegetation. An estimated 7,500 plant species grow in Japan, far more than the 1,600 in the United Kingdom and the 2,000 in New Zealand. The 3,000 species of mushroom growing in Japan account for more than 10% of the 20,000 species worldwide. There are 4,500 species of fish, compared to 300 in the United Kingdom and 1,300 in New Zealand.[1] Japan's biodiversity is truly notable in the global context.

The proximity of the mountains and seas where foodstuffs are harvested to the villages where people live has fostered an attitude of respect for ingredients. This respect is reflected in the words satoyama and satoumi, which express the idea that both the mountains and the seas are our home and must be managed carefully. In addition, the abundance of water has led to an obsession with cleanliness. The ikejime method of killing fish in a way that preserves freshness and the custom of eating fish and other foods raw are unmistakably derived from Japanese geography and climate. Our philosophy of honoring ingredients and not overcooking food, too, reflects an aesthetic rooted in terroir.

---

1 Data from *Relationships between Nature, Ingredients, and Washoku*, the official guidebook for "Washoku: Nature and Culture in Japanese Cuisine," a special exhibit at the National Museum of Nature and Science, written by Kenichi Shinoda, deputy museum director.

Masters of umami

In 2013, washoku was added to the UNESCO register of Intangible Cultural Heritage.

Around that time, overseas chefs began to explore the depths of Japanese cuisine. An increasing number visited kombu producers in Hokkaido, wasabi fields in Izu, tea plantations in Shizuoka and Uji, kombu wholesalers in Fukui, and sake breweries and miso factories throughout Japan. A prime example is Copenhagen's noma, which has topped the World's 50 Best Restaurants ranking five times. When noma opened a pop-up restaurant in Tokyo in 2015, Chef René Redzepi and his staff went to the Shirakami Mountains and the forests of Nagano, visited farmers and fermentation rooms, and ate vegetarian food at a temple in Kamakura to experience Japanese food from the perspective of place and history. They tried to understand "the simple art of Japanese cooking" from a broader context. Chefs were no longer just interested in the superficial use of soy sauce and wasabi.

Why is it that simple ingredients, prepared in a simple way, are so captivating to the diner? Why is it that the composition and seasoning seem so stripped down, yet bring a deep sense of satisfaction? They found one answer in the techniques used to produce umami, such as dashi and fermentation.

Can Japanese food save the world?

By controlling umami through the use of dashi and fermentation, food can be made more satisfying without the use of animal products such as meat and butter. I believe chefs all over the world find hope in this strategy, because it is also linked to the problems our planet faces today.

The United Nations estimates that the total population of Earth will reach 9.7 billion by 2050. Can the planet support that many people? The rapidly expanding exploration of new foods, such as insects and cultured meat, springs from fears of crisis.

We often hear the term "plant-based" these days, referring to a plant-centered rather than meat-centered diet. Although vegetables take center stage as they do in vegetarianism and veganism, plant-based diets are more forgiving and do not exclude all animal products.

When discussing the food crisis, livestock production is always on the chopping block. One pound (.45 kilo) of beef is estimated to require almost 6 pounds (2.7 kilos) of grain to produce. Some people believe it is more efficient for humans to eat the grain themselves, pointing out that the greenhouse effect of the methane gas contained in cow burps is also 25 times greater than that of carbon dioxide. Livestock production is under intense scrutiny, and marine resources are also declining. As the search for sustainable alternatives becomes more urgent, a plant-based approach may be inevitable, especially given that it is more likely to gain widespread support than strict veganism.

The traditional Japanese diet, with its history of excluding meat consumption, is similar in many ways to a plant-based diet. In part because an economic system based on rice was established in the Edo period, rice, soybeans, vegetables and fish have long been central to our diet. Japanese cuisine has the building blocks for a plant-based diet that can be practiced without difficulty or sacrifice. Dashi and fermentation can also help make plants that have not been fully utilized as foodstuffs in the past into a tasty part of our diet. Not a few chefs believe that the carefully honed culinary wisdom of the Japanese people can play a part in overcoming the challenges facing our planet.

Insights for the future

More and more, I'm hearing foreign chefs say they sympathize with the Japanese veneration of nature and belief that the gods dwell in all things.

In Western fountains, water shoots up from below. By contrast, the water in Japanese gardens flows from high to low places. The plants in the gardens of the Palace of Versailles are trimmed in geometric patterns while the Japanese garden is designed to reflect the natural landscape. The former is said to symbolize the conquest of nature by humans, while the latter indicates the symbiosis between humans and nature. The torrential rains, wildfires, and other disasters that climate change is causing around the world are a testament to the awe-inspiring power of nature, which we should regard with reverence. Our planet is in dire need of help, and the situation is drawing new attention to Japanese views of nature.

The world has begun to think that Japanese cuisine, built as it is on coexistence with nature, might have a future. The focus on our foods and the culture surrounding them is more intense than ever.

Resources

The Art and Science of Sushi: A Comprehensive Guide to Ingredients, Techniques and Equipment by Jun Takahashi, Hidemi Sato, and Mitose Tsuchida (Tuttle Publishing, 2022)

A Beginner's Guide to Japanese Fermentation: Healthy Home-Style Recipes Using Shio Koji, Amazake, Brown Rice Miso, Nukazuke Pickles & Much More! by Hiroko Shirasaki (Tuttle Publishing, 2023)

A Beginner's Guide to Japanese Tea: Selecting and Brewing the Perfect Cup of Sencha, Matcha, and Other Japanese Teas by Per Oskar Brekell (Tuttle Publishing, 2022)

The Book of Urushi: Japanese Lacquerware from a Master by Matsuda Gonroku (Japan Publishing Industry Foundation for Culture, 2019)

Chopsticks: A Cultural and Culinary History by Q. Edward Wang (Cambridge University Press, 2015)

A Dictionary of Japanese Food: Ingredients and Culture by Richard Hosking (Tuttle Publishing, 2015)

Etiquette Guide to Japan: Know the Rules that Make the Difference! by Boye Lafayette De Mente (Tuttle Publishing, 2015)

The Fine Art of Japanese Food Arrangement by Yoshio Tsuchia (Kodansha International, 2003)

Food Artisans of Japan: Recipes and Stories by Nancy Singleton Hachisu (Hardie Grant, 2019)

Introduction to Japanese Cuisine: Nature, History and Culture by the Japanese Culinary Academy (Shuhari Institute, 2016)

Japanese Kitchen Knives: Essential Techniques and Recipes by Hiromitsu Nozaki (Kodansha International, 2013)

The Japanese Sake Bible: Everything You Need to Know About Great Sake by Brian Ashcraft (Tuttle Publishing, 2020)

Japan's Cuisines: Food, Place and Identity by Eric Rath (Reaktion Books, 2016)

Japan's Urushi Craftsman: Can Old World Artistry Survive in the 21st Century? by Bruce Rutledge (Chin Music Press, 2020)

Koji Alchemy: Rediscovering the Magic of Mold-Based Fermentation by Rich Shih and Jeremy Umansky (Chelsea Green Publishing, 2020)

Oishii: The History of Sushi by Eric Rath (Reaktion Books, 2021)

Preserving the Japanese Way: Traditions of Salting, Fermenting, and Pickling for the Modern Kitchen by Nancy Singleton Hachisu (Andrews McMeel Publishing, 2015)

Rice as Self: Japanese Identities Through Time by Emiko Ohnuki-Tierney (Princeton University Press, 1994)

Seaweed: A Global History by Kaori O'Connor (Reaktion Books, 2017)

The Story of Rice by Xiaorong Zhang (Outskirts Press, 2022)

Tsukemono: Decoding the Art and Science of Japanese Pickling by Ole Mouritsen and Klavs Styrbaek (Springer, 2021)

Online Resources

Japan Eats! Podcast: https://heritageradionetwork.org/series/japan-eats

Japanese Food: The Podcast: https://en.bentoandco.com/pages/japanese-food-the-podcast

The Washoku Way: Japan's Nuanced Approach to Food. Ministry of Agriculture, Forestry and Fisheries: https://www.maff.go.jp/j/shokusan/gaisyoku/pamphlet/pdf/washoku_english.pdf

Hiroshi Nagashima

Born in Yokohama in 1946, Nagashima became executive chef of Shisui Japanese Restaurant at Tokyo's Tsukiji Honganji Temple in 1990, and in 2009 took on the role of executive managing director. In 2015 he became executive chef at Tokyo Airport Restaurant. He was named a Master Craftsman of Edo in 2003, a Contemporary Master Craftsman in 2008, earned a Yellow Ribbon Medal from the Japanese government in 2013, was named Goodwill Ambassador for Japanese Food in 2015 and Cool Japan Ambassador in 2016, and received an Order of the Rising Sun, Gold and Silver Rays in 2019. His publications include *The Art of Japanese Vegetable Carving* (Shibata Shoten; English edition by Kodansha International), *Shojin Ryori: Making the Most of Vegetables and Dry Ingredients* (Shibata Shoten), *Japanese Cooking: A Handbook for Weddings, Funerals, and Other Occasions* (Shibata Shoten) and *Surinagashi Recipes* (Seibundo Shinkosha).

Sawako Kimijima

Sawako Kimijima is the editor-in-chief of *The Cuisine Magazine*. Born in Tochigi Prefecture, she worked for Parco Co. and as a freelance writer before joining the editorial staff of *Cuisine Kingdom* magazine, where she was editor-in-chief starting in 2002. In 2006 she founded *The Cuisine Magazine,* an online publication about food. After serving as senior editor, she assumed her current position in July 2017. She is a member of the selection committee for the Shizuo Tsuji Food Culture Award. She has also contributed to *Nikkei The Style*, the Sunday morning edition of Nihon Keizai Shimbun, and has written columns for the design magazines *AXIS* and *And Premium*. She is the author of *Eating Out 2.0* (Asahi Press).

Published by Tuttle Publishing, an imprint of Periplus Editions (HK) Ltd.

www.tuttlepublishing.com

ISBN 978-4-8053-1762-4

MANGA DE WAKARU NIHON RYORI NO JOSHIKI
© 2021, Hiroshi Nagashima, Harumi Yaguchi
Illustrations © Megumi Osaki
English translation rights arranged with Seibundo Shinkosha Publishing Co., Ltd.
through Japan UNI Agency, Inc., Tokyo

English translation © 2024 Periplus Editions (HK) Ltd
Translated by Makiko Itoh

Staff (Original Japanese edition)
Editing and Writing Harumi Yaguchi
Illustrations Megumi Osaki
Cover and Interior Design Akira Sato
Photography Miwa Kumon
Cooking Assistant Jun Okada
Editorial Support Akiko Kamiyama; Japan Surinagashi Association
Proofreading Mie Shida
Photographs courtesy of Urushi Rocks Inc.
With support from Yamacho Shoten Co., Ltd.

Distributed by:

North America,
Latin America & Europe
Tuttle Publishing
364 Innovation Drive
North Clarendon
VT 05759-9436 U.S.A.
Tel: (802) 773-8930
Fax: (802) 773-6993
info@tuttlepublishing.com
www.tuttlepublishing.com

Japan
Tuttle Publishing
Yaekari Building 3rd Floor
5-4-12 Osaki Shinagawa-ku
Tokyo 141 0032
Tel: (81) 3 5437-0171
Fax: (81) 3 5437-0755
sales@tuttle.co.jp
www.tuttle.co.jp

Asia Pacific
Berkeley Books Pte. Ltd.
3 Kallang Sector, #04-01
Singapore 349278
Tel: (65) 6741-2178
Fax: (65) 6741-2179
inquiries@periplus.com.sg
www.tuttlepublishing.com

Printed in Singapore   2401TP

28 27 26 25 24   10 9 8 7 6 5 4 3 2 1

"Books to Span the East and West"

Tuttle Publishing was founded in 1832 in the small New England town of Rutland, Vermont [USA]. Our core values remain as strong today as they were then—to publish best-in-class books which bring people together one page at a time. In 1948, we established a publishing outpost in Japan—and Tuttle is now a leader in publishing English-language books about the arts, languages and cultures of Asia. The world has become a much smaller place today and Asia's economic and cultural influence has grown. Yet the need for meaningful dialogue and information about this diverse region has never been greater. Over the past seven decades, Tuttle has published thousands of books on subjects ranging from martial arts and paper crafts to language learning and literature— and our talented authors, illustrators, designers and photographers have won many prestigious awards. We welcome you to explore the wealth of information available on Asia at **www.tuttlepublishing.com**.